PRAGMATICS OF NATURAL LANGUAGES

SYNTHESE LIBRARY

MONOGRAPHS ON EPISTEMOLOGY,

LOGIC, METHODOLOGY, PHILOSOPHY OF SCIENCE,

SOCIOLOGY OF SCIENCE AND OF KNOWLEDGE,

AND ON THE MATHEMATICAL METHODS OF

SOCIAL AND BEHAVIORAL SCIENCES

Editors :

PRAGMATICS OF
NATURAL LANGUAGES

Edited by

YEHOSHUA BAR-HILLEL

HUMANITIES PRESS / NEW YORK

*Published under the auspices of the Israel Academy of Sciences
and Humanities*

SOLE DISTRIBUTORS FOR U.S.A. AND CANADA
HUMANITIES PRESS / NEW YORK

Library of Congress Catalog Card Number 77–159653

U.S.A. SBN 391 00130 2

PREFACE

In June 22–27, 1970, an International Working Symposium on Pragmatics of Natural Languages took place in Jerusalem under the auspices of The Israel Academy of Sciences and Humanities and the Division of Logic, Methodology and Philosophy of Science of the International Union of History and Philosophy of Science.[1]

Some thirty philosophers, logicians, linguists, and psychologists from Israel, U.S.A., West-Germany, England, Belgium, France, Scotland, and Denmark met in seven formal and a number of informal sessions in order to discuss some of the problems around the use and acquisition of language which in the eyes of an increasing number of scholars have been left under-treated in the recent upsurge of interest in theoretical linguistics and philosophy of language.

More specifically, during the formal sessions the following topics were discussed:

The validity of the syntactics-semantics-pragmatics trichotomy
The present state of the competence-performance issue
Logic and linguistics
The New Rhetoric
Speech acts
Language acquisition.

The participants in the Symposium distributed among themselves reprints and preprints of relevant material, partly in advance of the meeting, partly at its beginning. Each session was introduced by one or two moderators, and summaries of each day's proceedings were prepared and distributed the next day.

The participants were invited to submit papers after the symposium, written under its impact. The eleven essays published here are the result.

It is probably not exaggerated to state that it was, at the end of the meeting, the consensus of the participants that the pragmatic aspects, or at least some of them, of communication through natural languages have to be treated by linguistic theory proper, just like its syntactic and semantic aspects, and that this treatment can only be delegated to some other field with a considerable loss to linguistics itself, contrary to the well-known thesis of Katz and Fodor in their well-known 1963 article. But there was little consensus on much else. The question whether a serious borderline can be drawn between semantics and pragmatics remained as open as the corresponding question with regard to syntax and semantics. The relation between the classical trichotomy syntactics–semantics–pragmatics and the more recent dichotomy competence-performance was somewhat clarified, but only somewhat. The status of the speech act conceptions of Wittgenstein, Austin, Searle, and Grice was pinned down, but only to a degree. How much light is thrown on the issue by the New Rhetoric remained uncertain. The connections with automata theory, cybernetics, and the like were scratched, but just barely.

Some of these issues are treated in the essays assembled here. If they do contribute to further clarification and perhaps also contain some substantial progress, it is not unlikely that part of this is due to the enlightenment that some of the participants may have drawn from the meeting under the clear and sunny skies of Jerusalem.

THE EDITOR

NOTE

[1] Supported in part by the Air Force Office of Scientific Research through the European Office of Aerospace Research, OAR, United States Air Force, under Contract F 61052-68-C-0036.

TABLE OF CONTENTS

TABLE OF CONTENTS

LEO APOSTEL

FURTHER REMARKS ON THE PRAGMATICS
OF NATURAL LANGUAGES

I. INTRODUCTION

In his *Foundations of the Theory of Signs*[1] Charles Morris, followed in this respect by Rudolf Carnap, divided the study of language into three parts: syntax, the study of relations between signs among themselves, semantics, the study of the relations between signs and objects, and pragmatics, the study of the relations between signs and their users, the speaker, hearer, writer, or reader. It is obvious that any development of pragmatics along Morris' suggestions (even if, as appeared during the Working Symposium 1970 of Jerusalem, Morris' conception is neither clear nor unique) should be able to define what is a producer and what is a receiver, either of oral or of written language. This demand, simple as it might look, was repeatedly raised by Professor Staal at the mentioned Symposium.

The paper we present here is an attempt (or rather a succession of attempts) to fulfil this demand. In doing so, we evidently have to develop a typology of the physical and social contexts of use, which any speaker or hearer takes into account in producing and understanding speech acts. Thus, a family of related concepts, 'speech act (or act of writing), production of a speech act, understanding a speech act', has to come under scrutiny. Staal's demand proves to be crucial, as is shown by Morris' definition itself.

Our paper is an outcome of the Jerusalem Symposium and of the intellectual interaction that took place there. It consists of the following parts: (a) We start by asking ourselves how the concept of 'producer' should be defined in the framework of Richard Montague's Pragmatics[2] (very obviously a 'pragmatics of formal languages' and not a 'pragmatics of natural languages' – even though he might doubt the relevancy of the distinction); (b) the next part is a study of Grice's analysis of the concept of producer, and we observe, having read with attention Hintikka's *Knowledge and Belief*, that the basic concepts of that book will be needed to continue Grice's work; (c) finally, having gone through the very heavily 'intensional' definition of producer suggested by our own idiosyncratic continuation of Grice, we try to go in the radically opposite direction and

Yehoshua Bar-Hillel (ed.), Pragmatics of Natural Languages, 1–34. All Rights Reserved.
Copyright © 1971 by D. Reidel Publishing Company, Dordrecht-Holland.

ask what type of interaction between abstract automata would be called a speech act (this last direction of research was our original one, and was represented at our Symposium by Helmut Schnelle).

We try to connect our three certainly very insufficient attempts towards a definition of 'communicator' and 'addressee', by studying the types of occurrences that would confirm or disconfirm hypotheses of the form, 'In situation S, A is a communicator, and B is an addressee'.

Developing all three attempts we must stress the differences between 'formal languages' and 'natural languages'. It will be obvious to the reader of the present volume that in the preparation of this paper we have greatly benefited from the other contributions to the Jerusalem Conference.

II. SPEAKER AND HEARER IN MONTAGUE'S PRAGMATICS

Let us consider a language L, the features of which we specify later. Montague[3] gives the following definition of L:

A possible interpretation for a pragmatic language L is an ordered triple (I, U, F) such that 1. I, U are sets, 2. F is a function with domain I, 3. for each symbol A in L, F_A is a function with domain I, 4. whenever P is an n-place predicate in L, and i is in I, $F_P(i)$ is an n-place relation on U, 5. whenever A is an n-place operation symbol in L and i is in I, $F_A(i)$ is an $(n + 1)$-place relation on U, such that for all $x_0 \ldots x_{n-1}$, there is exactly one object y in U such that $(x_0 \ldots x_{n-1}y)$ is in $F_A(i)$, 6. whenever N is an n-place operator of L and i is in I, $F_N(i)$ is an n-place relation on the set of all subsets of I.

Some comment on the definition is perhaps not out of order. The Tarski model method is obviously taken as a point of departure. But a set I of points of reference is added to the language and the set U upon which the language is mapped by the semantic interpretation function, and the mapping of L on U by F is made to depend upon the elements i of I.

In order to preserve the largest generality possible, no structure is imposed, at least not in the general part of Montague's pragmatics, (a) either on the set I, (b) or on the relation between I and U (it is neither required nor excluded that I and U are disjoint, or that I is included in U). Afterwards various specializations of I are introduced and compared with each other.

We mention this important work because of the fact that it seems suitable to start our search for the definition of the language user (speaker and hearer, writer and reader) from the work on pragmatics that has the clearest and strongest formal structure. We shall consider the various specializations for I mentioned by Montague in order to find out (a) whether I has some specificity after all and, if so, (b) whether by means of a combination of those specializations, the concepts we look for can be adequately defined. The specializations are the following ones:

1. The i can indicate moments of time, either strongly structured (the structure of real numbers) or weakly structured (Cocchiarella's simply ordered time).

2. The i can indicate names of persons or locations in space, and each i may be a sequence: when this is done[4], not one set of reference points is added to the model, but several. Such sets and their cartesian products are used.

3. The i can indicate possible worlds, among which one may or may not consider the Kripke-Hintikka accessibility relations (possible worlds with non-reflexive accessibility relations among them would be the objects of generalized deontic logics according to Montague). Various combinations are possible.

A remarkable feature of this system – we mention it because it has some relevance for our problem – is that intension is distinguished from extension: the intension of a symbol will be the function that maps it upon its extensions in the various models. If we construct a metalanguage MPL of PL in which the mapping functions of PL are to be found among its objects, we can talk about intensions and indeed develop an intensional logic, as Montague claims to have done.[5]

Are the speaker or the hearer mentioned somewhere in this framework? They are, on pp. 112–13. There we find, first: "(a) Let an individual constant c be part of L, (b) let the set of i be a set of speakers, and let, for every element of I, $F_0(i)$ be the class having as its only element i itself." It is then asserted that "the accommodation of several demonstratives and personal pronouns at once presents no problem: we should employ several distinguished individual constants and take sequences of corresponding length (considered for example as composed of the speaker, the person addressed, and the object at which the speaker is pointing) as points of reference".

As an impartial reader we can only say that "pragmatics" in the sense of Morris has not been obtained, *since the concept of speaker is presupposed and not constructed.* But Montague's conception is a much too important extension of Tarski's theory of models to be neglected. We shall try to use it to obtain what we shall call M-pragmatics (Morris-pragmatics) in which the study of the relations between signs and their users can be begun after the concept of the speaker has been explicitly defined.

M-pragmatics will obviously be a specialization, and perhaps also a modification, of the framework given here.

We start from the following supposition: for a given language L, we have a multiplicity of models U, and L is mapped upon a given U according to a specific type of reference points i, i.e., *among the n sets of reference points, there is a privileged set that determines the way in which the other reference points determine the mapping of L upon the selected U.* The same remark can be made by using for a given L not a multiplicity of U's but a multiplicity of F's. And again, there will be a privileged set of reference points that will determine which F will be used to map L upon the now unique U.

Formally, we could state this as follows: we have an M-pragmatics if we can add to the sets $I_1, I_2, \ldots, I_n, U_1, \ldots, U_n, F_1, \ldots, F_n$ (for any of the second and the third type of sets we may have only one element; but for the I sets we must necessarily have a multiplicity in number and in kind) a function G such that G has as its domain a particular set I_i of reference points and as its range either the set $F_i(L, U)$ or the set $F(L, U_j)$, both sets being sets of functions determined either by the i or the j parameter.

The intuitive justification of this proposed modification should be clear. The G function shows the way in which the same language is differently interpreted by different users and so specifies to a degree the role of the language user (speaker, hearer, etc.). It is interesting to remark that the i's of the domain of G will also be present in the domain of F. No postulate of exhaustiveness can be imposed.

M-pragmatics will have: (a) a G dependent upon the speakers and also upon the time of utterance, (b) for each speaker reference point, there will be different time reference sets. Global PL time and local speaker time must not necessarily be identical. This remark makes clear that a certain reflexiveness will be introduced into the model by means of the global time of the language in which the pragmatics of L is expressed and the local time of the speaker referents that determine the interpretation of L in as far as in L names for all speaker-reference points are available. Some complicated relationships must necessarily be postulated between the n local times and the global time.

It was important to stress that the time reference set (with weak or strong structure) must be present in the domain of G, because of the fact that though we did perhaps make a first step in the direction of defining the speaker set, we did not yet introduce in any sense the speaker-hearer relation. Again we shall try to stay within Montague's framework. It is evident that we can express the fact that at a given time point the interpretation of L by a given speaker i changes. We only have to say that there is at least one symbol of L that before this time point was mapped upon some object (individual, class or sequence) of U and after that time point upon some other object of U. And this change has to be dependent upon a given i, that is moreover a speaker (namely, in M-pragmatics, in the domain of G). But there has to be more: we have to introduce a relation C among the i's that are speakers, a relation that has the effect of changing after some time the interpretation of L by one i at least, leaving it unchanged in one other i at least. This relation is neither reflexive nor irreflexive (one can, but need not, talk to oneself). In this language there must be a function H mapping the time reference points upon the F(L, U, I) in such a way that for later time points the F is different for at least one speaker reference point, under the condition that the C relation held earlier. The relation C is neither symmetric nor asymmetric (if a speaks to b, it is possible but not necessary that b speaks to a), and neither transitive nor intransitive (if a speaks to b, and b speaks to c, it is possible, but not necessary, that a speaks to c). C is not connex over I_s (the speaker set), and many-many over I_s.

A hearer is then such that one or more other speakers (hearer = potential speaker) modify the hearer's own interpretation of the language L after an occurrence of the C relation between the latter and the former. We are aware of the fact that not enough structure has been given to the C relation.

Our analysis of the speaker-hearer relationship assumes that every speech act modifies the interpretation of the language in the hearer. In some subtle sense, this is possibly true. But most of us will probably prefer to have a definition of speaker and hearer allowing communication to occur without the interpretation of L to be changed, i.e., simple information transmission, although even this could be construed as interpretation change. A sentence mapped on 1 is mapped on 0, or a sentence mapped on 'undecided', if such a value is introduced, is mapped on either 1 or 0. We could introduce into L, as it is defined by Montague, a set of theorems, and we could make this set of theorems depend upon a time reference point. A communication that changes information without changing the interpretation of L would be a modification of the theorem set. This addition to Montague's ideas seems quite natural: if we make the semantic rules depend upon reference points, it is certainly allowed to consider syntactical sets in relation to reference points.

Before continuing, let us stipulate that if, as a consequence of an occurrence of the C relation, either the interpretation or the theorem set of some speaker is modified, L must allow the speakers i and j involved to state the occurrence of C as true. It might be pointed out that nothing in what was said so far implies this last fact; so we add: L must include C and its grammar.

Our definition of speaker and hearer, by means of a privileged set of reference points and a meta-function G will lead us towards definitions of the indexical terms of the language differing from those of Montague. We must say that, elegant as his solution may be, we must look for yet another analysis for the personal pronoun 'I'. Why? Montague's arbitrary singling out of the constant c, without even having the possibility to demonstrate that 'c exists', sins against a condition for adequacy that could be formulated as follows: "Any analysis of 'I' should yield that 'f(I)' (in direct discourse) implies 'I exist'". In traditional grammar we know of such an analysis. "'I', as used in any statement made at any time or place, designates the speaker making the statement in which 'I' occurs as constituent part." This analysis entails 'I exist' if it is true that every speech act has a speaker. Before developing our M-pragmatics and in order to test its adequacy, we should like to formalize this analysis of 'I'. It will also determine, as is well known, the analysis of past and future, of 'you' and 'he', of 'mine' and 'yours', of 'this' and 'that', etc.

L must contain n-place predicates, enabling us to express that a certain succession of speech events occurs at given moments (again the reference to time is essential). L must also contain (1) predicates defining parts of speech events and (2) classes of speech events characterized by the presence in them of certain parts. L can then express the fact that the speech event belongs to the class K of speech events, characterized by the presence in them of a part belonging to a given class, the 'I' class.

Our crucial definition then becomes:

Let the existence of the C relation between some i and some j have as a necessary condition the occurrence of some speech act belonging to the 'I' class; then 'I' shall designate *that participant whose F function is not modified as a result of the speech interaction C.*

This definition will be of use only if it is possible to characterize the concept of 'speech event' independently of the concept of speaker or hearer. This means that a speech event should be a specific type of physical or of psycho-social sequence. This possibility is neither proved nor disproved but must have the consequence that among the n-place predicates of L certain specific types of predicates occur whose nature cannot yet be specified. This involves a further specification of M-pragmatics. It is an important specification, though, because the other points of reference are for the most part definable on the basis of the concept 'I'. We could even be as bold as to say that the points of reference 'possible world' are for each 'I' the set of mappings of U on this 'I'.

So we come to an alternative proposal for Montague's own definition of intension. For him the intension (or meaning) of a symbol is the function that for a given point of reference maps this symbol upon its extension in U.

It seems to us that we must take into account the empirical fact that in many cases the intension is known and the extension unknown. On the other hand the intension certainly must have an important role in the determination of the extension. It seems to us, moreover, that the concept of intension has its most suitable definition in M-Pragmatics and not in Montague's general framework: the intension after all is a function of the modifications produced by communicating the symbol to the various hearers. There is, though, no incompatibility between this last intension (call it M-intension) and Montague's own concept. The following two remarks lead us towards two different definitions of 'intension'.

Remark. The intension of a symbol A is the set of all characteristic functions of its extension set, to which a heuristic strategy for given reference points of the speaker and non-speaker type is added. By this strategy a non-zero chance is induced to find the extension if the symbol is given. We use the concept of 'characteristic function of A' in the traditional sense: a function taking as elements of its domain the elements of U and having as its value 1 if the element is in the extension of A, and 0 if it is not. Even weak characteristic functions which are not everywhere defined can be admitted. Giving thus a decision procedure for 'being in the extension of A' is presumably not enough to determine the extension. This is why we add a set of heuristic strategies to find out if something is in Ext(A) when A is given. We do not know if this proposal is adequate (in fact, for our taste, it still defines too strongly intension by extension). But it seems a first step in the right direction.

As we see it, this definition remains in the spirit of Montague's pragmatics. Even though it becomes a trifle complicated, it gives some expression to our basic intuition that a symbol acquires its meaning by the causal chains in the central nervous system caused by that symbol in all the contexts in which it appeared. This rich intuitive concept, to which only a developed neurology can give some substance, seems to us to be approximated by the concept of intension in M-pragmatics.

So, finally, we end up in M-pragmatics with several concepts of intension that can all be explored and that are not incompatible with each other and with Montague's first definition.

We thought this idea important enough to look closer into it in M-pragmatics, because we believe, with Montague, that intensional logic could and should be developed on these foundations.

The same may be said about the concepts of consequence and validity. In Montague's pragmatics a sentence on L is a consequence of a set of sentences in L if it is true, for all points of reference, that whenever the antecedents are true in U at a given point of reference, then the consequence is equally true at that point. In M-pragmatics, we have introduced, by means of the metafunction G, a privileged set of points of reference; as a consequence of this decision it seems natural that the consequence and validity relation become dependent upon this privileged set also: we can have, for a privileged i constant, at all other points of reference, that when p is true in U at i, q is also true in U at i. We then have i-consequence. There will be two general consequence relations: the intersection and the union of the i-consequence relations. But neither of them must necessarily coincide with the consequence relation of Montague. In i-consequence we take each time one special type of reference constant, and let all the others vary freely. Neither the union nor the intersection of the consequence relations so obtained will necessarily be identical with the one obtained when we let all the reference points vary together freely, without the restrictions introduced by the metafunction G.

All the remarks made before can be made to apply to formal languages. But we want to apply them here to natural languages. In order to do so, we have to construct a formal model of a natural language.

We can make some steps in that direction.

1. A natural language contains vague terms. So we have to be able to study vagueness in M-pragmatics if we are to apply it to natural languages. A vague term can be defined in Montague's pragmatics as a term mapped by F upon a vague class (a class with an indeterminacy region), as a term associated with a sequence of mappings at different space, time, or speaking reference points.   This means a sequence that does not converge to a non-zero limit (this is one particular way of taking up a suggestion made by David Harrah during an unofficial discussion on vague terms in the Jerusalem Symposium).

2. In natural languages, one might want to work (following a suggestion by Bar-Hillel) with a partial ordering relation "more-grammatical-than" over the set of strings of that natural language.

If we allow this relational conception to prevail on the syntactical level it obliges us to ask many questions we are not used to, for instance: if a is more grammatical in L than b, and if P is less grammatical in L than Q, what can we say about P(a) and Q(b) in this respect? It is then natural to introduce this relation also in the definition of U (where U is then to be defined by an ordering R on a superset U' of U) and in the definition of the reference sets (where I is again defined by means of an ordering on a superset I' of I).

Let us compare two triads of pairs:

I: reference set 1
I': reference set 2 $(I \subset I')$
U: model set 1
U': model set 2 $(U \subset U')$
L: language set 1
L': language set 2 $(L \subset L')$.

Let T designate the degree of acceptability in a given system (either L, U, or I). This degree must not be necessarily quantitative, but can be ordinal. We could formulate requirements for elements m, $l \in L'$, i, $j \in I'$, $o \in U'$ of the following type:

If $T(i) \Rightarrow T(j)$, then, for *most (non-standard quantifier)* l and o, it is true that if $T(l, i) \Rightarrow T(m, i)$, then $T(o, l, i) \Rightarrow T(o, m, i)$; if $T(i) \leqslant T(j)$, no requirement is imposed.

T occurs first as a monadic, then as a dyadic, finally as a triadic function. This anomaly can easily be overcome by indexing. In the requirement taken as an example, the reference set is privileged. Other choices are possible.

3. A natural language is not a unique language L but a set of related languages called idiolects (Lieb[6] has offered the first axiomatization of this concept we know of). So instead of a mapping of L on U determined by I we must consider a mapping of a union of L's (all containing orders of grammaticality and vagueness). It then becomes important to know when a set of idiolects is a language. In first approximation it would seem that speakers of the various idiolects understand each other, at least sometimes, if not always. The definition of understanding we use is that the mapping of each idiolect upon its U can be changed as a consequence of the existence of the communication relation C between the speakers of the idiolects i and j. This definition can only be given if we consider the union of the pragmatic metalanguages of the various idiolects and if, in this language-union we can define the C relations between elements of the I sets of different languages. The definition will be more easily acceptable if we stipulate (1) that the dialect-concept is the one to be defined, (2) and that a language is simply a socially privileged dialect.

This restriction imposed on a union of languages, in order for them to be natural languages, is certainly not sufficient. Other types of relations are needed. But we claim that it is at least a necessary condition.

4. In Montague's 'Pragmatics' (*op. cit.*), various specializations of the I set are taken into consideration. We claim that a natural language is characterized by the fact that, for the sake of interpretation as well as of syntactical analysis, for various types of sentences various types of contexts are to be taken into consideration. It is thus not enough, as we have done, to single out by means of a metafunction one type of i's that determine the way in which other i's determine the F's. Among the other i's there still must be some which, in isolation or in combination, make other reference points either completely dominant or completely irrelevant, or mildly dominant or irrelevant. This hierarchization again must both determine the analysis of the global sentences in parts and their aggregation in classes as well as the mapping of these sentences upon the elements or sequences of U.

5. A natural language must be able to contain its own pragmatic metalanguage. It is certainly too soon now to ask what consequences ensue from the fact that an L contains its own M-pragmatics.

6. Finally, a natural language is a process in time. This means that we must consider another union of languages as our starting point, but now an ordered union, the order being related to the order upon the time

moment reference set. The way in which various stages of a language (another concept examined by Lieb[7]) are related to each other is different from the way in which various idiolects are related to each other. It is difficult to make a statement on the level of generality in which we find ourselves here.

7. Perhaps the most important addition to the ideas developed until now has been suggested to us orally by H. Van den Enden and E. Vermeersch: the speaker is a complicated function of groups of persons and of languages. The set of groups to which the person producing the speech acts belongs, the set of groups that are his reference groups, i.e., the groups whose norms are considered by the speaker as his own, and the functions this individual performs are involved (better still, the tasks in which the individual and both his membership and reference groups are engaged).

The functions that are the speaker and the addressee should be interdependent and dependent upon the communication relations.

If we really want to have a pragmatics of natural language, this seems to be a very important requirement. Our aim here would be to express this requirement in terms of Montague's framework. We have to start with the set I of reference points. We can define subsets of this set, and we can define functions of these subsets. The subsets of time moments, space locations and matter distributions over space locations are needed in order to be able to define the concept of task (if we had the opportunity, we would relate this to Rescher's *The Logic of Commands*[8] and von Wright's *Norm and Action*[9]). The set of 'persons' will have to be defined as the set of 'agents' (rather than the set of speakers, because our aim here is to define the set of speakers). An agent in this case is simply the performer of a task, the executor of a transformation upon the distribution of matter in space-time. We also have to introduce structured sets of agents (membership groups and reference groups, and their interaction) and can say that a speaker is a function of the place of the agent in the global and local transformation process.

What type of function of these very complicated variables will a speaker be? We cannot even give the beginning of an answer. We state the problem, adding that we now stipulate that only the just mentioned functions can be elements of the domain of the G-metafunction. Our rather empty result is thus that certain yet to be specified functions of sets of reference points are to be the elements of the domain of G in the M-pragmatics of natural languages.

It is our hope that the many complications we have been compelled to introduce to reach the concepts whose analysis is our aim do not lead us outside the Montague project and that further extending the Tarski model approach in a natural fashion is a major step in the right direction.

It remains to stress that a natural language is typically a context- (both linguistic and extra-linguistic) dependent language, in which contexts are *used* though not always explicitly *expressed*. When I point at something I use a visual image without verbally expressing its characteristics. Montague's attempt is to explicitly mention, in the pragmatic metalanguage, all the environmental features upon which the meaning of statements is dependent. This seems to be the necessary and natural thing to do; but it is certainly needed to prove that there exists, for some or all natural languages, a method by means of which, in a recursive and even boundedly finite way, all the controlling context features can be mapped upon elements of the I set in some pragmatic metalanguage (and preferably, at least according to us, into some M-pragmatic metalanguage).

III. SPEAKER AND HEARER IN AN EPISTEMIC REFORMULATION OF GRICE'S IDEAS

We start from Grice's basic article, 'Utterer's meaning, sentence meaning and word meaning', *Foundations of Language*, **4**, 1968, 225–42. We shall read it with the same intention as before, viz., to find a definition of speaker and hearer. We make this second attempt at a definition because it seems to us complementary to the first. The latter (inspired by Montague) tries to use extensional concepts; the former, as Grice himself stresses in his 'concluding note' (pp. 241–2), claims "that intensionality is embedded in the very foundation of the theory of language". Grice himself keeps an open mind as to the ultimate reducibility of intension to extension.

I think we should start here with the definition of an actual speaker as a system making a statement, and of a potential speaker as a system having the ability to make a statement. We understand a statement as an event located in space–time, a particular human action. One could perhaps construct classes of statements and formulate laws upon statements.

Both, however, belong strictly to the science of pragmatics, for the following reason: one of the ingredients of the statement Grice concentrates on is the utterance; it is the externally perceptible part of the statement event, and, if we are nominalists, it is a concrete sequence of acoustic changes, perceived or not perceived – a token, in Peircian terms; from this token we can abstract by some complicated eqivalence relation the type, a class of isomorphic tokens. Another part of the statement is the internal state (for indicative statements perhaps a belief), and here again we can concentrate upon the token or upon the type. The concept of proposition is presumably some abstraction of the type of the internal correlate of the statement. The concept of sentence is presumably some abstraction from the external token of the statement.

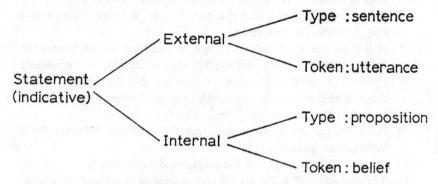

But it is basic for pragmatics to start with the statement and to define the speaker by means of the statement. Grice's formulation gives, in a way which is natural for every empirically inclined scientist, a privileged position to the utterance. He presents (pp. 230–1) an improved version of his earlier definition of the meaning of an utterance. From our point of view, this applies to the global act, a statement, as well.

Let us try, following Grice, to explain the following assertion: 'The speaker A addresses himself by means of the utterance U to the hearer B'. For the sake of simplicity, U is taken to be indicative. This would mean that by producing U, A intends B to think that A believes something (the content of U).

In most cases, A also intends that B should believe something (the content of U); A intends all this by means of producing in B the recognition of A's intentions.

Let us give the following specifications:

1. A causes the complex event $E = (e_1, \ldots, e_n)$.
2. B perceives the complex event $E' = (e'_1, e'_2, \ldots, e'_n)$.

3. $E' = f(E, x)$ (at the limit $E = E'$).

4. A knows that B perceives a function of E' (or weaker: has a large enough probability to perceive a function of E, not too different from the identity function; another possible weakening: replacing knowing by believing).

5. A wants, or desires, or wishes, or intends, that B should have the perception mentioned in 4.

6. B knows that it was A who caused the event that B now perceives (this condition could be weakened in 'B believes that . . .').

7. A knows (or believes) that if B perceives E', B knows (or believes) that A knows (or believes) p.

8. If B perceives E', B indeed knows (or believes) that A knows (or believes) that p. (This condition 8 is not needed if the first epistemic operator in 7 is 'knows' (in view of the law that Kxp implies p) but it is needed if we have the epistemic operator 'believes' (as we do not have that Bxp implies p).

9. A intends (or desires, or wishes) that B knows that A knows (or B believes that A believes) p.

10. A causes E because A has the intention described in 9.

11. The perception of E' causes the epistemic state in B about A because B believes that E' belongs to a set of events $\{E'\}$ whose structural description is such that only systems behaving in accordance with certain rules R (speaking a certain language) will produce elements of $\{E'\}$. Moreover B believes that these rules are such that only believing p and wishing others to know f(p) will produce E'.

12. Normally, the following two propositions should also be true: (a) A behaves according to the rule R; (b) A indeed believes the proposition that B believes A believes. But they can be false. Even if they are false, misunderstanding need not result. There is only misunderstanding (I shall now use the weakest epistemic operator, namely: 'believes') if B believes that A believes p, while A intends B to believe that A believes q, where q and p are neither equivalent nor synonymous. This includes the case where p and q are parts of each other (either a stronger belief or a weaker belief is imputed: in both cases of 'misunderstanding' condition 8 is not fulfilled).

Our list of conditions is already so long and still there seems to be something lacking: "The basic requirement for fully linguistic comprehension of a typical natural language is the ability to perceive language as instrumental".[10] To formulate this requirement in our language we should add:

13. B knows (or believes) that A produced E' as a means towards realizing the epistemic state in which B believes that A believes p.

We are not certain that this is the right description of the 'instrumentality' requirement, but we do not see a better one in the present language.

In this list of 13 requirements we shall now leave out 12, that is provisional anyway, and 8, as we must allow for lying, pretending and misunderstanding. But we shall keep all the others and say that A speaks to B by means of the statement E — E' (emitted-perceived) if these requirements are satisfied. The addressee of the speech act of A is the B mentioned in the various requirements. It is obvious that both A and B can be classes of persons.

A speaker is a person who can speak, i.e., who can initiate the complex interaction of propositional attitudes just described.

The reason for giving this very long paraphrase of what we take to be the intent of Grice's definition of speaker, inferred from his analysis of utterance meaning, is the following one: we see that in this definition a complex interplay occurs of 'x causes y', 'x perceives y', 'x intends y', 'x knows y', and 'x believes y', and we know that recently knowing and believing have begun to be studied; we also know that the logic of perception has begun to be analysed[11]; in an article to appear shortly we try to present a new model of causal implication. The study of the logic of 'intending' or 'aiming at' is still in its first steps. It thus seems that Grice's definition could receive a formal structure by means of these efforts.

It is not possible, in the scope of this article, to present and combine all these various formalisms. The only thing we can claim to do is to show that (1) certain points in the already extant logics of knowledge and belief are relevant for the properties of the speaker mentioned before; (2) Grice's concept of 'conversational implicature' can be related to Hintikka's 'doxastic and epistemic implication'.

Let us try to establish the first point. On pp. 62ff of *Knowledge and Belief*, Hintikka compares 'knowing' (K) and 'believing' (B) as to their transmissibility. This is immediately relevant for the communication act. Conditions 7 and 8 for instance are essentially different if we formulate them by means of the B or K operator, and if we admit the Hintikka properties. Indeedt he statement 'KaKbp I Kap' is considered in the book mentioned to be self-sustaining. This is very important. A proposition is called by Hintikka self-sustaining if it is immune to certain types of criticism (if it can be shown that there are no types of arguments an addressee would accept that would lead from premises he also accepts to the negation of the proposition mentioned). This concept is a dialogical (Lorenzen[12]) or a rhetorical (Perelman[13]) concept. The author of the present paper tried to present a formalization of the rhetorical situation in a contribution to appear in *Philosophy and Argument* (Pennsylvania State University, 1971). If now indeed Hintikka's statement is self-sustaining, then in condition 8, in its epistemic version, 'B knows that A knows that p' implies that 'B knows that p'. In the doxastic version where we have the belief operator, this consequence does not follow, as 'BaBbp I Bap' is not (Hintikka, p. 63) self-sustaining.

Another theorem that has received wide attention (as is shown by a recent number of *Synthese*, entirely devoted to its discussion) is 'Kxp I KxKxp'. It seems to us that the relation between condition 11 and the conditions mentioned before depend upon the truth or falsity (a) of this theorem and (b) of certain theorems referring to the relations between knowledge and belief. [Indeed only if the belief in the structure of E as analysed by B is accompanied in A by a knowledge of B's belief and certainly if A's knowledge about this structure is accompanied by the knowing in A that A is knows it that this knowledge can be used to obtain a belief in B.] This is perhaps a rather rationalistic conception of 'skill' and if this knowledge or belief can be used to obtain in others knowledges or beliefs without explicit awareness of the fact that I have this knowledge or belief about my statements, then this very simple fact about the speaker-hearer relation would be a counterexample to the thesis Kxp → KxKxp. Anyway, whether by being a special case of the thesis or by being a counter-example of its truth, the thesis is relevant for our reformulation of Grice's definition of speaker and hearer.

The epistemic axiom [Kx(p I q)] → [Kxp I Kxq] can naturally be applied to the statement [(x produces E) → (y believes q)] to obtain [Kx(x produces E)] → [Kx(x believes q)].

We cannot go through all of Hintikka's *Knowledge and Belief* to show the importance and applicability of its content to Grice's concept of speaker. We think that our definition itself and the few hints given just now must suffice to show that here a whole new field is opening up for pragmatics (if and when we obtain a good analysis of some other modal expressions, whose study has barely begun: *perceived, caused by, intended*).

This is not only a remark concerning the contingent fact of possible combinations of Grice's and Hintikka's work. We think that Grice's attempt is representative of a wide class of possible definitions of speaker and hearer, a class in a sense complementary, as we said, to Montague's. In the former the mentalistic and intensional features are dominant. It is significant that this intensional class, in which other important definitions of speaker and hearer should exist, can and should be formalized.

Our second way of relating Grice and Hintikka was the attempt to show that Grice's conversational implicatures could be related to the doxastic and epistemic implications of Hintikka.

Let us first define these two concepts:

P doxastically implies q if the belief in (p and not q) is indefensible;
p epistemically implies q if knowing (p and not q) is indefensible.

The definitions are only clear in as far as the concept of "defensibility" is clear. We must admit that only by means of a combination of Hintikka's work with our formalization of Perelman's (quoted before) can we really understand it. But let us for the moment accept that we have some intuitive grasp of the meaning of "defensibility".

We now give some of the conversational maxims that Grice mentions in his work without deducing them from any underlying principles. It certainly would be a good thing for our approach if we could obtain them as consequences of the definition of the speaker-hearer relation.

The maxims are the following ones:

1. The statement made should be relevant for the topic under discussion.

2. The statement should obey some minimum condition: it should contain no more information than is necessary for the discussion at that moment.

3. But if the possibility exists to make many statements, at a given moment of the discussion, the statement made should be the strongest one possible, and should be interpreted by the hearer as being the strongest possible (both these requirements should be in line with maxim 2).

I myself would add a dynamic feature:

4. The statement should help the dialogue to continue as a developing whole (or be a natural conclusion).

We know, consulting Grice's article on the causal theory of perception, some applications of these maxims.[14]

The assertion of the statement (p ∨ q) by a speaker x for a hearer y implies that it is not the case that x believes that y believes p, and also that it is not the case that x believes that y believes q. If the contrary were the case, then the communication p ∨ q would be irrelevant for the conversation (adding only knowledge already at the disposal of the participants). Applying another axiom we might add that this communication of a disjunction conversationally implies 'x wants y to believe that x does not know q'. If indeed y did not come to this conclusion but, to the contrary, would believe that x knew one of the alternatives to be true, then y would come to the conclusion that x did not apply the conversational maxim 3 (under the strongest interpretation put upon it).

Other examples could be given but this example already makes it clear that the application of the maxims is again based upon the interplay of the beliefs and knowledges of the speaker and hearer that are necessarily involved in the definition itself of these roles.

Let us now examine the main concept involved in the maxims, *relevancy*. A statement is relevant if believing it or knowing it partially or completely answers some questions that are being asked. As we cannot, in the scope of this article, use the logic of questions, we can replace this definition of relevancy by another one: a statement p is relevant if the belief in p is held to be logically connected with some statement that occurred not too long before, or that will occur not too much later.

All four maxims are deducible very easily from very simple conditions on the efficiency of action. This means: the fact that a speech act is an instrument used to cause some belief allows to apply to it the conditions of efficiency that can be imposed upon all instruments; and the fact that the totality of a conversation is as a whole an action allows to apply to its parts the maxims of efficiency that can be applied to all parts of actions.

If this point of view is taken, the maxims can be easily deduced: (a) the statements should be relevant, i.e., they should all contribute to the final state of belief aimed at, (b) they should not contain too much; at every stage of the process of belief production, the most economical means should be used; (c) but they should further the task as much as possible; so be as strong as possible at any point, while preparing the following stages of the process of belief production.

The fact that at all points the maxims can be cancelled means (a) that at all points lower levels of efficiency or other definitions of efficiency can be imposed, or (b) that at all points the aims of the belief producing process can be changed.

This deduction of the maxims is in some weak sense a deduction from the definition of speaker and hearer. We did not get into the deduction any reference to epistemic and doxastic implication. For this reason we should like to make yet another attempt.

Is the statement 'I assert that p and I believe that p has no consequences in the issue under discussion' either doxastically or epistemically defensible? Perhaps we should select a formulation in which the concepts of 'belief' or 'knowledge' are explicitly present. Such a formulation would be 'I as speaker assert p for you as hearer and, moreover, I assert that your hearing of p cannot produce any belief or knowledge different from the ones you have'. This statement can certainly be immediately attacked from the very definition of a speaker as a person aiming towards the production of belief. So it is neither epistemically nor doxastically defensible. Analogous constructions could be made for all the other maxims. Let us only take, by way of example, maxim 4. The statement would be 'I assert p, and I moreover assert that I disregard the assertions possible after p, either making them impossible, or, if not doing so, making them irrelevant, or, if not doing so, not relating my assertion to any possible one of them'. If my aim is to produce a belief (this being the definition of a speaker) then I can be attacked making this statement by the remark that I lower my chance to produce beliefs while it is my aim as a speaker to heighten this chance.

It is remarkable that the degree of defensibility of the statements denying the conversational maxims is different, and it is equally remarkable that the concept of 'defensibility' must necessarily be related to an audience and a context. This has not been done by Hintikka; but it has been done by Perelman. We think, however, that in addition to the rhetorical theory of knowledge of Hintikka (even though he is not explicitly aware of this feature) it is worthwhile to look for a non-rhetorical one in which I express the specific features of a semi-rational belief that is only an approximation to complete rationality, and in which for the third time we try to deduce (weakly) the conversational maxims of Grice. Let us state the following axioms (for such a semi-rational belief).

A1. For most propositions p, if a person x believes p, then there exists a proposition q, such that x also believes q, and such that x moreover believes that all persons holding q are obliged to believe p (or, in a weaker version: for most propositions p, and for most persons x, if x believes p, then there also exists a proposition q, such that x believes q and such that x believes that the truth of q implies that it is permitted to believe p). This is a postulate of foundation.

A2. A postulate of the search for, or the acceptance of, additional reasons (a reason for a p being any q having, with reference to that p, the relations mentioned in A1), again for most persons and most propositions.

A3. A postulate of defensibility: for most persons x and most propositions p, there exist propositions $s_1 \ldots s_n$, such that the belief in one of these s_i commits the believer to the rejection of p and such that the believer x accepts some reasons for the rejection of these s_i.

A4. A postulate of relevance: for most propositions p, and most persons x, if x believes p, there is at least some proposition q, such that either q is preferable to non-q, or non-q is preferable to q, and such that either p implies the possibility of q, or p implies the impossibility of q.

As a weakened deduction rule, if we combine it with the logic of questions, we can perhaps propose the following: 'If x has been asked if q is true, and if x believes p, and if p implies q, then x believes q' (a further weakening would mean the introduction of an operator suggested to me orally by D. Batens: "If x has been asked if q is true, and if there are some relations between p and q about which x has thought (the logic of the T (=thought) operator has still to be worked out), and if p I q and x believes p, then x believes q."

We think it to be a useful task to apply this belief logic (which is, as far as we know, the first attempt to construct a belief logic that is not only some fragment of classical logic), to the doxastic formulations of the definition of speaker and hearer. Our conjecture is that very few of the properties of the means-end relation (the foundation stone of our first deduction of the conversational maxims) are needed in combination with this axiom set to obtain the Gricean maxims. It seems clear in general that the maxims should not be collected haphazardly like flowers in the field but that they should be deduced from the speaker-hearer relation, and we have seen that this speaker-hearer relation is heavily dependent upon doxastic and epistemic logic.

It would now be our task to stress that we are interested in the pragmatics of natural languages. We should ask ourselves if either the definition given by Grice implies the properties of natural language we have mentioned, or if, to the contrary, the definition has to be modified in order to be applied to natural languages. Some essential point must be lacking in the definition of speaker and hearer given. As far as we can see, it does not enable us to deduce anything about the specific nature of the rules according to which the events E, the vehicles of the speech act, are produced, from the fact that they are intended to produce knowledge about knowledge or beliefs about beliefs. And the distinction between formal (or constructed) and natural languages is a distinction that concerns the type of rules on E. Naturally we can make some additional assumptions: we can say that a belief can never be immediately transmitted but only through an assertion. So that the relationship between assertion logic, epistemic logic and doxastic logic becomes the focal point in the understanding of the peculiarities of natural language. If we add explicitly that it is false that Bxp implies Asxp (x asserts p) and that it is moreover false that Asxp implies Bxp then we have eliminated any simple relationship, and we have before us the real search for a much more complicated one. It would be ill advised to say that every natural language is a structure that must be learned by a probabilistic mechanism and thus that the relations between beliefs and assertions, having been learned by a probabilistic mechanism, are probably (a) many-one (vagueness) and (b) exhibiting degrees of grammaticality and (c) many minor forms of divergence (idiolects). This is stipulating too much from the beginning. In the present state of research we know enough to reject any isomorphism between assertion logic and doxastic logic, but it would be avoiding the problem and not solving it to deduce the properties of natural languages by postulating a probabilistic learner for the relations between beliefs and assertions. The type of learner and the learning process should be deduced and not postulated. It is important to stress that the study of relations between the properties of languages and the properties of language users (speakers and hearers) becomes here a chapter in the coordination of doxastic and assertion logic.

Before finishing Section III of our paper we want to stress that the concept of conversational implication compels us to make a clear distinction between the logic of knowledge and belief and the logic of statements declaring in natural language 'I believe p'. The statement 'I believe p' conversationally but not logically implies that (a) I believe p to be contested,

(b) I do prefer p over non-p. If I say 'I know p', I conversationally but not logically imply that (a) I did not always know p, (b) there are reasons for doubts to have arisen about my attitude towards p, (c) I have the wish to eradicate completely these doubts. It is even natural to say 'I know p, but I cannot believe p' (while yet certainly 'Kxp I Bxp' must be a theorem), because of the fact that by saying the last sentence I convey the thought that there are reasons, though not necessarily overwhelming ones, for my not knowing p, if they were not counterbalanced by other reasons.

These remarks have only the following purpose: the theory of the speaker-hearer relation, to be expressed in epistemic and doxastic logic, makes statements about knowing and believing that have conversational implications different from the conversational implications of statements in which explicitly the words 'believing' or 'knowing' are used. It was necessary to point this out before leaving a wide open field in which, through Grice's example and Hintikka's help, much work on pragmatics can be done.

IV. ABSTRACT AUTOMATA THEORY AND THE SPEAKER-HEARER RELATIONSHIP

What kind of automaton would be a speaker? What kind of automaton would be a hearer? What type of inputs and outputs of automata would be speech acts? These are the questions we finally tackle now, in the last part of this paper.

It is known that through the work of Chomsky, Schützenberger, Bar-Hillel, Rabin and others[15] many theorems have been proved about the equivalence between certain types of machines and certain formal representations of languages. As a word of warning we must say that our intention here is completely different. We ask ourselves another question: what type of automata would produce and use structures such as natural languages. Most probably these automata, if they exist, will have to be quite different in structure from natural languages. In an earlier paper, published in *Communicatie en Cognitie*, called 'The pragmatics of natural languages',[16] we tried to use the extant formal structures of the Chomsky school and to apply them to themselves: a language user would be a tree whose nodes are trees, or a tree having a set of trees, taken together with their mutual mappings, as nodes. Such an approach is not unreasonable but, so it seems to us now, not fundamental enough. It was sufficient, however, to show that a PS grammar whose elements are themselves PS grammars is formally very different from the first structure.

Our method will thus be as abstract and deductive as we can make it: we start out with the concept of an automaton and then, by considering various specializations and combinations of automata, we try to reach a more or less adequate model of the language producer and the language consumer (the speaker and the addressee).

Let us then give a definition of an abstract automaton. An automaton is a quintuple of three sets and two functions:

1. The set of possible states of the automaton: set S
2. the set of possible inputs of the automaton: set I
3. the set of possible outputs of the automaton: set O
4. a function l mapping the cartesian product of I and S upon S: the function that gives for all pairs of inputs and states the next state
5. a function d mapping the cartesian product of I and S upon O: the function giving the output dependent upon the input and the internal state.

In order to have the speaker-hearer situation we must naturally introduce interaction between several automata. Later on we shall have to describe the type of automaton having the ability to engage in this interaction. But first the interaction must be specified.

At least the following conditions must be satisfied:

1. Some of the outputs of automaton S must be some of the inputs of automaton H: $O(S) \cap I(H)$ (the intersection of the two sets) must be different from the empty set.

2. In order for this intersection to contain signs we must have the representation or symbolization relation: in automata terms, this means that some of the outputs of S that are also inputs of H must provoke in H either an output, or an internal state, that belongs to a certain family of outputs, or internal states, also provoked by another input of H. We don't yet specify anything about the relations the members of the family must have towards each other.

Formally this means: for every element of the set of internal states of H (or at least for some elements of this set), the sign-input, output of S, must provoke either a state of H (eventually a sequence of states or a relation between later states), or an output of H, that is not identical to, nor even part of, nor even analogous to, but rather some complicated function of, the set of states or the output induced by at least one other input of H.

3. In general, we can demand that not all inputs of H satisfy the condition 2. The H automaton must be a many-input – many-output automaton at every moment. But it is not excluded that the output of S, that is a sign-input to H, can also be induced by another input of S.

As a historical remark, we think that this definition is a generalization of Morris' own definition[17]: he thought, using Hull's concept of a habit family, that the sign should provoke an initial segment of the action sequence provoked by the thing signified. It seems to us, however, that this is too special a case; in general, there need not be any common part between the reaction towards the sign and the reaction towards the thing signified, but there has simply to be some functional dependence of the one action sequence upon the other action sequence. We realize that on the other hand it seems desirable not to be as general as that and to put some restrictions upon that function F.

4. The object signified by some sign received by H as input must also belong to the input set of the automaton S. It is not at all necessary that the transfer function of S maps this input upon the same sequence of S's internal states as the transfer function of H maps the sign-input upon (there need not even be functional dependence).

5. Both automata S and H must be retroactive automata (in other words they must tend towards certain simple or multiple equilibrium points). This means that some of their outputs must also later become inputs. And the transfer function must be such that some function of the relation between the sign input of H and the state sequence following it is a prerequisite for at least one equilibrium position of S. This means that the connected complex automaton (S, H) must itself be retroactive as a whole so that some outputs of H are also inputs of S.

Just as the speaker must want to be understood, so the hearer must want to understand (at least in some cases). This means that for H some relation between the sign outputs of S and the inputs of S they are connected with must be an equilibrium condition. This means that in order to have the speaker-hearer relationship between automata, we must have at least four cycles: the cycle (S, S), the cycle (H, H), and the cycles (S, H, S) and (H, S, H).

6. As a consequence of the requirement 5, it seems to us that the automata S and H must themselves be complex automata, in which subauto-

mata exist having the following features: (a) the input of the M (model) subautomaton of S (MS) is a function of the input of S (more precisely, a function of equivalence classes over the set of subsets of the input set of S); the output is a category, in the sense of Eilenberg,[18] a representation of the input set of S upon itself. This subautomaton has as its equilibrium point (one among many, presumably) a state in which the nearest possible approximation to isomorphism exists between the class of inputs of S and the class of outputs of MS. In consequence of the fact that outputs from H are inputs to S, in MS there will also be a representation (more or less complete) of H. It is only by means of the existence in S of this partial representation of H that S can control its action in such a way as to reach in H a given relation between sign inputs and sign outputs (the relation required in the first part of 5).

(b) In H a model subautomaton (MH) must also exist having again as one of its equilibrium points as good a mapping as possible of H's inputs (and as part of this, as good a mapping as possible of S). Only by using this representation can H tend to represent the relation between the S inputs and the S sign-outputs that are also H inputs.

We must now correct our requirement 6. The demand that MS or MH reach as isomorphic a representation as possible is the expression of a Wittgensteinian theory of knowledge we do not share ourselves. We are convinced of the fact that understanding is not reproducing, that the aim of knowing is not the production of an isomorphic model of the object known, but we do not have at our disposal another precise definition of the aim of knowing. For this reason, we used the familiar term of approximate isomorphism. But we want to be on record as rejecting the Wittgensteinian ideal. To know is to transform but nobody knows what transformation is meant. The reader, if he knows more, should fill in, whenever he encounters in the text 'approximate isomorphism', whatever suitable and formally useful description of the aim of knowing he is acquainted with.

These six conditions seem to us to be the essential ones to represent the speaker-hearer relationship. Pragmatics should now deduce from the definitions given some properties of the sign outputs and sign inputs of S and H, i.e., some properties of languages. Then it will be constituted as a science.

In order to see if this is possible, we try to connect the complex S-H automaton we just described with some fundamental concepts and problems of automata theory.

Before doing this we still want to make two remarks:

(a) Some sign-outputs are context dependent in the sense that the effects they produce in H are codetermined by the simultaneous and earlier non-sign inputs. They will be strongly context dependent if this relation is indeed also part of the S equilibrium-presuppositions.

The assumption, sometimes made but convincingly refuted in a recent study by Asa Kasher,[19] implying the impossibility of developing a theory of non-linguistic context dependency means nothing more than the assumption that no natural classification of automata inputs, determining in any sense the sign effects, can be made. We see no reason to assume such a negative attitude, though we recognize that very little has been achieved yet.

(b) The remark that the speaker is a complicated function of various groups to which he belongs should be treated in this automaton model as follows: the S and H automata are not characterized by only one transfer and only one output function but, on the contrary, by sets of such functions. These functions determine other sign-sets (inputs producing outputs that are functions of the outputs produced by other inputs, or producing state sequences that are functions of state sequences produced by other inputs), and determine other types of retroactions. In order to make the speaker a function of a speaker set, we have to add that there are privileged inputs that transform the automaton guided by one transfer function into an automaton guided by another transfer function; both transfer functions being distinct from each other in the way in which the sign effects are dependent upon the denotatum effects and different in the way in which S wants to influence H and H wants to understand S (to use mentalistic language, in part 3 in which it has been on purpose as strongly avoided as it was encouraged in our second section).

These remarks being made, we now try to show the relevancy of some topics in basic automata theory to the definition of the speaker-hearer relation.

It is obvious that Glushkow's[20] chapter 5 (*Theorie der Abstrakten Automaten*), 'Komposition von Automaten' must be relevant for the definition of speaker-hearer interaction. It is strange that the study of compositions of automata, that would be of the highest interest here, receives so little attention in the literature we have consulted. We used the textbooks by Starke, Salomaa, and Ginzburg[21] but did not find a chapter on composition. We shall have to introduce the relevance of the basic distinctions mentioned in these textbooks, however Glushkow is also incomplete in the sense of not developing the theory of quasi-machines of Ginzburg. Here another essential idea for the definition of speaker is presented, namely the introduction of a structure on the set of inputs and outputs. Glushkow is incomplete for another reason: the thorough attention given to stochastic and non-deterministic machines in Salomaa and Starke is absent. We shall claim that the speaker-hearer automata should be non-deterministic automata having a next-state function that is many-valued, or in the strongest case stochastic automata giving, for pairs of states and inputs, probability distributions over the set of next states and over the set of outputs. Our reason for claiming this is the following one: S speaks to H and H listens to S only if S supposes that H can do many different things in the future (non-deterministic, stochastic) and that these things can be influenced by means of the sign-input, while H supposes that S can give many different sign outputs and wants to know which one will be selected. Both suppositions imply the non-deterministic and/or stochastic character of the speaker-hearer automaton. *What seems to be needed, however, is a combination of the theory of automata composition with the theory of stochastic and non-deterministic automata.*

Let us now, having thus set our aim, return to the concrete matter of Glushkow's chapter 5. It is manifestly inspired by Seiti Huzino's *Theory of Finite Automata* (1962).[22]

We start by considering the following composition (*direct sum*): take n automata with the same input and output sets and with disjoint internal states. Then form an automaton having as its set of states the union of all the states, and as transition and output function of a given state, the special transition function of that state. This composition may have some use for the formalization of the speaker-hearer relationship, but not much; we can naturally schematize the members of a speech community as automata having the same environment and the same abilities, but internally different, and we can then conceptualize the total speech community as the direct sum. But in general these co-requirements are too strong; the input–output sets are not strictly identical for all the members of a speech community (in fact, communication often occurs because of the fact that this condition is not realized), and the internal states are not strictly disjoint. An operation with weaker requirements could have some use in defining a speech community.

It is an interesting fact that no speaker or hearer is allowed to be a strongly connected or simple automaton because, for such automata, there are possible inputs that can lead from every possible internal state to every other possible internal state. The fact that speaker and hearer have a finality built into them prevents this. Neither can a speaker or hearer be a reversible automaton (in Huzino's sense) even though if we were to believe Piaget's work in the psychogenesis of intelligence, the intellectual component of any goal-directed automaton should be a reversible automaton (in Huzino's sense).

The second composition considered is the *direct product*. We take here again n (finite) automata and we define as input set the set of sequences of inputs having one element out of every input set. The same cartesian product operation is applied to the set of outputs and the set of internal states. The transfer function for the composite automaton gives a composite next state, each element of which is the next state produced by the first input on the first state of the first automaton and so forth. The same holds for the output function. There is no useful application of this direct product because there is no interaction introduced. But Glushkow's def. 23 (p. 61) is much more important for our purpose. We introduce two functions: φ and ψ, φ mapping the cartesian product of the n states and n input sets upon the cartesian product of the n input sets (a retroaction) and ψ mapping a cartesian product of the n input and n state sets upon the set of outputs (an output function of the combined set). All elements of the input sets of the product automaton are in the range of ψ.

We can say that one of our requirements implies that every speaker and hearer is a direct product under functions φ and ψ, and that the composite automaton that is the union of S and H must also be a direct product under functions φ and ψ

But we can find in Glushkow still more material to give a formal framework for our definition of speaker and hearer. On p. 64 the *superposition* of two automata is considered. We quote: "Die Superposition läuft praktisch darauf aus, dass die Ausgabesignale eines Automaton als Eingabesignale eines anderen Automaton verwendet werden."

The superposition of two automata, classically defined as a quintuple, has the following features: (a) the set of states is the cartesian product of the set of states, (b) the input set of A_2 is the output of A_1, (c) the transfer and output functions are the following ones: $d(a,x) = (d_2(a_2,l_1(a_1,x)), d_1(a_1,x))$ and $l(a,x) = l_2(a_2,l_1(a_1,x))$.

Having at our disposal the concept of superposition, we say that the speech act is at least a partial superposition of automata (we cannot say that all the outputs of A_1 are identical with all the inputs of A_2, but we must have partial identity; there should be overlapping), and of automata that are themselves direct products under functions φ and ψ. This is not satisfactory as a formal characterization, but it shows the way.

The next important step is to represent as an automaton operation the sign-denotatum relation. Again, the theory puts no ready made tools at our disposal but allows us to go somewhat in the right direction.

In order to do this, we think we have to combine the theory of representation of events in automata with the theory of homomorphisms, equivalence and reducibility of automata.

We can say that every S or H is an automaton having an initial state. We can also consider relatively initial states (defined as initial states in given sets).

Let us say that a relativized initial state automaton is able to represent a certain event if and only if there is a real subset of the set of states in which this event, as input, maps the initial state (definition of Medwedjew, Glushkow 31).[23]

To this definition of representability we now add the definition of reducibility. It requires first the definition of equivalence of automata. Two automata are equivalent if they map the same inputs on the same outputs; an automaton is reduced when there is no subautomaton with fewer internal states that is equivalent to it. If I were of the opinion that the sign provokes the same reaction (= output) as the denotatum, then I should say that every speaker-hearer automaton should be unreduced (as two equivalent inputs exist for it: the sign, and the denotatum), and were the automaton to the contrary reduced, one of the two equivalent inputs would be erased. But, as the reader well knows, we are not of the opinion that the sign provokes the same reaction as the signified, but only that there exists a functional dependence between these reactions we do not know how to specify. To express this fact as a generalization of the concepts of reducibility and of representability, we say that an automaton is reduced with reference to a function f if and only if there are no pairs of representable events in that automaton, such that it is the case that the representation of e_1 is a function f of the representation of e_2. Where f is identity we have the usual case of being reduced. Let us now require in general that a speaker or hearer automaton be not f-reduced. Then we have done some step towards building in the sign-denotatum relationship. We use fundamental concepts (representation, equivalence, reducibility) of automata theory and we can go on looking for specifications of f.

Combining our last remarks we now stipulate that *a speaker or hearer is to be a non-f-reduced automaton that is itself the direct product under* φ *and* ψ *of a set of automata and that stands in a partial superposition relation to another automaton equally not f-reduced, and equally a direct product under* φ *and* ψ.

Pragmatics, if we accept this definition of the speaker-hearer relation, is the study of the structure of the intersection of the output set of S and the input set of H, as a consequence of the existence of the relations and requirements in this definition.

It will be obvious to the reader that this is only the beginning of a theory. Many other Huzino operations should be tried out; it should be made clear what is the exact relation between the regular languages that define the set of events representable in finite automata, and the natural languages that satisfy the requirements we have started to formulate here.

Moreover – and this is fundamental – as said before, we should apply to non-deterministic and stochastic automata the definitions just given.

Things look difficult but still hopeful.

V. RELATIONSHIPS BETWEEN OUR THREE DEFINITIONS OF SPEAKER AND HEARER

It is certainly possible, within Montague's 'pragmatics', to insert part of the structure of automata theory into model theory. We can stipulate that the speaker reference sets should refer to automata of a given type, e.g., the ones whose partial definition we tried to give above. It is also certainly possible to use model theory to interpret doxastic logic; a proposition is believed, in the sense of Hintikka, if it is true in a given set of models whose properties can be specified. Finally, the reader will have seen that we often try to express in automata theory language the same notions (aiming at, believing-representing) that we try to express in our intensional logic of belief.

There is some reason for this threefold attempt to define 'speaker' and 'hearer'.

The first attempt starts out from the general concept of 'language' and defines the speaker in terms of a model theory of language. This point of view is neutral with reference to the difference between introspective or extrospective ways of speech. The second attempt is uncompromisingly introspective and subjectivistic without abandoning, however, the claim to rigour. The third attempt is equally biased in the mechanistic-materialistic direction (but again, without abandoning the claim to rigour). It seems to us that there is a systematic reason to continue building up a suitable speaker-hearer definition in these three directions. In some sense, we think that the three together should give us the complete picture.

But the reader will be aware of the fact that (a) M-pragmatics is in an even more inchoative state than pragmatics itself, (b) the combination of ill-known modalities, needed to express the intensional definition, is to be built up, and (c) many modifications have to be introduced in abstract automata theory in order to define the speaker-hearer relation.

At the present moment, we are not really in a position to determine the relation between the three definitions. For this reason, we must simply be content to hint at possible relationships without being able to show their nature.

VI. HOW TO DISCOVER WHO IS THE SPEAKER OR THE HEARER, THE AUTHOR OR THE PUBLIC?

We have now presented three incomplete attempts of defining the basic concepts of pragmatics. Only by applying inductive logic in some form to the definitions we have constructed can the problem 'How can we confirm that the speaker of the sentence p is the person A?' be solved. It is however impossible to present, at the moment, a combination of any type of theory of confirmation with M-pragmatics, with a complex logic of epistemic modalities or with a modified theory of automata. We simply want to pose the question, postponing its answer for later work.

Even if the assignment of preparing an inductive logic for pragmatics is premature, we can make some remarks of the following topics: (a) If, as in the case of Sebeok in his 'zoosemiotics', we find ourselves placed before an unknown species, behaving in strange ways, on the basis of what facts do we come to the decision that communication takes place and that a certain animal is the speaker and another animal the hearer (the problem is the more interesting for our topic, if the media of communication are not the ones we normally use, sounds and visual data, but rather chemical or electrical stimuli)?

(b) If we find ourselves in a speech community the mores and the language of which are unknown to us (the situation Quine analysed in *Word and Object*), how do we discover that communication takes place, and that a given person is the speaker, another the addressee?

We reconstruct hypothetically as follows (but the practitioners of the art should be consulted to decide if the reconstruction is adequate):

1. We subdivide the behaviour of the species in two classes: actions that lead immediately or mediately (without intervention of other organisms) to need satisfaction (a model of the needs should be provided), and actions that do not lead to need satisfaction without the cooperation of other organisms. The speakers must certainly be organisms that produce behaviour of the second type.

2. We make a second subdivision: behaviour that is stereotyped against non-stereotyped behaviour. The speaker must produce stereotyped behaviour. The concept of stereotyped behaviour can be defined but we presuppose its meaning known to the reader.

3. Our third subdivision is the creation of two classes of actions: those that are lawfully or regularly followed by actions if other organisms have perceived them, and actions that do not possess this last property.

4. The fourth division will be the subdivision between actions that only occur when certain other stimuli are either present or have been present a certain time before, and actions that are not regularly related to specific sets of external stimuli.

5. Finally, we distinguish between actions that have subactions that can and do occur in other actions of the same type, and actions that do not have this property.

I now call a speaker *an organism that is observed to initiate stereotyped action, linked to clear sets of stimuli in the present or past, having subactions used in other actions of the same type elsewhere, not immediately need satisfying but, when observed by other organisms of the same type, regularly producing action that is need satisfying.* I call a hearer *an organism that has the ability to perceive such speaker action and to use it for need satisfaction.*

We are certain that many problems remain unsolved in this description, and we should not like to be a behaviourist by using this description as a definition of the speaker or hearer but as a vague description of the type of strategy to be followed to discover the speaker and the hearer.

I think the reader could easily apply our distinctions to the question 'Why did von Frisch come to the conclusion that the bee dance is an act of communication?' As to the Quine situation, we again make the remark that introduced this paragraph: its adequacy should be measured by an empirical study of the work of the lexicographer, and anyway the problem asked should be formally solved by the application of inductive logic to the speaker-hearer situation. *Most emphatically we should not use these data in the definition of S–H itself but they are sorely needed to see whether the proposed definitions are adequate or not.*

It is suitable, at the close of such a paper, to define the status of the propositions that it contains. We think that this paper proposes hypotheses to be confirmed by deducing their consequences. Our own attempt would be: There are statements about the existence of language universals.[24] Are these statements derivable or not from the definitions present in this paper? If they are not derivable, are they derivable from small additions to the definitions given? Or, on the contrary, are they incompatible with part or all of the definitions given?

The paper has no cognitive status (we accept in this respect the empirical meaning criterion of our deeply regretted late teacher, Rudolf Carnap), if it cannot be either confirmed or partially refuted by the facts known about language universals.

At the present moment, we must present its content as a succession of hypotheses, neither proved nor disproved.

When we think, however, about the doubts that were voiced, during the Jerusalem Working Symposium, about pragmatics having a definite set of questions, techniques and methods, our conclusion is: as a development and modification of existing formalisms, the theory of the relation between the language users and the language structure really does exist, as an independent field of study.[25,]

University of Ghent

NOTES

[1] *Encyclopedia of Unified Science*, Chicago University Press, Vol. I.
[2] 'Pragmatics', in R. Klibansky (ed.), *Contemporary Philosophy*, Florence 1968, pp. 102–22.
[3] *Ibid.*, p. 106.
[4] *Ibid.*, p. 113.
[5] 'Pragmatics and Intensional Logic', *Synthese* 22, 68–94 (1970) (cf. also 'English as formal language I', in B. Vizentini *et al.*, *Linguaggi nella societa e nella tecnica*, Milan 1970, pp. 189–224; and 'Universal Grammar', to appear in *Theoria*).

[6] Hans-Heinrich Lieb, *Communication Complexes and Their Stages*, The Hague 1968.
[7] *Ibid.*
[8] N. Rescher, *The Logic of Commands*, London 1966.
[9] G. H. von Wright, *Norm and Action*, London 1963.
[10] D. M. Mackay, 'The Growth of Knowledge: Computers and Comprehension', in M. Kochen, D. M. Mackay, M. E. Maron, M. Scriven, and L. Uhr (eds.), *The Growth of knowledge*, pp. 232.
[11] J. Hintikka, *Models for Modalities*, Dordrecht, 1970.
[12] P. Lorenzen, *Metamathematik*, Mannheim 1965.
[13] Chaim Perelman, *Traité de l'Argumentation*, Paris 1958.
[14] P. H. Grice, 'The Causal Theory of Perception', in *Proceedings of the Aristotelian Society*, suppl. vol. XXXV (1961), 121–52.
[15] See Y. Bar-Hillel, *Language and Information, Selected Essays*, Addison-Wesley, Reading, 1964.
[16] In *Communicatie & Cognitie*, No. 7, Ghent, 1970.
[17] Ch. Morris, *Signs, Language and Behavior*, Chicago University Press, Chicago, 1964.
[18] S. Eilenberg, *Proceedings of the Conference on Categorical Algebra, La Jolla 1965*, Springer-Verlag, Berlin, 1966.
[19] Sent to the author in MS form, in September 1970.
[20] N. M. Glushkow, *Theorie der Abstrakten Automaten*, V.E.B. Deutscher Verlag der Wissenschaften, Berlin, 1961 (from Russian original).
[21] Peter H. Starke, *Abstrakte Automaten*, Berlin 1969, pp. 1–392; A. Salomaa, *Theory of Automata*, Pergamon Press 1968; S. Ginzburg, *An Introduction to Mathematical Machine Theory*, Addison-Wesley, Reading, 1962.
[22] S. Huzino, 'Theory of Finite Automata', *Mem. Fac. Sec., Kyusyu Univ.* Serie A, **15** (1961), No. 2.
[23] J. T. Medwedjew, quoted in N. M. Glushkow (Russian), *op. cit.*, p. 31.
[24] J. H. Greenberg, (ed.), *Universals of Language*, MIT Press, 1963.
[25] We wish to thank our colleague and friend, Dr Jan Buelens for his help in making this text somewhat more readable. Professor Bar-Hillel's suggestions to that effect are gratefully acknowledged.

NIELS EGMONT CHRISTENSEN

REMARKS ON LOGIC AS UNIVERSAL SEMANTICS

Some, or perhaps all, of those who met in Jerusalem in June 1970 to discuss
the pragmatics of natural languages may have wondered what they, in their
particular capacity, could contribute to this kind of study of language. At
least such wondering is a natural and happy result of the challenge offered
by different approaches to the same subject. The following will contain
reflections stimulated by this challenge to me as a participant in my capacity
as a philosopher.

During the conference I often felt that it was the philosopher who had
the greatest difficulty in showing what he could contribute to our understanding of language, or at any rate the greatest difficulty in getting such a
message across to the others. And for good reasons, indeed. Psychology
and linguistics are respectable empirical sciences, both in fruitful development, and no one will doubt that we are able to understand things better
by their help. Similarly, the amazing development of logic in this and
the previous century is ample proof of the need for logicians. But are
philosophers, who neither use empirical methods nor mathematics, as
do today's logicians, at all in a position to add to our knowledge of
language?

There are two possible answers to this question that we must consider
before trying to give a third and, I hope, more informative one. First, it
could be argued that psychology, linguistics, and logic, like all other
sciences, have their philosophical problems and that these problems are
exactly identical with those within the philosophy of language that are
worthwhile to pursue. But even if there is a considerable amount of truth
in this suggestion, it is not very helpful. It makes the clarification of the
philosopher's task dependent upon a general clarification of the relation
between science and its philosophy, and thus tempts us to answer concrete
and pressing questions by abstract considerations.

Second, it could be said, as a complementary rather than as an alternative
answer to the first one, that there is really no sharp difference between
philosophical and scientific concern with language. So there is no purpose
in trying to delimit the philosopher's task by rigid boundaries. Again there

Yehoshua Bar-Hillel (ed.), Pragmatics of Natural Languages, 35–49. All Rights Reserved.
Copyright © 1971 by D. Reidel Publishing Company, Dordrecht-Holland.

is much truth in this point of view, in particular in so far as we are thinking of the fundamental, conceptual part of science, where it is hard, if not impossible, to tell where science stops and philosophy takes over or vice versa. Still, any form of cooperation of the kind we tried to bring about in Jerusalem will profit from some division of labour; therefore it is not amiss to try to tell, in outline, what, if anything, philosophy and only philosophy might bring to our understanding of language as an answer to our query above. And as always it will be better to give a few examples instead of abstract and programmatic formulations.

In this task I feel greatly helped by some, admittedly tentative, remarks made by Bar-Hillel concerning logic as a kind of universal semantics. It is obvious that the philosopher *qua* philosopher is interested in what will hold for any language and not what holds only for particular languages. Consequently the idea of a universal semantics is bound to make him cock his ears and inquire if there is sufficient foundation for the idea of such a semantics. In view of the difficulty of the matter I shall not try to reach sweeping conclusions; all I want to do is to argue for further investigation of Bar-Hillel's proposal and to defend it against some of the more likely objections. But first let us see how the notions are introduced.

According to Bar-Hillel, the "meaning rules can be separated into two parts: one that is specific for a given language such as English, and one that is universal, holding for all languages, or, rather, is language-independent. That *is as old as* and *is older than* form a quasi-order is, of course, peculiar to the English language, is a rule of specific English semantics; but the fact that, if they do, then *is as old as* is symmetrical, *is older than* is transitive, and so on, has no longer anything to do with English specifically. This implication belongs with 'universal semantics' or 'logic', depending upon the department you belong to."[1] When one comes to the crucial point of specifying the criteria for including some features in universal semantics, we learn that "it might be useful to propose not to treat the terms 'general semantics' and 'universal semantics' as synonyms, but rather to make use of the opportunity and, by fiat, give those terms, *qua* technical terms, different meanings. Whereas, I propose, *general* should be used to denote 'accidental allness', *universal* should be reserved for 'necessary allness'. Whereas generality should therefore allow of degrees and enable us to say that certain linguistic phenomena are more or less general, or that such and such a feature occurs generally in all the Indo-European languages (but perhaps not in Semitic languages), universality would be absolute. A given linguistic feature would be termed universal, rather than just general, not simply because the state of affairs was such and not otherwise, but rather because we would not want to call something a language unless it contained that feature, in other words, if the occurrence of that feature was necessitated by the very meaning of the term 'language'."[2]

Though I have no doubt that such a distinction between 'accidental allness' and 'necessary allness' is called for, it seems to me that we must be more careful in making it. Talking about what is necessary for something to be a language will arouse the suspicion of all empiricists, and not without reason, as Bar-Hillel is himself clearly aware; to overcome their suspicion we shall have to show that there are problems about language that are neither solved by observation nor by calculation, but by reflection, philosophical reflection. Since we are thus at the very heart of the justification of the philosopher's task in regard to language, our analysis cannot stop by saying that we do not want to call something a language if it does not contain this or that feature, right as it may be. For which criteria are we using in such a decision? And is it a decision at all? If we are not able to answer or suggest answers to these questions our position as philosophers is endangered.

It is not impossible, however, that an argument of long standing in philosophy should turn out to be respectable enough to help us out here. Kant's transcendental reasoning has no immediate appeal to the modern mind, but nonetheless it seems that such a kind of argument is what we need here. By a transcendental method Kant understood a method that aimed at establishing the necessary or logical conditions for experience. Applying such a transcendental method to language will mean asking if there are conditions that language has to fulfill, if we are to be able to use it for the purpose of communication in the way we do.

Putting the question in this form immediately suggests that there are such universal conditions and that we are able to formulate at least some of them by application of the transcendental method. How, on the other hand, universality in the sense of 'necessary allness' could be established without the use of some such method is a bit more difficult to comprehend. No one will deny, however, that in using this method we tread on dangerous ground, and that we may easily be tempted to irresponsible use of a powerful argument. But provided we move carefully, we shall see that there are transcendental arguments relating to language, arguments that do not appeal to decisions, purposes, worthwhileness, and the like, but are in a sense definitive.

Since universal semantics is identified with logic, it is to be expected that logic will furnish us with some examples where transcendental arguments may profitably be used. Our expectations are not disappointed. The basic logical principles, the law of contradiction and the law of excluded middle, seem to be formulations of universal conditions for communication by language. Since, however, this statement goes counter to the conventionalistic, instrumentalistic thinking that is *en vogue* in philosophical logic, it will need a little defense.

By the law of contradiction I do not refer to some such law of propositional logic as '$\neg(p \wedge \neg p)$', but to the metalogical principle that a proposition cannot both be true and not true (false), and similarly the law of excluded middle is understood as stating that a proposition is either true or false. Formulated in this way, the semantical character of the two principles is evident, and it is exactly this character on which their universality is founded. So these principles belong to universal semantics if any do.

In order to show this, we have to make use of Tarski's important semantic conception of truth;[3] according to him, for a truth definition to be adequate it must turn out that 'p' is true if and only if p. Tarski rightly observes that such a view of truth is in line with the classical correspondence theory of truth. But if truth essentially consists in a relation between a proposition and a corresponding fact, we should have no difficulty in understanding why a proposition cannot be both true and false and must be one or the other, and why communication will break down if we try to violate these principles.

Let us imagine a person saying that it was both true and false that the train left at 11.15. We should simply not understand what he intended to convey; no information about anything would be communicated by such a strange statement; so it is just as though nothing had been said. It might be worth noting this, in a sense, obvious fact, the more so since contradictions are often banned for the doubtful reason that they are said to imply anything. However, even if we reject this reason, contradictions do not become more attractive for that. Similarly, we should not understand what was meant by saying that it was neither true nor false that the train left at 11.15, for the obvious reason that either there will be a correspondence between that statement and the train leaving at 11.15, or not.

All this is, or should be, commonplace, but in fact is far from being so.

After the appearance of the so-called many-valued logics, due to Łuka-siewicz and others, reasoning like the above is no longer felt to be univer-sally valid, perhaps even worse, it is no longer felt to be respectable. This, however, seems to be due to confusion and the failure to understand the importance of transcendental points of view.

The situation in the philosophy of logic has been compared to the situa-tion in mathematics after the discovery of non-Euclidean geometries; just as these geometries freed us from *a priori* transcendental arguments of the Kantian type, many-valued logics should remind us that any *a priori* validity cannot be claimed for classical two-valued logic. The analogy is thoroughly misleading, however, and for more than one reason.

First, the choice of a geometry, Euclidean or non-Euclidean, is in some sense dependent upon the subject matter to which we want to apply the geometry; it is dependent upon empirical considerations. But in no similar sense are there facts to which we apply logic; at least it is entirely unclear what could be meant by such an empirical application of logic, and there is certainly no unanimity concerning this, even among those who are in-clined to view logic wholly or partly as a descriptive empirical science.

Second, as pointed out by Rescher, "the development of a geometric system is unfettered and free of involvement with presystematic geometric principles, while that of a logical system requires the use of a pre-systematic logic."[4] Consequently there will always be some presystematic logical principles upon which we work out our more articulated logical systems.

Some of the facts that could tempt us to apply a new logic are the facts about the future. And historically it were indeed reflections concerning these facts that prompted Łukasiewicz to work with a three-valued logic. But the explanations he himself gives about this logic are more apt to convince us of the universality of two-valued logic than of the opposite. In asking what the third truth value is he admits that he has no suitable name for it, but nonetheless he maintains "that there are propositions which are neither true nor false but *indeterminate*. All sentences about future facts which are not yet decided belong to this category."[5] The immediate question about this explanation concerns, of course, the meaning of 'decided'. Decided as what? Apparently there can be no other answer but 'as true or false'.

This, however, will not constitute a break with two-valued logic. Cer-tainly it is an important thing to know about a proposition that it is not

known whether it is true or false, but the very formulation of this epistemo-
logical insight seems to contain a warning against introducing this indeterminateness as a truth-value on a par with truth and falsehood.

We can accept this and still acknowledge that the proposition 'it is
indeterminate that p' has a useful purpose. This also holds of 'it is known
to be true that p' and 'it is known to be false that p'. And the meaning relations between propositions with these prefixes and compounds of such
propositions may also be interesting and worthy of a calculus. Similarly
there are relations worth studying between propositions with prefixes such
as 'it is possible that', and 'it is necessary that', and between 'it is obligatory
that', 'it is permitted that', and 'it is forbidden that'.

In this way, many-valued logic, modal logic, and deontic logic are
looked upon as studies of the meaning relations of the relevant notions.
Whether or not we want to call these important studies logics is a verbal
matter, as long as it is quite clear that they are in principle different from a
logic dealing with truth and falsehood. We had a feeling of this difference
from the way Łukasiewicz introduced the third 'truth-value', and it is
possible to give further arguments to this effect. For it holds universally
that, whenever we state that it is indeterminate, obligatory, or necessary
that p, this statement is either true or false, but not both. In other words,
whenever we ascribe a value, modal, deontic, or whatever it may be, to a
proposition, the proposition will either have this value or not, in the
exclusive sense of 'or'. So I propose never to call these values truth-values
and never to use 'truth' and 'falsehood' for any particular value, but to
find more suitable names. It is difficult to see which studies would be
barred by such a terminology. If the proposal is followed, there will be only
one logic based on two truth-values, and this logic will be universal in the
sense that it will be applicable to all propositions, including the propositions of the other 'logics'.

One could argue against my proposal that what I am doing amounts to
presupposing in the metalanguage a two-valued logic and that this is
nothing but a prejudice, due to my upbringing and education. In order
to counter such an argument it must be shown that the two-valuedness of
the metalanguage is no accidental matter, but follows from the fact that
the principles of contradiction and excluded middle are necessary and
universal conditions for communication. The difficulty now is to show this
without presupposing these principles. Since they are universal conditions,
the task is, of course, strictly speaking as impossible as to raise oneself by

one's hair. Nevertheless it seems possible to give some sort of transcendental argument that, without being flatly circular, will make us understand
why these principles are necessary metalinguistic principles.

The curious thing about this argument is that we, as it were, are forced
to move outside language and base the logical principles on facts after all,
but facts of a very peculiar sort. These facts or rather this fact is found in
the very nature of the linguistic sign as a discrete unit. For the purpose of
communication such a sign, owing to its physical character, may be either
produced or not produced. When saying so, we do not presuppose the very
laws we want to 'prove'; we point to an empirical fact, inherent in the use
of a language that consists of discrete signs, and therefore forming a universal condition as long as language has this nature. Since there are only
two possibilities with respect to a sign, either to produce it or not, every
sign in language in a sense divides the world into one part where it applies
and another where it does not.

Since the sign effects such a bipartition of the world, we should not
understand what could be meant by it if we violated the principle of contradiction and said that the sign both applied and did not apply; in an obvious
sense this would destroy or annul the bipartition and thus deprive the sign
of its meaning. So contradictions are from this point of view meaningless.
In a similar way the bipartition universalizes the law of the excluded middle
not only with respect to the sign in question but, since any discrete sign will
effect such a bipartition, with respect to all signs.

Presumably it will help us to understand this if we try to envisage a
language that does not consist of discrete signs or not only of discrete
signs, say, one in which we refer to some continuous concepts, such as
height, by some corresponding continuous variation of whistling, or, to
take a more familiar example, if we imagine the way we can express
differences in richness by varying the intensity of the word 'rich' (in spoken
language) when we say 'he is rich'. For this latter sentence the law of
excluded middle would fail or perhaps rather not apply; it would not be
correct to say that either it was true that he was rich or else it was false;
for richness is capable of varying by degrees, and we express this variation
by varying the intensity of the spoken word 'rich' accordingly. However,
as soon as we try to express the different degrees by ordinary linguistic
signs in some way or another, we shall be reverting to the principle
mentioned above; each time we introduce a sign, either a simple one or a
composite one, to talk about a specific degree of richness, this sign could

be produced or not, and accordingly the specific degree of richness either could be expressed or not.

If we reflect for a moment on this and similar examples, we shall understand also why there can be dissatisfaction with two-valued logic; in a certain sense it is not adequate to the facts, or at least not adequate to all facts. Whenever we come across properties that may vary continuously, such as 'height' or 'richness', we do not match these properties by our discrete signs. Irrespective of the number of signs we introduce to express difference in richness, each such sign will, as a consequence of its physical character, apply or not.

Further, we understand why a metalanguage is essentially two-valued. Since a sign in the object language will apply or not, this will be reflected in the metalanguage and give rise to the universal semantical principle that a proposition is either true or false. Now we may also, of course, talk about linguistic matters such as propositions and say, for instance, that a particular proposition is indeterminate. But since "indeterminate" is obviously a discrete sign, it will apply or not, and two-valued logic accordingly will hold for all propositions concerning indeterminateness. That similar reasoning is possible with respect to all other propositions within many-valued, modal, or deontic logic is too obvious to need demonstration.

The contention that a metalanguage is essentially two-valued is called by Rescher 'entirely erroneous'.[6] And, of course, he is right in holding that in a formal way we may so develop many-valued logic autodescriptively that such a logic serves as its own metalanguage. It is unclear, however, how such a metalanguage could be used for communication. In so far as this metalanguage is a language at all, it must contain propositions, and if we are to understand a particular proposition, we must either take it to be true or false, or be told that it has another value; if the latter alternative shall be informative, it must have this value or not, and we are again in a two-valued framework.

Another question is if it is possible to apply our reasoning above with respect to 'true' in the sense that either it is true or not that a proposition is true. Of course it is, but what is interesting here is rather another matter. Since the dichotomy of true and false merely reflects in the metalanguage an essential property of the object language, 'true' and 'false' are, as noted by Ramsey,[7] eliminable with respect to particular propositions; that 'p' is true is equivalent simply to p. In contrast to this it is worth noting that if we say that a proposition is indeterminate, possible or obligatory, such a classification is never eliminable. This remarkable distinction between the truth-value 'truth' and other values is another reminder of their basic difference and the unique position of two-valued logic.

Taking for a moment the historical point of view, it is interesting to remember the old saying of logical empiricism that logic contained linguistic and not factual truths. If our reasoning above is correct, the principles of contradiction and excluded middle are truths based not on facts (the facts may even be in a certain contrast to them), but on language, on the way we talk. This way of talking, however, is no arbitrary convention; it follows from the fact that we, in order to express our meaning, use discrete signs that we either produce or not.

Having now tried to show how by philosophical, transcendental reasoning we can argue in favour of at least some universal semantical principles, the next question will be if we can extend our argument to cover other principles as well. And so it seems, with due and proper attention to the dangers inherent in transcendental reasoning. Thus it is a universal condition for communication that we know where and when our signs apply, in simpler words, what we are talking about. Strawson[8] has made important contributions to the formulation of these conditions, though one need not agree with all his points.

The conditions we have dealt with so far are truly universal in the sense that they will hold for anything we should want to call a language. Some of the examples Bar-Hillel mentions in the quotation above do not seem to be universal in quite that sense. For instance, it is not evident that we should refuse to use the term 'language' for a communication system in which one could not express the concepts *is as old as* and *is older than*. On the other hand, it is clear enough that if they form a quasi-order, the fact that *is as old as* is symmetrical and *is older than* transitive is not an English fact, but a necessary universal truth.

It seems to be an open problem, however, if a transcendental argument could be of use in establishing such a truth. Though we may not have the slightest doubt about it, it is not so easy to tell exactly how we shall proceed when challenged by a sceptic here. Can we refute him without admitting that there are necessary conceptual relations, that if *is as old as* and *is older than* did not behave as in our universal semantics, they were simply concepts different from the ones we usually express by these words? I, for one, would not suffer sleepless nights by such an admission, but in view of its importance we should perhaps be frank about it.

At any rate we are on safer ground, or so it seems to me at least, when we claim universality for two-valued logic. Nonetheless this claim will probably seem appalling to many and it is not hard to understand why. Logic has in this century developed into a study of formal systems of great variety and the really interesting results are due to concentration on such formal systems and their properties. But something has been lost on the way, as has repeatedly been pointed out by Black and Bar-Hillel,[9] among others. It is as if the preoccupation with different formal systems has led to a certain loss of interest in the problem of application, or at least to a very conventionalistic view of this problem: any system will be more or less artificial, so we simply choose the one most convenient for the purpose at hand.

It has not been an obstacle to this view that the usual truth-functional bivalent logic is in itself a highly artificial system, perfect from the formal point of view, but hardly a logic in the sense that it covers the reasoning we use in daily life or in mathematics for that matter. In order to cause a little uneasiness, if possible, among logicians, I shall try briefly to argue this case. Should the result be renewed interest in matters concerning the application of logic, it will be worth the attempt.

Whatever view we take of logic, it must be systematic and general; whether our logic is nothing but a few rules about valid inferences or a full-fledged formal calculus, the rules or the calculus must be applicable in a general way to particular instances. So if we develop a logical formalism, there must be some rules that bring this formalism to bear upon examples of actual reasoning in mathematics or daily life or both if possible. Otherwise the formalism could not be called a logic in the traditional sense, though it may be interesting and worthwhile from many other points of view.

Presumably such a demand for rules of correspondence between the formal logic machinery and the language we use in reasoning and inferring will also be considered a reasonable demand by most logicians. They will only insist, and rightly so, that we cannot expect any one-to-one correspondence between a systematic logical formalism and unsystematic language in its full richness. So if logic is to be a science, it will have to make idealizations and leave out something, like all other sciences. Still, these idealizations must conform to the idea of generality; if logic fails in its application, we cannot make do with ad hoc explanations for that particular case. Exactly at this point mathematical logic as we now know it seems to be in trouble.

These troubles are an immediate consequence of the truth-functional character of the usual propositional logic. But since this truth-functionality is an essential feature of that logic, we are in trouble provided I am right. Most of us have been taught that in logic we regard 'or' and 'if-then' as truth-functional connectives, or perhaps rather regard '∨' and '⇒' as truth-functional connectives that correspond more or less to 'or' and 'if-then', which we, for the purpose of their logic, may regard as truth-functional connectives.

In itself this is a very respectable view. By our formalism we should not strive to catch the full meaning of the propositional connectives, but only what is necessary for their logical content. So if the truth-functional sense is sufficient for this, no better defence of a truth-functional '∨' and '⇒' could ever be given. The question is only whether they are sufficient or, after all, too weak to do the job. I shall argue in favour of the latter alternative by showing that from the very weakness of the truth functional '∨' and '⇒', it follows that mathematical logic is, in a sense, both inferentially insufficient and, what is worse, inferentially harmful in leading from truth to falsehood.

Some of the inferences we want to be covered by our logic are the obviously valid so-called hypothetical and disjunctive syllogisms. The usual opinion is that they are covered by the tautologies $(p \wedge (p \Rightarrow q)) \Rightarrow q$', '$(\neg q \wedge (p \Rightarrow q)) \Rightarrow \neg p$', '$(\neg p \wedge (p \vee q)) \Rightarrow q$' and '$(p \wedge (p \veebar q)) \Rightarrow \neg q$' that enable us to justify the corresponding inferences. But if we take a look at, say, the first disjunctive inference in a natural setting, a curious thing appears. We conclude from two premisses to a conclusion:

$$\frac{\begin{array}{c} A \vee B \\ \neg A \end{array}}{B}$$

If we are not permitted to put more sense into '∨' than the truth-functional, we are unable to understand how we can add to '$A \vee B$' another premiss and deduce something interesting by its help. For if '∨' is truth-functional, '$A \vee B$' says nothing more than that 'A' is true and 'B' is false or, alternatively, that 'A' is false and 'B' is true, or (being non-exclusive) that 'A' is true and 'B' is true. It does not say – a fact that is well worth noting – that if the first alternative did not hold then the second would, for this would establish a connection between 'A' and 'B' that is foreign to the truth-functional '∨'. But if this is so, the role of the second premiss in the inference is difficult to understand. If the first alternative holds, 'A' true and 'B' false, the second premiss is inconsistent with the first. If, on the other hand, the second alternative is the case, 'A' false and 'B' true, the second premiss is superfluous, and if the third alternative holds, 'A' true and 'B' true, the second premiss is both inconsistent with the first and superfluous.

Since this argument may have an air of hocus-pocus, let me explain in passing how another sense of the non-exclusive 'or' that is altogether different from the truth-functional one does not run into the same difficulties. If by '$A \lor B$' is meant that it is excluded that both components are false, whereas it may be that the first is true and the second false, or the first false and the second true, or both true, we understand easily how this will function in a deduction. For if we add to this that '$\neg A$' is true, it is clear that we can deduce 'B'. The information in the second premiss excludes two of the three truth-possibilities for '$A \lor B$' and thus leaves only one, and this determines the truth-value 'true' for 'B'.

This is not to say, however, that '$(\neg p \land (p \lor q)) \Rightarrow q$' with a truth-functional '$\lor$' is false but rather that the disjunctive inference depends upon a stronger sense of '$\lor$' than the truth-functional one; but since the just-mentioned propositional schema is valid and contains all elements in the inference in their proper order, one may well ask if truth-functional logic has not just done what is required of logic, namely, to leave out meaning in order to preserve only what is necessary for inference. This is a rather strong counterargument since all we can say is that by a truth-functional '$\lor$' we do not understand how the premisses are equally necessary for deduction. That a '$\Rightarrow$' and '$\mathbb{W}$' will leave us in similar doubt about the other inferences mentioned can, of course, be shown by arguments analogous to the one above.

What these arguments, however, may lack in ultimate force, they regain if we combine them with arguments to the effect that '$\lor$', '$\Rightarrow$' as truth-functional connectives may lead from truth to falsehood, a rather unhappy consequence of an alleged logic. We are able to perform such a combination, since we base our reasoning upon the admitted weakness of the truth-functional connectives. For if we negate something that is too weak, we are bound to end up with something too strong, and this is exactly what happens.

Let us imagine that we hold, for instance, that if it will be raining tomorrow, it will also be blowing, and someone wants to take issue with us and deny this by saying 'no'. Using the truth-functional conditional here, we arrive, by negation, at the statement that it will in fact be raining tomorrow but not blowing, since '$\neg(p \Rightarrow q)$' is truth-functionally equivalent to '$p \wedge \neg q$'. Clearly the man saying 'no' will not be wrong if it so happens, but he is by his negation definitely not committed to this inference. It may perfectly well not be raining, and yet incorrect to say that if it were raining, it would also be blowing, for the simple reason that such a connection between rain and wind does not exist. So we have here an unambiguous instance where we may, by mathematical logic, deduce a falsehood from a truth. For it could be true that it is not the case that if it is raining, it is also blowing, but false that it is raining.[10] The example was one drawn from colloquial language, but apparently similar ones could be found wherever we use 'if-then' to express some connection and we deny the existence of such a connection. For instance, in mathematics we may express a deductive connection between A and B, based on a purported proof, by saying 'if A then B'. Someone who has found the flaws in this 'proof' may deny the connection without thereby committing himself to 'A and not B'.

We cannot get around this difficulty in the way so many other objections against mathematical logic are countered, viz. by urging the truth-functional character of the connectives in question and explaining the divergences from ordinary language as due to the particular truth-functional sense. For 'and' is used truth-functionally not only in logic but also in ordinary language; so there is no special sense to help us out here. There are, however, a number of other likely objections we must deal with.

First, it could be said that no one in his right mind would apply logic as we have done; so it is only a foolish application of logic that has led us from truth to falsehood and there is no need to blame logic itself. To be sure, the inference will not occur, but it seems that the only thing which prevents it is some prelogical intuitive notion of what counts as a logical inference and what not. And if it is such prelogical intuitions that prevent misapplication of a formalism, one may well wonder in what sense the formalism is a *general* systematization of inferences. We must do better than just say that we use our formalism if we go right and do not use it when we go wrong.

A more serious attempt at getting round the difficulty would be to show how exactly we have misapplied the formalism and how, in general, examples such as those above should be handled. One could argue, for instance, that propositional logic was incapable of covering them and that we need other means; we could not do justice to these particular examples in propositional logic, but have to use predicate logic or some other stronger logic.

This may well be so, but it leaves us with a problem concerning the truth-functional 'v' and '⇒'. Which natural 'or's and 'if-then's do they cover? Logic is in an unsatisfactory state, if we cannot answer this better than by repeating as above: those where we do not go wrong. Also it seems to be too casuistic to say that '⇒' covers the connective we use expressing a conditional from which we infer hypothetically, and afterwards refuse to let the very same arrow cover the very same conditional, since now we are denying this conditional. At least we have to produce arguments better than that we are just not willing to accept the logical consequences of such a denial. Without some rules, and general rules, concerning the application of 'v' and '⇒', and all other signs in the formalism, our logic remains in our intuitions.

One could try to argue, of course, that denying a conditional is not a truth-functional operation and that the difficulties stem from this mistake. In this way one might keep the conditional as truth-functional to be covered by '⇒'. Though negation may not be truth-functional, I do not think this is a correct diagnosis, but I shall refrain from arguing so here and merely point out that the difficulties for propositional logic are not allevi-ated by such a hypothesis. For evidently negation is truth-functional all right in the usual logic systems, so a revision of logic would be necessary anyhow.

A revision would be necessary provided that the reasoning above is sound and that logic is necessarily truth-functional. The last provision is inescapable, however. Tautological schemas such as '$p \Rightarrow (p \lor q)$', '$p \Rightarrow (q \Rightarrow p)$', and $p \Rightarrow (\neg p \Rightarrow q)$' force us to a truth-functional interpreta-tion of 'v' and '⇒'. This will be evident from an investigation of their meaning; the first one allows us to move deductively, under preservation of truth, from a truth to the same truth to which we adjoin any proposition whatever. If this adjoinment is taken to be disjunction, it follows that a dis-junction will be true as soon as one component is true, and this is, in fact, the definition of truth-functional disjunction. A similar 'proof' of the necessarily truth-functional character of '⇒' is possible by use of the two other schemas above.

So either these schemas, and a number of others, will have to go, or the argumentation in the latter part of my paper must be shown to be wrong.

If there is, on the other hand, some truth in it, it is no wonder that Bar-Hillel's ideas about logic as universal semantics have not won immediate universal consent; for if logic shall be universal, this logic has not as yet made its way into the abundant textbooks of modern logic.

Det Filosofiske Institut – Aarhus Universitet

NOTES

1 *Aspects of Language*, Jerusalem 1970, pp. 187–8.
2 *Op. cit.*, p. 190.
3 Non-technically expounded in his 'The Semantic Conception of Truth', *Philosophy and Phenomenological Research*, Vol. IV, 1944, a paper reprinted in various collections.
4 *Many-Valued Logic*, New York 1969, p. 219.
5 'On Determinism', in Jan Łukasiewicz, *Selected Works*, Amsterdam 1970, p. 126.
6 *Op. cit.*, p. 229.
7 *The Foundations of Mathematics*, London 1927, p. 143.
8 Mainly in his *Individuals*, London 1959.
9 Black convincingly in his 'Logic and Ordinary Language', *Contemporary Philosophic Thought: The International Philosophy Year Conferences at Brockport*, New York 1970, and Bar-Hillel in 'Argumentation in Natural Language', *op. cit.*, pp. 202–5.
10 A longer and detailed version *Truth Functions or Not* is planned for publication.
11 Benson Mates has a similar example, though apparently he is not seriously troubled by it. See his *Elementary Logic*, London 1965, p. 76.

L. JONATHAN COHEN

SOME REMARKS ON GRICE'S VIEWS ABOUT THE LOGICAL PARTICLES OF NATURAL LANGUAGE

In the earlier part of a stimulating series of William James Lectures at Harvard in 1968 Professor H. P. Grice drew the attention of the philosophical public[1] to a most intriguing hypothesis about the familiar logical particles of natural language 'not', 'and', 'if ... then ...', and 'either ... or ...'. I shall henceforth call this the Conversationalist Hypothesis. What it asserts is that those particles do not diverge in meaning, or linguistic function, from the formal-logical symbols, '~', '&', '→', and 'v' respectively, as standardly interpreted by two-valued truth-tables, and that wherever they appear to diverge from truth-functionality the appearance is due to the various standing presumptions with which natural language utterances are understood. On the whole Grice argued in favour of this hypothesis, though he confessed to having no answer to one particular objection to it. I shall argue in this paper that the objection to which Grice refers is not, *pace* Grice, a serious one, but that there are good reasons for preferring an alternative account, which I shall call the Semantical Hypothesis, to the Conversationalist Hypothesis. According to the Semantical Hypothesis many occurrences of these particles do differ in significance from their formal-logical counterparts and many do not, and both kinds of occurrence are best explained within the bounds of an adequate semantical theory for natural languages and without recourse to a theory of conversational presumptions.

Grice in fact also included such expressions as 'all', 'some', and 'the' within the scope of the hypothesis that he was supporting. But he offered no arguments about these expressions. So, like him, I shall confine my remarks on the subject to the level of propositional logic. The question of quantification-theoretic idiom is also an interesting one, but it can be left for another occasion.

No doubt philosophers have sometimes mistakenly attributed to the meaning of a word or the analysis of a concept some feature that is more correctly regarded as a condition for the appropriateness of certain utterances involving that word or concept. Such philosophers have been struck, for example, by the oddity of discussing whether or not an action is

Yehoshua Bar-Hillel (ed.), Pragmatics of Natural Languages, 50–68.

voluntary when the action itself is a perfectly satisfactory one; and then they have mistakenly traced this oddity to the meaning of the word 'voluntary' instead of to the conditions for there being some point in remarking of a (voluntary) act that it was voluntary. No doubt there are a number of philosophical errors than can thus be corrected by paying a proper regard to the presumptions of normal conversation. But it is also possible for the pendulum to swing too far in this direction. What is better accounted a feature of linguistic meaning may sometimes be put down to conversational presumptions. This, I shall argue, is what the Conversationalist Hypothesis does in regard to the logical particles of natural language.

One can easily see why the Conversationalist Hypothesis is so tempting. If there are divergences of meaning between 'not', 'and', 'if ... then ...', and 'either ... or ...', on the one hand, and their familiar formal-logical counterparts, on the other, the task of representing the logic of natural language becomes more complicated. If this representation is to be accomplished within a formal theory one or other of two things has to be done.

On one alternative some tailor-made non-truth-functional system has to be constructed with temporal connectives, intensional conditionals, and so on. But at best such a system achieves fidelity of representation in a certain area of language only at the cost of sacrificing conceptual economy and computational facility. More commonly the system throws up its own, more subtle, divergences from natural language.

On the other alternative, the formal theory is offered as a reconstruction, rather than as a description or replication of natural language, and divergences are explained away as being unimportant for logical purposes. For example, if 'if ... then ...' is always reconstructed as the truthfunctional '... → ...', most intuitively valid patterns of deductive inference that involve conditional statements, like modus ponens, can be reproduced, and no inference from true premises to false conclusions will ever be validated. But then the system also throws up inferences that seem to have no counterparts in natural language, like that from 'q' to '$p \to q$'.

To avoid either alternative, and thus escape through the horns of the dilemma, one has to surrender altogether the search for a formal representation and be content with informal descriptions of ordinary usage. But this is to sacrifice all the rigour of treatment, and opportunities for insight, that formal systematisation can provide. No wonder, then, that the Conversationalist Hypothesis should be so tempting. All these difficulties loom over us as a result of our assuming that 'not', 'and', etc. commonly differ in meaning from their familiar formal-logical counterparts. If that assumption could be safely abandoned, the classical truthfunctional systems of Frege and Russell would afford an accurate and economical representation of the fundamental features of the logic of natural language.

Unfortunately, however, tempting though the Conversationalist Hypothesis may be, there are good reasons for rejecting it in favour of the Semantical Hypothesis. I shall discuss each of the four main particles in turn.

I. NOT

According to the usual two-valued truth-table definition of '$\sim$', '$\sim p$' is false whenever 'p' is true. But there are several dialects or natural languages in which 'not', or its counterparts, do not behave in this way. In several London dialects of English, for example,

(1)   You won't get no beer here

is an emphatic reformulation, not a negation, of

(2)   You'll get no beer here.

I.e., in these dialects (1) is true, not false, when (2) is true. Similar emphatic uses of the negative particle occur in Italian (e.g., 'Non fa niente'), in Spanish and in Homeric and classical Attic Greek.[2] How could the Conversationalist Hypothesis be defended against such *prima facie* counter-examples? One possible move would be to say that the Hypothesis is not to be construed as making a claim about natural language in general but only about some dialects of some natural languages, e.g., Standard English. But not only is this not how Grice apparently envisaged the hypothesis that he was discussing. It also substantially weakens the claim that is made. The claim now is that some natural languages or dialects are fundamentally truth-functional, rather than that all are. Instead of purporting to express a general truth about the logic of natural language, it now does no more than describe an idiosyncrasy of vocabulary that is allegedly present in some languages and absent in others.

Another possible move would be to say that the Conversationalist Hypothesis is to be construed as making a claim not about the negative particle 'not', and its counterparts in other languages, but rather about the phrase 'it is not the case that' and its equivalents. It may well be that those phrases do conform to the usual truth-table definition of the formal-logical constant ' ∼ '. However, this is again not how Grice himself apparently envisaged the hypothesis that he was discussing. And in any case the claim made is substantially weakened. It applies only to certain phrases in which 'not' occurs rather than to that word in general.

So perhaps a third possible defence would be offered, viz., that the apparent equivalence between (1) and (2) is not an equivalence of sentential meaning, but an equivalence in force of utterance, due to the bearing of conversational presumptions on our assertions. Now, Grice held that, *ceteris paribus*, participants in a conversation will be expected to observe a general principle that runs roughly as follows: "Make your conversational contribution such as is required, at the stage at which it occurs, by the accepted purpose or direction of the talk-exchange in which you are engaged." Several more specific maxims, on Grice's view, will yield results more or less in accordance with this general principle, e.g., ' Make your contribution as informative as is required', 'Don't say what you believe to be false', 'Don't say what you lack evidence for', 'Be relevant', 'Avoid obscurity, ambiguity or unnecessary prolixity', and 'Be orderly'. It is conceivable therefore that in every case in which, in some dialect or other, someone utters a double negative as in (1) with the purport of a single negative like (2), the speaker should be construed to be speaking ironically. That is, we have to presume his obedience to the maxim 'Don't say what you believe to be false', and should therefore infer, from the obvious falsehood of what he says if taken literally, that he must be speaking ironically. There is an implicature, as Grice calls it now,[3] of irony: i.e., one has to assume irony in order to maintain the supposition that the cooperative principle and maxims are being observed. If this were the case, the negative particle in (1) would have its usual meaning, in accordance with the truth-table definition of ' ∼ ', and the equivalence between (1) and (2) would not be an equivalence of sentential meaning, but the kind of equivalence that exists between an ironical utterance of 'He's a fine person to trust' and a non-ironical utterance of 'He's a bad person to trust'.

But the defence of irony will not work here. First, it doesn't fit the facts. It assumes a quite incredibly wide prevalence of ironical speech. Indeed it implies the use of irony on very many occasions on which the hearer has no reason to believe that in its literal meaning what the speaker says is false, and therefore no adequate reason to believe that he is talking ironically. Secondly, the defence of irony will be even less plausible when the emphatic double negative occurs in a subordinate clause, as in the antecedent of a conditional or in indirect speech. Compare, e.g.,

> If I won't get no beer here, I'll have a cider instead

or

> They've tried to fix it so you won't get no beer here.

But, if irony is not at work here, it is very difficult indeed to see in what other way conversational presumptions could lead to the equivalence of uttering (1) with uttering (2) when 'not' is purely truth-functional. Indeed it looks as though this equivalence stems from an equivalence of sentential meaning between (1) and (2).

II. AND

Perhaps it will be said that at least Grice's own dialect is one in which 'not' always functions in accordance with the truth-table definition of '~', and never just adds emphasis to another negative. But what about 'and'? Let us look at some of the data.

Two facts seem incontestable. On the one hand, in some cases the utterance of two sentences conjoined by 'and' asserts more than just the truth of both statements. For example, there is an important difference between what is implied by an assertion, *tout court*, of the sentence

(3)   A republic has been declared and the old king has died of a heart attack

and what is implied by an assertion, *tout court*, of the sentence

(4)   The old king has died of a heart attack and a republic has been declared.

The order of events implied by an assertion of (3) is the converse of that implied by an assertion of (4). On the other hand, in some cases the assertion of two sentences conjoined by 'and' implies no more than the truth of both statements, as in

(5)   The old king has died of a heart attack and a republic has been declared, but I don't know which of these two events preceded the other nor do I wish to suggest some connection tends to exist between two such events.

In these latter cases every bit of additional information that might have been conveyed by the utterance of 'and' is somehow cancelled or deleted. (Compare too the patent truth-functionality of 'It is the case that . . ., and it is the case that . . .'.)

But, though both facts seem incontestable, their interpretation is highly controversial.

According to the Conversationalist Hypothesis, which Grice favours, the meaning or linguistic function of 'and', even in (3) and (4), is just the same as that of the truth-functional constant '&', and the implication of temporal sequence that is conveyed by uttering (3) or (4) derives from a presumption that people's discourse obeys the maxim 'Be orderly'. This presumption may be rebutted, as in (5), and then no sequence or connection will be implied (or implicated, as Grice calls it). But when the presumption is not rebutted, it will always operate, as in isolated assertions of (3) or (4).

According to the Semantical Hypothesis, however, the meaning or linguistic function of 'and', as a clause-concatenating particle, is rather richer than that of the truth-functional constant '&'. In addition to expressing the conjunction of two truths it also indicates that the second truth to be mentioned is a further item of the same kind, or in the same sequence, or of a kind belonging to the same set of commonly associated kinds of item, or etc. etc., as the first truth to be mentioned. Hence an implication of temporal sequence arises in cases like (3) or (4), or of connectedness in cases like

(6)   Tom has a typewriter and he types all his own letters.

But this additional feature in the meaning of 'and' and of its equivalents in other languages is subject to cancellation or deletion in certain contexts, as in (5). I.e., according to the Semantical Hypothesis what is cancelled is a feature that is one of those features which should be listed in any adequate dictionary entry for the word, whereas according to the Conversationalist Hypothesis what is cancelled is a presumption of human discourse in general – a presumption that it would be out of place to state in the description of any particular natural language.

Now how are we to choose between these two quite different theories about the correct interpretation of utterances asserting sentences like (3), (4), or (5)?

Note first that neither theory has any advantage over the other in respect of lexicographical simplicity. At times Grice seems to suggest that anyone who opposes the Conversationalist Hypothesis about 'and', 'if . . . then . . .', etc. must be prepared to accept at least two dictionary meanings for such logical particles – a stronger meaning that is not purely truth-functional and a weaker meaning that is. But such a suggestion would be incorrect. The Semantical Hypothesis accords just as well as the Conversationalist Hypothesis with Grice's excellent recommendation not to multiply senses beyond necessity. Both assign only one dictionary sense to 'and', as a word in the language. But the one theory assigns a weaker sense to the word and fills out this analysis by invoking a deletable conversational implicature of orderliness, while the other theory assigns a stronger sense to the word and allows a certain feature of this sense to be deleted on occasion, in the process of composing the meaning of a compound sentence out of the meanings of its constituent words and clauses.

Moreover, while the two theories disagree about the nature of the deletion or cancellation that has to be imputed to assertions of (5), each type of deletion is certainly realized in some other, relatively uncontroversial cases. For example, if Professor X is asked his opinion of Professor Y's abilities and replies

(7)   He is a very competent bicyclist,

he implicates, without its being part of his sentence's meaning, that Professor Y is not so competent in academic matters; and this implicature would be cancelled or deleted if Professor X added

(8)   But I do not wish to suggest that he is not also very competent at his work.

On the other hand, the statement

That is a flower

implies, in virtue of the meaning of the word 'flower', that the object in question forms or formed a part of a plant; and this implication is cancelled or deleted if the word 'plastic' is put before 'flower'. In that respect the phrases 'stone lion', 'well-painted hand', 'sub-vocal speech', etc. are all rather similar: in each case part of the normal meaning of the noun is cancelled or deleted by the adjacent adjective.[4] Dictionaries do not need to list both a strong sense of 'flower', in which we speak of flowers as growing, and a weak sense in which we speak of 'artificial flowers', 'plastic flowers', or 'toy flowers'; and similarly the Semantical Hypothesis does not need to suppose both a strong and a weak sense for 'and'. In other words, while we can regard the Conversationalist Hypothesis as assimilating the interpretation of (5) to the paradigm of (7) + (8), we can regard the Semantical Hypothesis as assimilating it to the paradigm of

> That is a plastic flower.

Is there any reason for preferring one pattern of assimilation to the other? A marginal advantage seems to be gained by the Conversationalist Hypothesis because it treats locutions like 'I do not wish to suggest that . . .' as accomplishing the same type of deletion or cancellation in both (5) and (7) + (8). However, the assumption of this argument is that similar expressions should perform similar roles and on that assumption there is an argument of about equal strength for the Semantical Hypothesis. The particle 'but' obviously has an adversative, and not merely conjunctive, function in such sentences as

> Tom has a typewriter but he prefers to write all his letters.

So, by analogy, it seems reasonable to suppose that the particle 'and' has a connexive, and not merely conjunctive, function in (6). Indeed the temptation to treat 'and' as being like 'but' in this respect (i.e., in being not merely conjunctive) becomes stronger when we consider cases like

> Tom picked up a stone, and threw it, but missed the tree, and hit a window, but the window did not break, and Tom's father was not angry,

where connection seems to alternate with opposition. It seems a little strained to suppose that in uttering such a sentence the connection conveyed by each utterance of 'and' is a consequence of conversational maxims while the opposition conveyed by each utterance of 'but' is a consequence of linguistic function. However, though it is a little strained to suppose this, it is not very difficult, just as it is also not very difficult to suppose that locutions like 'I do not wish to suggest that . . .' accomplish different kinds of deletion in (5) and (7) + (8), respectively. So this line of reasoning does not seem to be conclusive in either direction.

But there is at least one type of 'and'-occurrence that the Conversationalist Hypothesis can hardly be stretched to fit at all. This is where 'and' occurs in the antecedent of a conditional and the truth of the statement made by asserting the conditional depends on the precise sequence of events suggested by this occurrence of 'and'. Consider, for example,

(9)   If the old king has died of a heart attack and a republic has been declared, then Tom will be quite content

where Tom might not be at all content if a republic had been declared first and then the old king died of a heart attack.[5] Of course, it would be open to Grice to extend or adapt his theory of implicatures in such a way that anyone who asserts a conditional like (9) would normally implicate that the truth of the conditional as a whole is partly dependent on a condition of temporal sequence that is conveyed, in virtue of conversational presumptions, by the utterance of the antecedent. But this would hardly be consistent with the claim made by the Conversationalist Hypothesis, which Grice supports, that 'if ... then ...' has just the same purely truth-functional meaning as the standard formal-logical connective '→'. For, if the truth of (9) as a whole is just a function of the truth-values of its antecedent and consequent, and if 'and' is purely truth-functional, so that the truth-value of (9)'s antecedent is just a function of the truth-values of its constituent conjuncts, it follows that the truth of (9) cannot depend at all on any condition of temporal sequence that may be conveyed, in virtue of conversational presumptions, by the utterance of the antecedent. That is, the truth-functionality of 'and' in cases like (9) could only be maintained at the cost of sacrificing the truth-functionality of 'if ... then ...' (and accepting a good deal of extra complexity into the theory of implicatures). Hence, so far as the purpose of maintaining the truth-functionality of 'and' is to defend the Conversationalist Hypothesis, there seems to be no point in maintaining it: the Conversationalist Hypothesis seems incapable of being defended in this way.

Perhaps it will be claimed instead that utterance of (9) implicates the order of the conjoined clauses in the antecedent to be somehow essential to the relevance of one part of the indirect evidence for (9). (By 'indirect evidence', for a conditional, is meant evidence other than the truth-values of the conditional's antecedent and consequent.) But that would amount to claiming that an assertion of (9) implicates the existence of more indirect evidence for its truth than is necessary on a purely truth-functional account of the meaning of 'and'. It would be as if to say that the truth-functionality of 'if ... then ...' can only be maintained at the cost of sacrificing the truth-functionality of 'and'. The Conversationalist Hypothesis has again to be rejected.

III. IF . . . THEN

Grice suggested, in his Lectures, that there are some cases in which 'if . . . then . . .' quite obviously does not diverge in linguistic function from the standard formal-logical connective '→', other cases in which it may seem to diverge but can be shown not to, and yet other cases in which it seems to diverge and he, Grice, does not see how to show that it does not. Let us consider these cases in turn, as data to be taken into account in making a rational choice between the Conversationalist and Semantical Hypotheses. It should be borne in mind that on Grice's view, i.e., according to the Conversationalist Hypothesis, the assertion of an 'if . . . then . . .' sentence, while truth-functional in linguistic meaning, commonly carries with it a (cancellable) implicature that there is indirect, i.e., non-truth-functional, evidence for its truth. I suppose that this is because of the maxims requiring a speaker to have evidence and forbidding him unnecessary prolixity: e.g., if his only evidence for 'if p, then q' were the fact stated by 'q', he would do better to say just 'q'. On the other hand, according to the Semantical Hypothesis, a dictionary entry for the particles 'if . . . then . . .' should state that they indicate a connection between antecedent and consequent as well as performing the purely truth-functional role of ruling out the conjunction of the antecedent's truth with the consequent's falsehood, though the Hypothesis is quite consistent with finding certain occurrences of these particles where the context is such as to delete the connexive aspect of their dictionary meaning, analogously to 'and' in (5).

First, then, let us consider the cases in which 'if . . . then . . .', on Grice's view, quite obviously does not diverge from '→'. These are, on his view, the cases in which the alleged implicature of there being indirect evidence for the conditional is cancelled by the linguistic or environmental context of utterance.

Suppose, for example, two partners announced at the beginning of a game of bridge a special Five No Trumps Convention, whereby a call of 'Five no trumps' signified the statement

(10)   If I have the king of hearts, I also have a black king

as well as the usual undertaking to make five no trumps if there is no over-bid. Grice claimed that, on such an occasion, not only would (10) be

patently truth-functional, but also its utterance would not convey the usual
suggestion made by a conditional statement that there is some reason for
believing it other than knowledge of the truth-values of its antecedent and
consequent clauses. However, the trouble with this example is that the
speaker, by uttering the call 'Five no trumps', does give the other players an
indirect reason to believe in the truth of (10), as a statement in which 'I'
refers to himself. Even if what he said to the others was actually (10) instead of 'Five no trumps', he would still be giving them thereby an indirect
reason to believe in its truth. The only kind of utterance of (10) at the
bridge table that would not count as an indirect reason to believe in its
truth would be if a player said (10) silently to himself. But this he would
hardly be likely to do. So even if we grant to Grice that his indirect-evidence
implicature is normally cancelled when sentences like (10) are at issue,
that is not because the utterer of such a sentence does not convey clearly
enough to his hearers the existence of indirect evidence for the truth of his
assertion, but rather because he conveys this altogether too clearly: his
very utterance constitutes the evidence. Nevertheless, an assertion of (10),
in the specified circumstances, does seem patently truth-functional, when
contrasted with an assertion of, say

> If I have the king of hearts, I am lucky.

But this is not because there is no suggestion of indirect evidence, since
there is such a suggestion. Rather, it is because there is no suggestion of a
connection between antecedent and consequent. Hence the Semantical
Hypothesis fits such cases perfectly well. We simply have to suppose that
the connexive aspect of the linguistic meaning of 'if . . . then . . .' is deleted
or cancelled by the context of utterance. It is rather like pointing to something in the corner of an oil-painting and saying

> (11)   There's a hand.

The context of such an utterance of (11) would make it perfectly clear that
'hand' here did not mean flesh and blood.

Just the same is true of another example of Grice's – the kind of logical
puzzle in which you are given the names of a number of persons in a room,
their professions, and their current occupations, and a few clues as to
how these fit together, and then you have to determine which person belongs to which profession and is currently occupied in what. For example,
a sentence like

> (12)   If Mr. Tailor is a cobbler, Mr. Baker is currently gardening

may be given as a clue. But the very giving of it as a clue is a perfectly adequate indirect reason to believe in the truth of the statement it makes about the puzzle situation. At the same time the nature of the puzzle context is such as to delete or cancel the connexive aspect of the meaning of 'if . . . then . . .', if the Semantical Hypothesis is correct.

Similarly, if we consider a case in which according to Grice the implicature of indirect evidence is explicitly cancelled by the linguistic context of utterance, we shall see that the Semantical Hypothesis again fits perfectly well. Suppose someone says

(13)   I know just where Smith is and what he is doing, but all I will tell you is that if he is in the library he is working.

Grice's view seems to have been that by uttering the clause

(14)   I know just where Smith is and what he is doing

the speaker cancels the usual implicature that there is indirect evidence for the truth of the conditional

(15)   If Smith is in the library he is working.

But whatever happens to the implicature, according to Grice's theory, it is certainly true that by uttering (14) along with (15) a speaker would create indirect evidence for (15). And in any case, if the utterance of (14) deletes the assertion of a connection when (15) is uttered (and I am not sure that this deletion will always occur when (13) is uttered), this deletion can be explained in the usual way by the Semantical Hypothesis.

Thus far I have been agreeing with Grice that the assertion of certain conditional sentences may sometimes be wholly truth-functional in meaning, while arguing that the Semantical Hypothesis can cover all such cases. In this respect I class two other examples of Grice's along with (10), (12), and (13), viz.,

> If England win the first Test, they will win the series, you mark my words

and

> Perhaps if he comes he will be in a good mood.

Grice also cited two further sentences where he thought the implicature of indirect evidence would be either absent or cancelled and the assertion of the conditional would be purely truth-functional in character, viz.,

(16)   See that, if he comes, he gets his money

and

(17)   If he was surprised, he didn't show it.

But (16) and (17) are even worse evidence for the Conversationalist Hypothesis than (10), (12), or (13), because neither would commonly involve a purely truth-functional conditional. If the conditional in (16) were purely truth-functional, the instruction expressed by (16) as a whole would be fulfilled by seeing that the man got his money even if he did not come. But the employer who uttered (16), and thus told his cashier to pay the man if he came to work, might be inclined to dispute the view that the cashier had done his duty by paying the man even though he had not come to work. As for (17), what one has to ask, if (17) is alleged to be truth-functional, is why someone who accepts (17) because its consequent is true may nevertheless be reluctant to assert

If he was not surprised, he didn't show surprise

of which the consequent would also be true. The reason, surely, is that 'if' in (17) has the sense of 'even if', not of 'if . . . then . . .' as in (10), (12), or (13). You can put 'even if' in place of 'if' in (17) without changing the sense, but if you do this in (10), (12), or (13) you change the sense. 'Even if . . .' does not normally function to state a condition that, if it holds, generates a certain consequence, as in the ordinary conditional, but rather to state a condition that does (did, will) not prevent a certain consequence. Hence it looks as though (17) is not strictly relevant to the present discussion.

Let us now turn to cases where, on Grice's view, the implicature of indirect evidence is not cancelled. In these cases, according to Grice, the conditional 'if . . . then . . .' is purely truth-functional, and the suggestion of non-truth-functional reasons for accepting the conditional is carried not by the meaning but by the implicature that conversational presumptions generate. A typical case, I suppose, would be

(18)   If the government falls, there will be rioting in the streets.

Now, in the case of simple, straightforward conditionals like (18) there seems nothing to choose between the Conversationalist Hypothesis, favoured by Grice, and the Semantical Hypothesis which claims the stand-dard linguistic meaning of 'if' to be stronger than a purely truth-functional account can represent.

But consider what happens when (18) goes into the antecedent of another conditional like

(19)   If it is the case both that if the government falls there will be rioting in the streets, and also that the government will not fall, then the shopkeepers will be glad.

According to the Conversationalist Hypothesis, (19) would normally carry the implicature that there is indirect evidence of its antecedent's not being true without its consequent's also being true. But for the antecedent of (19) to be true, we must have both (18) true and the antecedent of (18) false. Hence, if (18) is to be understood as a truth-functional conditional, in accordance with the Conversationalist Hypothesis, its inclusion in the antecedent of (19) would be quite inessential. To discover the truth-value of the antecedent of (19) all we need to know is the truth-value of the ante-cedent of (18). For, if the antecedent of (18) is false, the antecedent of (19) must be true, in virtue of the law ' $\sim p \rightarrow ((p \rightarrow q) \ \& \sim p)$ '; and, if the ante-cedent of (18) is true, the antecedent of (19) must be false, in virtue of the law '$(p \rightarrow \ \sim ((p \rightarrow q) \ \& \sim p)$'. It follows that indirect evidence for the truth of (19) would be quite sufficient if it related the fate of the government to the feelings of the shopkeepers without having any bearing whatever on the causes and effects of rioting in the streets. But this is quite counter-intuitive since it assumes the truth of the consequent to be dependent on only one condition – the fate of the government – whereas in asserting (19) one would assert it to be dependent on two mutually independent conditions. There-fore, if we feel that the evidence for (19) must tell us something about the question of rioting, we cannot accept that the occurrence of 'if . . . then . . .' in (18) is purely truth-functional in meaning.

Perhaps it will be objected that because of the conversational maxim forbidding unnecessary prolixity there is a presumption that in uttering (19) no inessential clauses have been uttered. Accordingly, it will be said, there is an implicature that the content of (18), as well is its truth-value, is essential to the truth of (19). But that would make (19) not wholly truth-functional – contrary to what the Conversationalist Hypothesis asserts. So perhaps the objector will instead claim an assertion of (19) to implicate that the content of (18) is somehow essential to the relevance of part of the indirect evidence for (19). But that would amount to claiming that an assertion of (19) implicates the existence of more evidence for its truth than is necessary on a purely truth-functional account of (19)'s meaning. It would be as if to say that the truth-functionality of 'if . . . then . . .' in its occurrence as the main logical particle of (19) can only be maintained at the cost of sacrificing its truth-functionality in respect of its occurrence within one of the conjuncts in the antecedent of (19). For sentences like (19), as for those like (9), it looks as though the Conversationalist Hypothesis is indefensible. Only some vastly complicated, and correspondingly implausible, addition to the theory of implicatures could possibly save it.

Finally we come to the cases in which 'if . . . then . . .' seems to diverge in meaning from the ordinary formal-logical '→' and in which Grice sees no way of using his theory of conversational presumptions to show that this divergence is illusory. Consider, for example,

(20)   It's not the case that, if the government falls, then there will be rioting in the streets.

On Grice's view, if assertion of (18) normally carries an implicature of indirect evidence for the truth of a truth-functional conditional, (20) must normally carry a denial of that implicature. But someone might object that when an utterance is not absurd, if taken literally, a denial of it is standardly a denial of its literal reading, not of its implicature. For example, if you say ironically

(21)   He is a splendid fellow

and I reply

(22) He is not a splendid fellow

I must be saying, directly and feebly, just what you have, ironically, implicated. And to this objection Grice, in his Lectures, sees no answer.

But, compared with some of the other – above mentioned – objections to the Conversationalist Hypothesis, this one seems rather weak. The fact that although there are some cases like (21) and (22) in which denial of an utterance is not a denial of its implicature there are also other, non-absurd utterances in which it is. For example, if I say

(23)   *Someone* has not sent in a correct return

I implicate that I am unable or unwilling to tell the full story. But if I deny (23) by saying

Everyone has sent in a correct return

I also deny the implicature of (23). It looks as though Grice has over-generalized from the rather special case of ironical implicatures as in (21). Certainly, if we construe one of his conversational maxims as prescribing 'Don't say what you lack *adequate* evidence for', anyone who says *p* implicates that he has adequate evidence for *p* and anyone who denies *p* denies this implicature also. So, *pace* Grice, the objection under consideration looks as though it can be quite easily answered: whether or not the denial of a non-absurd assertion is also a denial of its implicature must depend on the nature of the assertion and the nature of the implicature.

Nevertheless there is a very obvious way in which (20) runs counter to the Conversationalist Hypothesis. That hypothesis holds that 'not' and 'if . . . then . . .' are truth-functional in meaning, though assertions of 'if . . . then . . .' sentences often carry with them implicatures of indirect evidence. But, if the meaning of (20) is such as to deny the truth of a truth-functional, it must logically imply both that the government will fall and that there will be no rioting; and as this implication is quite unacceptable (20) cannot be the denial of a truth-functional conditional. Grice's Lectures offered no viable rejoinder to this type of objection. It is no use rejoining that (20) should be construed as propounding a counter-conditional to (18), viz.,

(24)   If the government falls, there will not be rioting in the streets,

since (24) is not at all synonymous with (20). Nor is it any use rejoining that (20) has the effect of a refusal to assert (18), or of a denial of the implicature of (18). For, if by 'effect' here is meant 'implicature' or 'illocutionary force', the rejoinder does not meet the objection, which is about the meaning of (20). And, if by 'effect' here is meant 'meaning', then the Conversationalist Hypothesis is being sacrificed in respect of the meaning of 'not' in order to try and save it in respect of the meaning of 'if . . . then . . .'.

IV. EITHER . . . OR . . .

Analogous moves may be made against the Conversationalist Hypothesis in regard to 'either . . . or . . .' sentences, and I shall not go into much detail here. According to the Hypothesis assertion of such a disjunctive sentence normally carries with it an implicature that there is indirect evidence for the disjunction, though the implicature may be explicitly cancelled in certain cases as in Grice's example

(25)   The prize is either in the garden or in the attic, but I'm not going to tell you which,

where the speaker suggests that he knows the truth of the disjunction because he knows the truth of one of its disjuncts. But such cases are rather like (10) and (12). The speaker's utterance of (25) is an event that constitutes indirect evidence for the truth of the disjunction. Here too the speaker would not normally utter the corresponding sentence to himself, viz.,

> The prize is either in the garden or in the attic, but I'm not going to tell them which,

because from his point of view there is only direct (truth-functional), and no indirect, evidence for the disjunction. So even if we grant to Grice that his indirect-evidence implicature is normally cancelled when sentences like (25) – or (10) – are at issue, that is not because the utterer of such a sentence does not convey clearly enough to his hearers the existence of indirect evidence for the truth of his assertion, but rather because he conveys this altogether too clearly: his very utterance constitutes the evidence. Hence, though an assertion of (25), as of (10), would normally seem truth-functional, this cannot be because there is no suggestion of indirect evidence, since there is such a suggestion. Rather, it must be because there is no suggestion of any underlying fact or principle that limits the alternatives. Now, according to the Semantical Hypothesis, though such a suggestion is part of the dictionary-meaning of 'either . . . or . . .',[6] it is deleted or cancelled in certain contexts, just as the prefixing of 'plastic' to 'flower' deletes the suggestion of forming part of a plant. So the Semantical Hypothesis can accommodate sentences like (25) just as well as it can accommodate sentences like (10) or (12).

Moreover it is easy to construct 'either . . . or . . .' examples that present the same kind of difficulty to the Conversationalist Hypothesis as does (19). Consider

(26)   If the prize is either in the garden or in the attic, and in fact it is in the attic, the gardener will be glad.

On the truth-functional account the disjunction is quite inessential to the antecedent of (26). Indirect evidence for the truth of (26) would be quite sufficient if it related the prize's being in the attic to the feelings of the gardener without having any bearing whatever on the question where the prize would be if it were not in the attic. But this is quite counter-intuitive, because it assumes the truth of (26)'s consequent to be dependent on only one condition – the prize's being in the attic – whereas in asserting (26) one would assert it to be dependent on two mutually independent conditions. If therefore we feel that the evidence for (26) must tell us something about where the prize would be if it were not in the attic, we cannot accept that the disjunction in (26) is purely truth-functional in meaning.

Someone may object that (9), (19) and (26) are all special cases because they mention mental attitudes in their consequents. But it does not seem difficult to construct appropriate examples of other kinds such as, for (9),

> If a shilling is pushed into the slot and the red button is depressed, a bar of chocolate will fall into the tray

or, for (19),

> If it is the case both that if the wind blows the cradle will fall, and also that the wind will not blow, then the cradle is insecurely fastened but the wind will nevertheless not interfere with it

or, for (26),

> If it is the case both that he will either jump off the ice or fall through it and also that he will in fact jump off it, then he will have saved his own life.

I conclude that there are several rather stronger objections to the Conversationalist Hypothesis than the single objection that Grice himself was worried about in his Lectures. In general that hypothesis breathes the same spirit as earlier attempts to resolve philosophical puzzles about truth by reference to speech-acts of endorsing or conceding, or to resolve puzzles about goodness by reference to speech-acts of commending or commanding.[7] Such theories gain what support they seem to have from the consideration of relatively simple examples. Their weakness becomes apparent when more complex sentences are examined – especially sentences where the locution in question occurs within the antecedent of a conditional.

The Queen's College, Oxford

NOTES

[1] I do not know whether Grice still holds the views that he expressed in these lectures, and I certainly do not wish to imply that he does. In any case I hope that he will take it as a tribute to the interestingness of his ideas that I have not delayed my own discussion of them until the oral publicity of the William James Lectures has been compounded by a printed version. I have taken great care not to misrepresent the content of Grice's lectures as they have been reported to me. But if there are any details on which I have erred I do not think that they affect the main point I am trying to make.

[2] E.g. Euripides *Andromache*, line 986: "Ouk estin ouden kreisson oikeiou philou", literally 'There is not nothing better than . . .', meaning, in Standard English, 'There is nothing better than . . .'.

[3] Grice's concept of implicature was explained by him in 'The Causal Theory of Perception', *Proc. Aristotelian Soc.*, Suppl. vol. 35 (1961), 121–152, but there he still used the word 'implication' for it.

[4] Compare perhaps also 'He unintentionally insulted her' and 'The girl on the dust-cover is naked'. On the relation of such cancellations or deletions to other processes of semantic composition, cf. L. Jonathan Cohen and Avishai Margalit, 'The Role of Inductive Reasoning in the Interpretation of Metaphor', *Synthese* **21** (1970), 469 ff. It emerges that an order of relative importance has in any case to be supposed for the set of distinctive features that characterise a particular meaning. So the less important features will normally be the ones that are exposed to cancellation or deletion in literal usage: e.g. the prefix 'plastic' deletes the notion of growth implicit in the meaning of 'flower' but not the feature of outward appearance. Where one of the more important semantic features is deleted, we tend to regard the usage as metaphorical – e.g., in 'A child is a fragile flower'. Correspondingly it is the truth-functional core of meaning in the logical particles that is undeletable: we never ascribe such words a metaphorical usage.

Of course, it might be objected that every word for a representable object or event x should be assigned a second dictionary meaning as 'representation of x'. But anyone who was prepared to multiply dictionary meanings on this scale would hardly be entitled to jib at assigning a weaker (purely truth-functional) meaning to 'and', 'if . . . then . . .', 'either . . . or . . .', etc., in addition to a stronger (connexive) meaning. Also, presumably, the decision between listing one meaning or two in the dictionary entry for 'and' must be matched by a corresponding decision, in discourse analysis, with regard to the semantics of sentence concatenation.

[5] I have borrowed this example, in a modified form, from my *The Diversity of Meaning*, 2nd ed., 1966, p. 271.

[6] I am trying to suggest here no more than the general nature of the non-truth-functional element in the meaning of 'either . . . or . . .'. I am not offering, in this article, an exact lexicographical characterisation of 'either . . . or . . .', any more than of 'and' or of 'if . . . then . . . '. But I certainly do not wish to claim, as is sometimes claimed, that a dictionary entry for the locution 'either . . . or . . .' should mention as a feature of its meaning that it indicates the speaker's ignorance of which alternative is true. Where an utterance of the locution does indicate this, the indication seems to belong rather to what Grice calls the implicature than to the meaning.

[7] Cf. my 'Speech-Acts', in T. Sebeok (ed.), *Current Trends in Linguistics*, vol. XII (forthcoming).

DAVID HARRAH

FORMAL MESSAGE THEORY

I. INTRODUCTION

Formal communication is the sort of communication used in large organizations; the unit of formal communication is the formal message. Typically, a formal message indicates that it comes *from* a certain person (in a certain status, at a certain time), *to* another person (in a certain status, at a certain time), with an *aim* or *point* connected with previous messages; it has a *body*, and perhaps also an *interpretation intention* that includes a special glossary or other aids to interpreting the body.

Zermelo-Fraenkel set theory provides a natural framework for logical analysis of formal messages and formal communication. The first part of this paper is devoted to presenting such an analysis. We call this *message theory*; its main concepts are *standard message* and *standard message set*. Within this theory we define some concepts that we believe will be fruitful in formal studies of the human communication situation. E.g., we define *communicative force* and *pragmatic content*.

In the latter part of this paper we present the basis for a theory of utterances (roughly, an utterance is an entity that can be construed as expressing a message), and we discuss the relations between our message theory and the utterances of natural language. It will be obvious that our message theory can serve as a logic of utterances, and is at least indirectly relevant to explanatory theories of human language behaviour.[1]

Notation: We use 'iff' for 'if and only if.' Where there is no danger of ambiguity, we omit commas and outermost brackets from expressions of the form $\langle X_1, \ldots, X_n \rangle$. Thereby $XY = \langle X, Y \rangle$.

II. THE LANGUAGE L

To fix ideas, let us assume a standard language L with first-order predicate logic, identity, and descriptions. L has a finite alphabet, out of which are constructed denumerably many individual constants, individual variables, k-ary functors, and k-ary predicates (for every k). The *constants* of L are

Yehoshua Bar-Hillel (ed.), Pragmatics of Natural Languages, 69–83. All Rights Reserved.
Copyright © 1971 by D. Reidel Publishing Company, Dordrecht-Holland.

the individual constants, the functors, and the predicates. Terms and wffs are constructed in a normal way (depending on the theory of descriptions adopted). *Closed* terms are those with no free variables; *sentences* are wffs with no free variables.

The semantics of L is developed in the usual way: We take an *interpretation* to be a pair UV, where U is the universe and V is the interpretation function that assigns meanings to the constants of L. An *interpretation with assignment of variables* (or *model*) is a pair IA such that I is an interpretation and A is a function from the variables into the universe of I. For terms and wffs X we define $IA(X)$; roughly, this is the denotation of X in IA if X is a term, and the truth-value (0 or 1) of X in IA if X is a wff. We define satisfaction, holding, truth, validity, and implication in the usual way. If X is any constant, closed term, or closed wff, we let $I(X) = IA(X)$, where A is any assignment. If X is an open wff, with just n free variables, we let $I(X)$ be the extension of X under I (roughly, the set of n-tuples of things that satisfy X under I).

III. INTERPRETATION INTENTIONS

An *interpretation function* is a function whose domain consists of constants of L. An *interpretation intention* is a pair VW such that V is an interpretation function and W is a set of sentences of L. We say that V *interprets* the members of its domain, and we call W the *axiom set in VW*.

Given two interpretation intentions $H = VW$ and $H' = V'W'$, the *fusion of H and H'*, or $H + H'$, is the pair $\langle V \cup V', W \cup W' \rangle$.

An interpretation intention VW and an interpretation UV' *conform* to each other iff V is a subset of V' and all the sentences in W are true in UV'.

IV. THE INTERPRETATION INTENTION H^*

Suppose the alphabet of L has n letters. For convenience we shall here use 'Λ' to refer to the $(n + 1)$th individual constant of L, '$\frown$' for the first binary functor, '$\in$' the first binary predicate, and 'Com' the first ternary predicate.

We now assume that V^* is an interpretation function such that:

(1) If X is the i-th individual constant of L, and Y is the i-th letter of L, then $V^*(X) = Y$.

(2) $V^*(\Lambda)$ is the empty set.

(3) V^* is infinitely incomplete in all categories (that is, denumerably many individual constants and, for each k, denumerably many k-ary functors and k-ary predicates are not interpreted by V^*).

The *Set Theory* of L consists of the following axioms of Zermelo-Fraenkel set theory: Extensionality, Unit Set, Union, Sum, Power Set, Regularity, and Separation.

The *Con Theory* of L consists of axioms for the functor $^\frown$, plus the assertion that there is a set consisting of all the expressions of L. These axioms suffice for concatenation theory and syntax as formulated by Tarski.

The *Com Theory* of L consists of axioms for the predicate Com. Roughly, Com (x, y, z) says that x is a communicant in status y at time z. The axioms are:

(1) $(Es)(x)(x \in s \equiv (Ey)(Ez) \text{ Com } (x, y, z))$,

(2) $(x)(z)(\text{Com } (x, a, z) \supset F)$, and

(3) $(x)(z)(\text{Com } (x, a, z) \ \& \ (x)(F \supset F') \supset \text{Com } (x, a', z))$,

for every choice of x, z, a, a', F, and F' such that F and F' are one-place wffs with x as free variable, a is the concatenation name of F, and a' is the concatenation name of F'.

Let W^* be the union of the Set, Con, and Com Theories of L, plus perhaps other non-logical theories. We now define $H^* = V^*W^*$.

We do not need special axioms for the theory of statuses or times. A *statuswff* is a wff F of L such that, for some variable x, x occurs free in F but not bound in F, and no other variable occurs free in F. We identify *statuses* with statuswffs.

One letter of the alphabet is identified as the *tally mark*. A *tally* is a string of tally marks. We identify *times* with tallies. A time T *precedes*, or *is earlier than*, another time T' iff T is shorter than T'. The n-th *positive integer* is the set of tallies that begin the n-th tally. The *counting numbers* are the empty set, the positive integers, and the set of all tallies. A *sequence* is a function whose domain is a counting number.[2]

V. NORMAL INTERPRETATIONS

An interpretation UV is *normal* iff (1) UV conforms to H^*, (2) $V(^\frown)$ is a concatenation function, (3) $V(\in)$ is a set of pairs XY such that Y is a set and X is a member of Y, and (4) $V(\text{Com})$ is a set of triples CFT such that F is a status wff and T is a time. A *normal model* of L is a model IA such that I is normal.

Let H be an interpretation intention, F and G be wffs, and S a set of wffs. Then:

An *H-model* is a model IA such that I conforms to H.

A *normal H-model* is an *H*-model IA such that I is normal.

F is *H-valid* iff every *H*-model satisfies F.

F is *normally valid* iff every normal model satisfies F.

F is *normally H-valid* iff every normal *H*-model satisfies F.

S *H-implies* G iff every *H*-model that satisfies all the wffs in S also satisfies G.

S *normally implies* G iff every normal model that satisfies all the wffs in S also satisfies G.

S *normally H-implies* G iff every normal *H*-model that satisfies all the wffs in S also satisfies G.

$F \ldots$ *implies* G iff $\{F\} \ldots$ implies G.

Similarly for related concepts of consistency and equivalence. Similarly also for concepts of denotation. E.g., for terms X:

X *H-denotes* Y iff $IA(X) = Y$ for every *H*-model IA.

X *normally denotes* Y iff $IA(X) = Y$ for every normal model IA.

X *normally H-denotes* Y iff $IA(X) = Y$ for every normal *H*-model IA.

VI. MESSAGE THEORY

A *standard communicant-specifier* (or *com-spec*) is a triple GFT such that G is either a closed term or one-place wff, F is a statuswff, and T is a time.

An *individual constant com-spec* is a com-spec GFT such that G is an individual constant. (For these we write: NFT)

The *name in NFT* is N; the *time in NFT* or GFT is T.

The *com-correlate of* a com-spec GFT is:

(1) the wff Com (G, a, a'), where a is the concatenation name of F and a' is the concatenation name of T, in the case where G is an individual constant; and

(2) the wff $(x)(G \supset \text{Com} (x, a, a'))$, where a and a' are as above, in the case where G is a wff with x as free variable.

A *standard message origin* is a non-empty set of individual constant com-specs.

A *standard message distribution* is a non-empty set of com-specs.

A *standard message aim* is a set of pairs JK such that J is a set of standard message origins and K is a set of sentences.

A *standard message body* is a set of sentences.

A *standard message* is a 5-tuple $ODHAB$ such that:

(1) O is a standard message origin.

(2) D is a standard message distribution.

(3) H is an interpretation intention.

(4) A is a standard message aim.

(5) B is a standard message body.

(6) For each NFT in O and $GF'T'$ in D, T' does not precede T.

(7) If $H = VW$, then the domain of V consists of individual constants and includes all the names in members of O.

Hereafter we confine attention to standard messages M (assuming always that $M = ODHAB$, with $H = VW$), and sets S of standard messages.

M is *finitary* iff O, D, V, W, A, and B are finite, and, in each member JK of A, both J and K are finite and each member of J is finite.

M *conforms properly to I* (and *I conforms properly to M*) iff I is a normal interpretation and $H + H^*$ is an interpretation intention that conforms to I.

M is *origin-proper under I* iff M conforms properly to I, and, for each NFT in O, the com-correlate of NFT is true in I.

S is *origin-regular under I* iff:

(1) Every message in S is origin-proper under I.

(2) For any two distinct messages M and M' in S, if some NFT is in O and $N'F'T'$ is in O', and $I(N) = I(N')$, then $T \neq T'$.

(Intuitively: In such a set, each sender signs at most one message at any time.)

S is *aim-regular* iff, for each M ($= ODHAB$) in S, if JK is in A and O' is in J, then

(1) there is a message in S whose origin is O', and

(2) if NFT is in O and $N'F'T'$ is in O', then T' precedes T.

S is a *standard message set under* I iff:

(1) S is a non-empty set of standard messages.
(2) S is origin-regular under I.
(3) S is aim-regular.

S is a *standard message set* iff S is a standard message set under some I.
C is a *sender of M under* I iff there is an NFT in O such that $I(N) = C$.
M is *for C at T under* I iff M conforms properly to I and there is a GFT in D such that:

(1) G is a term and $I(G) = C$, or G is a wff and C is in $I(G)$;
(2) C is in $I(F)$.

M *refers to M' via A* iff the origin of M' is in J in some pair JK in A.
M is a *standard formal message* iff the domain of V is just the set of names in members of O.
S is a *standard formal message set under* I iff S is a standard message set under I, and every member of S is a standard formal message.
S is a *standard formal message set* iff S is a standard formal message set under some I.

(Intuitively: A standard formal message is purely verbal, in the sense that the acts of interpretation associated with V can be confined to acts of making signatures. A non-formal message, on the other hand, may have a V that has associated with it other kinds of act of interpretation – e.g., pointing, picturing, physical attachment, or the like.)

The following are some consequences of the definitions presented thus far:

The senders of M under I are in the universe of I. Also, if M is for C at T under I, then C is in the universe of I.

For many standard messages M (and in particular all the finitary ones), if M conforms properly to I, then:

(1) M is in the universe of I, and
(2) there is a closed term X of L that denotes M under I – that is, $I(X) = M$.

The notion of standard message set cannot be defined in L, but we can describe in L a set Z that has among its subsets all standard formal message sets, and from the axioms of the Set Theory and Com Theory of L we can prove that Z exists.

M cannot refer to itself via A. On the other hand, some M's can refer to themselves via self-referential sentences in B.

VII. MESSAGE CONTENT

The total meaningful content of M includes the assertions made explicitly by B and also certain assertions made implicitly by other components of M. The implicit content of M includes some justification or clarification of the aim of M, but the aim of one message might involve the implicit content of previous messages. Accordingly, we cannot define these various notions separately, but must define them simultaneously, by recursion, in terms of some ordering of the messages in the given set. For this purpose we cannot use any ordering based solely on the times of messages, because times alone do not order these sets well enough; but it will become clear that the times of messages, together with our requirements on A, give us just enough ordering to serve the purposes of our definitions. Viz:

An *assertion made by M* is a sentence that is in W or B. The *assertion set of M* is the set of all assertions made by M.

The *com-correlate of M* is the set of all wffs F such that F is the com-correlate of a com-spec in O or D.

Suppose A is empty. Then:

(1) The *clarification set for M in S under I* is the empty set.

(2) A *presumption of M in S under I* is a sentence that is normally H-implied by the com-correlate of M.

(3) The *presumption set of M in S under I* is the set of all presumptions of M in S under I.

(4) An *implication of M in S under I* is a sentence that is normally H-implied by the union of the presumption and assertion sets of M in S under I.

(5) The *implication set of M in S under I* is the set of all implications of M in S under I.

Suppose next that A is not empty. Then:

(1) For each sentence F in the K in each pair JK in A, G is a *clarification of F in JK in M in S under I* iff either:
  (a) F is false in I, but J is non-empty and there are conditionals $(F' \supset F)$ such that
    1. F' normally H-implies F, and

2. F' is normally H-implied by the union of the implication sets of the messages in S whose origins are in J; and G is such a conditional.

(b) F is true in I, or J is empty, or F is false in I, but there are no such conditionals $(F' \supset F)$; and G is F itself.

(2) The *clarification set for M in S under I* is the set of all sentences G such that, for some F in the K in a JK in A, G is a clarification of F in JK in M in S under I.

(3) A *presumption of M in S under I* is a sentence that is normally H-implied by the union of the com-correlate of M and the clarification set for M in S under I.

(4) The *presumption set of M in S under I* is the set of all presumptions of M in S under I.

(5) An *implication of M in S under I* is a sentence that is normally H-implied by the union of the presumption and assertion sets of M in S under I.

(6) The *implication set of M in S under I* is the set of all implications of M in S under I.

Roughly, the rationale of the foregoing definitions is this: Messages in S whose origins have the earliest time do not refer via A to other messages in S; so their clarification, presumption, and implication sets are determined separately, one after another. Later messages in S, if they refer via A to other messages in S, refer only to earlier messages in S, for which clarification, presumption, and implication have already been determined. Thus, for later messages, implication is determined in part by clarification, and clarification may be determined in part by the implications of other messages, but those other messages are earlier ones.

The next four definitions are intended to capture the notion of the logical force of a message, as distinct from the logical content on one hand and psychological force on the other.

The *communicative force of M in S under I* is the set of all triples XYZ such that X is a com-spec in O, Z is a com-spec in D, and Y is an implication of M in S under I.

The *expressive force of M in S under I* is the set of all pairs XY such that X is a com-spec in O and Y is an implication of M in S under I.

The *addressive force of M in S under I* is the set of all pairs YZ such that Z is a com-spec in D and Y is an implication of M in S under I.

The *connective force of M in S under I* is the set of all pairs XZ such that X is a com-spec in O and Z is a com-spec in D.

The *syntactic content of M in S under I* is the assertion set of M.

The *semantic content of M in S under I* is the implication set of M in S under I.

The *pragmatic content of M in S under I* is the union of the communicative, expressive, addressive, and connective forces of M in S under I.

We do not claim that the three preceding definitions accurately express the intentions of other theorists who have used the words 'syntactic', 'semantic', and 'pragmatic'. The rationale in our definitions here, of course, is that the syntactic content of M is the immediate, explicit sentential content of M; the semantic content is the total sentential content implied by M; and the pragmatic content of M is the communicative use made of the total sentential content of M. Occasionally we shall use 'assertion set' instead of 'syntactic content', and 'implication set' instead of 'semantic content'.

M is *presumptively proper in S under I* iff all the presumptions of M in S under I are true in I.

M is *true in S under I* iff M is presumptively proper in S under I, B is not empty, and all the assertions made by M are true in I.

M is *false in S under I* iff M is presumptively proper in S under I, B is not empty, and not all the assertions made by M are true in I.

Suppose we have an information function, a concept of the information in a set of sentences, and a concept of relative information. Then we may define the *explicit information in M in S under I* as the information in the assertion set of M, relative to the information in the presumption set of M in S under I (provided that M is presumptively proper in S under I? and zero otherwise?), and the *implicit information in M in S under I* as the information in the implication set of M in S under I (provided . . . ?).

For a logic of messages, we can define various containment relations between messages. Relations sensitive to the internal structure of M and M' can be defined in terms of containment between O and O', D and D', A and A', B and B', the presumption sets of M and M', the assertion sets of M and M', and the implication sets of M and M'.

For a logic of communicants, we can define the *commitments* of a sender (in S) in terms of the implications of his messages (in S), and we may call a sender *consistent* if his commitment set is consistent.

VIII. EXPRESSION OF MESSAGES

To fix ideas and simplify exposition, let us now assume that the alphabet of L contains the comma, parentheses, the two brackets '[' and ']', and the superscripted letters 'O', 'D', 'W', 'A', and 'B'. Assume also that these letters and square brackets do not occur in terms or wffs of L.

For any interpretation intention H, *normal H-expression* is defined recursively:

(1) If X is a term of L that normally H-denotes Z, then X is a normal H-expression for Z.

(2) If X is a sentence of L, then X is a normal H-expression for X.

(3) If Z is a set whose members are $Y_1, \ldots, Y_n$, and X_1 is a normal H-expression for Y_1, and
$$\vdots$$
   X_n is a normal H-expression for Y_n,
   then the expression $(X_1, \ldots, X_n)$ is a normal H-expression for Z.

(4) If GFT is a com-spec and
   X_1 is either G or a term that normally H-denotes G,
   X_2 is either F or a term that normally H-denotes F, and
   X_3 is either T or a term that normally H-denotes T,
   then the expression (X_1, X_2, X_3) is a normal H-expression for GFT.

(5) If JK is a member of a standard message aim, X_1 is a normal H-expression for J, and X_2 is a normal H-expression for K, then the expression (X_1, X_2) is a normal H-expression for JK.

(6) Nothing is a normal H-expression for any Z unless its being so follows from (1)–(5) above.

X is an *m-expression for M* iff M is a standard message $ODHAB$, with $H = VW$, and X is an expression of L of the form

$$[^{\alpha 1} X_1{}^{\alpha 1}{}^{\alpha 2} X_2{}^{\alpha 2} \ldots {}^{\alpha n} X_n{}^{\alpha n}]$$

where:

(1) For each i from 1 to n inclusive:
   (a) αi is either 'O', 'D', 'W', 'A', or 'B'; and
   (b) if αi is 'O', 'D', 'W', 'A', or 'B', then X_i is a normal H-expression for some subset of O, D, W, A, or B, respectively.

(2) For some j, there are j sets $O_1, \ldots, O_j$ such that:
   (a) O is the union of $O_1, \ldots, O_j$; and

(b) for each h, from 1 to j inclusive, there is an i $(1 \leqslant i \leqslant n)$ such that X_i is a normal H-expression for O_h and X_i occurs in X flanked by superscript 'O'.

(And analogously for D, W, A, and B.)

X is an *m-expression* iff X is an *m*-expression for some M.

Roughly speaking, our definition allows an *m*-expression for M to break up and rearrange the components of M, but requires it to express all of M. The definition also allows an *m*-expression to have the obvious and simple form:

$$[^O X_1{}^{OD} X_2{}^D {}^W X_3{}^{WA} X_4{}^{AB} X_5{}^B]$$

Z is an *m-expresser for* M iff Z is a pair XY such that X is an *m*-expression for M and Y is the interpretation function V in M.

Z is an *m-expresser* iff Z is an *m*-expresser for some M.

Note: Certain *m*-expressers can be effectively recognized as being *m*-expressers, and they effectively indicate the M's for which they are *m*-expressers.

IX. AN ANALYSIS OF UTTERANCES

Z is an *utterance-type* iff Z is either an expression X of L, an interpretation function Y, or a pair XY such that X is an expression of L, and Y is an interpretation function.

An expression X *can be projected into* an expression X' iff

(1) every letter occurring in X occurs in X', and
(2) if a letter Y precedes a letter Y' in X, then Y precedes Y' in X'.

An utterance-type Z *can be projected into* an utterance-type Z' iff(roughly) the X in Z can be projected into the X' in Z' and the Y in Z is a subset of the Y' in Z'.

A *standard construction on* an utterance-type Z is a triple MSI such that S is a standard message set under I, M is a member of S, and there is a pair XY such that XY is an *m*-expresser for M, and Z can be projected into XY.

A *strict construction on* an utterance-type Z is a standard construction MSI on Z such that Z is an *m*-expresser for M.

We are here dealing with utterance types rather than utterance tokens or events. To develop a theory of the latter, we should first develop a theory of tokens or events, and then develop constructions on tokens or events. Our guiding idea is that utterance tokens or events derive their rationale from utterance types, and utterance types derive their rationale from standard messages. In particular, utterance types derive their semantics and logic from the semantics and logic of messages. Thus, where Z is an utterance-type and MSI is a standard construction on Z, we define: Z is *true under MSI* iff M is true in S under I. Z is *false under MSI* iff M is false in S under I.

X. SOME CONSEQUENCES

Roughly speaking:

(1) It is always safe to utter sentences that are normally valid. Let Z be an utterance-type that indicates a non-empty B consisting of normally valid sentences. Then there is no strict construction MSI on Z such that Z is false under MSI.

(2) It is never safe to utter sentences that are normally inconsistent. Let Z be an utterance-type that indicates a non-empty B containing at least one sentence that is normally inconsistent. Then there is no strict construction MSI on Z such that Z is true under MSI.

(3) It is safe but futile to express a message whose point is normally inconsistent. Let Z be an utterance-type indicating an A that has in it a pair JK such that J is empty and K contains some sentence that is normally inconsistent. Then there is no strict construction MSI on Z such that either Z is false under MSI or Z is true under MSI.

(4) In the case of some utterance-types Z, whether or not Z has a truth-value under MSI depends on S.

(5) If you want to assert F, but it is probable that F is false in the receiver's interpretation I, your best strategy is to treat F as an a priori assumption rather than a negotiable assertion; it is best to put F between occurrences of the superscript letter 'W'. If F is false in I, and F is treated as part of B, then utterance-types Z containing F cannot be true under MSI (and might be false). If F is treated as part of W, then Z cannot be false under MSI, because MSI cannot be a standard construction on Z.

XI. PROVISION FOR PRONOUNS AND INDEXICALS

Let the alphabet of L contain some special letter α. Let us assume that with this letter we can form indefinitely many expressions $\alpha_1, \alpha_2, \ldots, \alpha_i, \ldots$ We assume that these expressions, which we call *abbreviators*, are effectively recognizable as such, and that they do not occur in wffs of L. These abbreviators may be used in a systematic way to abbreviate various parts of m-expressers, via rules like the following. (Note that these rules may be specific, as is the first one below, or general, as are the others.)

(1) α_1 is interchangeable with the term X, wherever X occurs.

(2) α_2 is interchangeable with N's in the parts of m-expressions that correspond to the com-specs in O (cf. the pronoun 'I').

(3) α_3 is interchangeable with N's in the parts of m-expressions that correspond to the com-specs in D (cf. the pronoun 'you').

(4) α_4 is interchangeable with T's (cf. 'now').

(5) If an abbreviator is interchangeable with X in any part of an m-expresser, then it is interchangeable with X in any other part (including the domain of the interpretation function in the m-expresser).

Hereafter, we shall use 'R' to refer to sets of such rules. Note that such an R might allow a given expression X to be abbreviated in several different ways, and allow a given occurrence of an abbreviator to be replaced by any of several different expressions X, so that such abbreviators are ambiguous under R. The purpose of R is to simplify the vocabulary by which messages can be expressed, and R achieves this sort of simplification by allowing this sort of ambiguity.

Let Z be any utterance-type. Then MSI is a *standard construction on Z via R* iff there is an utterance-type Z' such that MSI is a standard construction on Z' and Z comes from Z' by replacing zero or more parts of Z' by abbreviators via the rules in R.

Let Z be any utterance-type and MSI a standard construction on Z via R. Then Z is *true under MSI via R* iff M is true in S under I.

(And likewise for *false under MSI via R*, and so on.)

Areas for research include the following: (1) Relations between the occurrence (or non-occurrence) of superscript letters in an expression X and the ambiguity of the abbreviators occurring in X. (2) Criteria for evaluating different R's. (3) Optimality of R's with respect to economy and efficiency on the one hand and freedom from harmful ambiguity on the other. (4) Resemblance between various R's and the rules for pronouns and indexicals in natural languages. (5) Effect of changes in our treatment of time. The treatment of time presented above is the simplest one adequate for a theory of signed messages. A treatment that is more general but more complicated to develop is this: We assume tally theory as above, but we let the T in a com-spec be a term of L that normally denotes a set of tallies. We allow this T to denote a single time, or a finite time stretch, or a set of disconnected times, or whatever. Such a treatment should open up new possibilities for indexicals in particular and the theory of communication in general.

XII. APPLICATIONS

How widely applicable is this message theory? First, it seems clear that our analysis of formal messages, centred around the concepts of standard message and standard message set, is a good first approximation. As we extend and refine our ideas of what counts as formal communication, we may correspondingly extend and refine our theory of formal messages; but it seems plausible that this extension and refinement can be made within our already specified set-theoretical framework and by means of concepts similar to the concepts developed thus far.

Second, it seems clear that our theory of messages can accommodate many variations in the language L and the interpretation intention H^*. The particular content of L and H^* that we specified above was chosen in order to make it possible for the users of L to describe, within L, the expressions of L and certain set-theoretical entities, so that they can describe, within L, standard messages and message sets. This is needed where the users of L want to send messages by expressing the messages indirectly, by normal H-denotation. This particular content of L and H^* is not needed if the users of L are willing to confine themselves to finitary messages and are willing to send them by expressing them directly, not by normal H-denotation but by the procedures of normal H-expression that use direct display of the ingredients of the message.

We have assumed that every expression of L is finite, but it might be worth studying a development in which infinite expressions could exist at the level of messages, though only finite expressions would be used at the level of utterance-types. We have assumed that the alphabet of L contains a special tally mark, but this is not essential; any system of time-indication will do. We assumed a special set of letters to serve as punctuation marks in m-expressers; again, any system will do. Likewise, of course, for our abbreviators.

Now, regardless of how applicable our message theory is as a logic of human communication, is it relevant to empirical studies of human communication? Bar-Hillel has challenged semioticians to develop theories that can answer questions like: What did person P mean by sentence X at time T? Message theory is intended to be an advance toward answering such questions. It is clearly an advance on formal theories of meaning that can answer only the question: What does sentence X mean under the interpretation I? Message theory can answer not only this question but also questions like: What messages M are expressible by the utterance-type X? What are the presumptions of the message M in set S under interpretation I? What is the communicative force of M in S under I? What commitments does person P make by sending M in S under I?

While working toward the goals indicated by Bar-Hillel, we may take encouragement from the example of decision theory in economics. There the programme was: first to specify a general kind of situation, then to determine what is rational behaviour in that situation, and then to study human behaviour in light of the abstract theory. We approach the individual by way of the type; the actual by way of the rational. *De astris per aspera!*

Dept. of Philosophy, University of California at Riverside.

NOTES

[1] The work presented here was done during 1968 and 1969, and was supported by grants from the University of California.
    This particular paper is a revised version of the paper, 'Message Theory as a Basis for Pragmatics', which was distributed in advance to participants in this Symposium. Most of the revisions made here were stimulated (directly or indirectly) by comments made by various members of the Symposium; in this connection I am indebted especially to Professor Yehoshua Bar-Hillel.
[2] For Tarski's concatenation theory see 'The Concept of Truth in Formalized Languages', in Alfred Tarski, *Logic, Semantics, Metamathematics: Papers from 1923 to 1938* (Oxford 1956).
    The reader will note that, for the developments mentioned in the present paper, there is considerable redundancy in the logical and axiomatic basis assumed above. On the other hand, the reader has already thought of further axioms that we shall eventually want for Com Theory and other parts of message theory.

Note added in proof. In addition, further assumptions concerning the semantics of L should be specified and studied. For example, in a normal interpretation UV, the universe U is a standard transitive set, and $V(\in)$ is the membership relation restricted to U.

ASA KASHER

A STEP TOWARD A THEORY OF LINGUISTIC PERFORMANCE*

The *type-token-tone* distinction has reached a grand old age and is apparently dead. The purpose of this note is not to write another obituary, but rather to consider one chapter of the testament. It will be claimed that the *sentence-utterance-inscription* distinction, which is a young offspring of Peirce's trichotomy, should be promoted in order to grant it the status it deserves in linguistic theory, viz., as a small pillar in the theory of linguistic performance. This claim will be defended by clarifying the nature of the members of our triad, outlining their mutual relations within a theory of linguistic performance, and showing how this subtheory of linguistic performance is related to the theory of linguistic competence.

I. INSCRIPTIONS AND UTTERANCES

The most important reason for introducing the type-token distinction was to treat separately the *theoretical linguistic* entities, sentence- and word-types, and the *observational linguistic* entities, sentence- and word-tokens. But talking about linguistic observational entities is actually talking about *physical observational* entities in a *linguistic* setting. Our *inscriptions* are these physical entities described in isolation from their possible functions in linguistic settings. Marks of ink or chalk and sound waves are inscriptions.

Utterances are not inscriptions, but inscriptions-*cum*-appropriate-settings. Formally speaking, an utterance is an ordered *pair* whose first component is an inscription and whose second component is an *appropriate* setting. Given any inscription *ins*, not every setting can be its bedfellow. Only a setting in which a purported linguistic function is ascribed to *ins* can join it to constitute an utterance. Such a setting is characterized by the fact that a person p successfully applies to *ins*, during the time interval t, a set s of rules, which are rules of reception or production, related to a certain natural language l.[1] Given an utterance $u = \langle ins, c \rangle$, where $c = \langle p, t, s \rangle$, *ins* will be called 'the inscription' of u and each member of c will be called 'an index' of u.

Yehoshua Bar-Hillel (ed.), Pragmatics of Natural Languages, 84–93. All Rights Reserved.
Copyright © 1971 by D. Reidel Publishing Company, Dordrecht-Holland.

The result of an application of s to *ins* is generally a decision as to whether p is willing to ascribe to *ins*, on t, a linguistic function within l. Note that u is an utterance only if p answers in the affirmative.

Utterances have a peculiar methodological status. Let me explain. Clearly, an utterance is not an observational entity, because given a pair $u = <ins, c>$, one cannot always decide *observationally* whether u is an utterance. Where $c = \langle p, t, s \rangle$, one cannot decide observationally whether p successfully applies s to *ins* during t, unless one is p himself, being in the lucky state of applying s to *ins* during t.[2] Hence, $u = \langle ins, \langle p, t, s \rangle \rangle$ is an observational entity for p on t and is a theoretical entity for anybody else. We conclude that the term 'utterance' is, according to our explication of it, neither merely observational nor merely theoretical but, so to speak, intra-observational and extra-theoretical. It seems that the explication of any kind of intuitional activity – linguistic, logical, aesthetical, or what have you – will involve such methodologically peculiar terms.

Among the utterances some are more interesting than the others. Recall that u is an utterance in case p is *willing to ascribe* to the inscription of u (*cum* its indices) a linguistic function; p does not have either to *specify* or even to *be able to specify* any such purported linguistic function of that inscription. Any unclear handwriting supplies examples of these utterances. We are interested mainly in those utterances to the inscriptions of which p does ascribe certain linguistic functions within certain natural languages. In such a case, p relates the given utterance to a certain sentence, clause, word etc., which are all theoretical entities of certain languages. We shall say that p considers u, i.e., its inscription cum its indices, to be an *instance* of the corresponding theoretical entity. Now, let us consider these theoretical entities themselves.

II. SENTENCES

There is no simple answer to the seemingly simple question: What kind of an entity is a sentence? Aristotle's answer was: "A sentence is a significant portion of speech, some parts of which have an independent meaning."[3] This definition has found wide acceptance. Shades of it even recur in modern linguistic writings: "The unit of speech is . . . the sentence, i.e., a word or a group of words expressing a complete concept, each word composed of individual sounds, and the meaning of the single word . . . or the combination of meanings of the group of words conveying a unitary idea."[4]

These definitions may be evaluated by trying to apply them as a criterion for determining when what might appear to be two sentences are in fact one sentence. In doing so we shall find that the last definition is inadequate. It is clear that the series of sounds referred to in the definition is not to be considered as a series of observable entities, for otherwise every sentence could be uttered precisely once and its lifetime would be measured in seconds. A sentence can, however, not be defined as a given sound pattern, since the same sentence may be connected with totally different sound patterns, while different sentences may be associated with the same sound pattern. Secondly, according to the definition, the difference between a series of sounds that constitutes a sentence and one that does not is a matter of meaningfulness, but this is an oversimplification. Consider the series of sounds associated with the following examples:

(1)   Lamno wabe grimsey
(2)   Because what but what not what because
(3)   The man which came went
(4)   John is more of a son than Bill.

The reasons for (1)–(4) not constituting sentences lie in a variety of factors that are all relevant to the linguistic aspect of the matter. In the following explication we have tried to obviate these defects inherent in the classical characterizations.

The usage of the term 'sentence' in linguistics is highly ambiguous. When the syntactic ambiguity of the sentence *Visiting relatives can be a nuisance*[5] is considered, what is denoted by 'sentence' is a string of formatives with which two (or more) syntactic descriptions can be associated. Chomsky seems to adhere to this wording, talking about strings being sentences,[6] but his 'semantic interpretation' of a sentence is a semantic interpretation of a string of formatives *cum* a certain syntactic description of the string.[7] Similarly, when we describe the presuppositions a speaker has when using appropriately the sentence *He saw a beautiful girl's dress near the bank* we describe the string of formatives *cum* one of its possible syntactic descriptions *cum* one of its possible semantic descriptions. Furthermore, 'a complete linguistic description of a sentence' may be taken to mean something that includes information of a pragmatic nature, as well as syntactic and semantic information, e.g., a specification of the presuppositions a speaker is assumed to have when he uses the string of formatives *cum* fixed syntactic and semantic structures of it, appropriately.

Thus, we have several levels of representation of linguistic data. These levels are arranged in a hierarchy and each of them is itself possibly a hierarchy of sublevels.[8] In the lowest level we find strings of formatives, while in the highest level we find descriptions, each of which specifies completely one possible combination of syntactic, semantic and pragmatic data concerning one string of formatives. Naturally, we have to decide whether we take the explication of the common term 'sentence' to be an entity of the highest or of the lowest level of representation. Any other choice of an entity that belongs to an intermediate level or sublevel will of course be arbitrary. We prefer using 'string' for the denotation of entities of the lowest theoretical level, viz., strings of formatives, and using 'sentence' for the denotation of entities of the highest linguistic theoretical level. Indeed, one may adhere to another terminology, taking 'sentence' to mean a string of formatives and calling what we denote by 'sentences', say, 'linguemes'. Recall that Katz and Postal introduced the term 'sentoid' "to refer to a string of formatives with a unique associated syntactic description",[9] using 'sentence' for the strings themselves. Our preference is motivated by what seems to us to be the use of the locution 'an instance of a sentence'. If an utterance is to be considered an instance of a certain sentence, then it is not an instance of a string of formatives regardless of the linguistic descriptions it receives in the various levels of representation. It is rather an instance of a string of formatives *with* certain syntactic, semantic, and pragmatic properties. If I know just what string of formatives you have uttered, do I know what sentence you have uttered? According to our intuitions the answer is negative.[10] Anyhow, nothing below depends just on our terminology.

Formally speaking, we mean by 'sentence' an ordered pair, $\langle st, vc \rangle$, where st is a string (of formatives) and vc is a unique complete linguistic description of st within each of the various levels of representation.[11] (Our vc stands for *verbal context*.) Any verbal context can only be presented against the background of the appropriate linguistic theories that provide the corresponding levels of representation. Accordingly, to present a sentence properly means to require a proper representation of the related linguistic theories, which amounts to a proper representation of a considerable part of the language. To cite Wittgenstein: "Roughly: understanding a sentence means understanding a language."[12]

Not every pair $\langle st, vc \rangle$ is a sentence. Developed linguistic theories will provide measures of the well-formedness of such pairs. Let us call these pairs 'expressions'. Assume that a given measure assigns each expression a number between 0 and 10. We can take only those expressions to which the number 10 is assigned to be our sentences. In this case, some other expressions – say, those to which 7, 8, or 9 is assigned – will also be linguistically interesting, as the following examples show:

(5)   David Ben-Gurion was a king of Israel
(6)   The man has dissipated
(7)   Five of the three disputants agreed with me
(8)   One square is round, cautious and smiling.[13]

The importance of taking expressions which are not sentences into our linguistic considerations lies also in the domain of diachronic theories and acquisition theories. It seems reasonable to conjecture that in the shift from one stage of linguistic historical development to the next stage the degree of well-formedness of expressions, sentences included, varies in a universally restricted way. A similar hypothesis also applies to certain aspects of the linguistic development of children.[14]

III. OUTLINING PERFORMANCE

After having presented roughly the trichotomy *inscription-utterance-sentence* and some related linguistic concepts, we would like to consider them within the context of a possible linguistic theory of performance.

We shall introduce several performance-theoretical classes and functions. The following notation will be used for that purpose: *UT* is any non-empty set of utterances, relative to a fixed natural language *l*. It may be the set of all such utterances or a subset thereof. *INS* is the set of all the inscriptions of the utterances of *UT*. *STR* is the set of all the strings of the language *l*.

DEFINITION 1. *F* is an *internal function* if and only if:

(a) it is a function from the set *INS* of inscriptions to the set *STR* of strings[15];

(b) it is a homomorphism with regard to the concatenation operation, i.e., if ins_3 is the concatenation of ins_1 and ins_2, then $F(ins_3)$ is the concatenation of $F(ins_1)$ and $F(ins_2)$.

Informally speaking, an internal function corresponds to certain 'clear' inscriptions of utterances appropriate strings. These inscriptions may be regarded as instances of the corresponding strings.

Let F_0 be a fixed internal function.

DEFINITION 2. An utterance *u* belonging to the set *UT* is a *deviant* utterance if and only if the inscription of u does not fall within the domain of the internal function F_0.

The internal function F_0 correlates strings with inscriptions of non-deviant utterances. How are the inscriptions of deviant utterances related to the strings?

DEFINITION 3. G is an *amplifier* if and only if:

(a) G is a function from INS to the power set of INS, i.e., G (ins), if defined, is a subset of INS;

(b) The domain of the internal function F_0 is a proper subset of the domain of G, and where $G(ins)$ is defined all its elements belong to the domain of F_0;

(c) Where $F_0(ins)$ is defined, G (ins) contains as an element ins itself.

Accordingly, an amplifier is a function correlating with the inscriptions of certain utterances sets of inscriptions which are 'clear' and related straightforwardly to strings. Thus an indirect relation is established between 'unclear' inscriptions and strings. Let G_0 be a fixed amplifier.

DEFINITION 4. An utterance u is *amplifiable* if and only if the inscription of u falls within the domain of G_0. It is *strongly amplifiable* if and only if it falls within the domain of G_0 but not within the domain of F_0.

Now, let SNT be the set of sentences of the natural language l. As stated, every sentence is an ordered pair whose first component is a string.

DEFINITION 5. H is a *simple instance function* if and only if:

(a) H is a function from UT to SNT;

(b) If H is defined for the utterance $u = \langle ins, c \rangle$, the first component of $H(u)$ is a string that belongs to the set $F_0(G_0(ins))$.[16]

A simple instance function therefore is a function from the given set of utterances into the given set of sentences. This function correlates to an utterance in its domain, a sentence to whose string it is connected by means of its inscription, the internal function F_0 and the amplifier G_0. Let H_0 be a fixed simple instance function.

DEFINITION 6. The utterance u is a *simple instance* of the sentence snt if and only if $H_0(u) = snt$.

DEFINITION 7. The utterance u is *defective* if and only if it does not fall within the domain of H_0.

Let EXP be the set of all the expressions of the language l, i.e., all the strings of l paired with their verbal contexts. Clearly, SNT is a proper subset of EXP.

DEFINITION 8. *H* is an *instance function* if and only if:

(a) *H* is a function from *UT* to *EXP*;

(b) if *H* is defined for the utterance $u = \langle ins, c \rangle$, the first component of $H(u)$ is a string that belongs to the set $F_0(G_0(ins))$.

It is clear that any simple instance function, relative to F_0 and G_0, is also an instance function, relative to the same internal function and amplifier.

Let H_1 be a fixed instance function.

DEFINITION 9. An utterance *u* is an instance of the expression *exp* if and only if $H(u) = exp$.

DEFINITION 10. An utterance *u* is *hollow* if and only if it does not fall within the domain of H_1.

The following picture emerges from these definitions: the instance function divides the utterances into two sets – the set of hollow utterances and the set of utterances that are instances of sentences or other expressions. To give a simple example of a hollow utterance: We notice a piece of paper and after picking it up we find that there are some inscriptions on it, which seem to be Roman letters. "Well," we say to ourselves, "there is something written here in English." At this stage we have an utterance. Now we say to ourselves – "Let us read what is written here." In doing so we are trying to find out what is one possible linguistic function of the inscription of the utterance, under its indices. But assume our attempt to do so fails. We then say "This is a mere jumble of inscriptions" and conclude – "Nothing is written here in English." By this stage we have found that the inscriptions on the piece of paper, to the best of our discretion, fulfil no linguistic function whatsoever. The utterance in question therefore is not an instance of a sentence or another expression, but a hollow utterance.

Within the set of utterances that are not hollow, we must distinguish between different types of utterances, according to their inscriptions. There are clear inscriptions, which unambiguously reflect certain strings. Many written inscriptions, mainly the printed ones, and fewer sound inscriptions are clear. The transition from these clear inscriptions to the corresponding strings is expressed by the *internal function*. The presentation of this function for a certain natural language seems to be the task of certain linguists, e.g., phoneticians and phonologists.

When the inscription of a given utterance is such a clear inscription, it is generally an instance of a sentence or of a non-sentential expression, whose string is that which the internal function assigns to the given clear inscription. A clear inscription may be the inscription of different utterances and may therefore be associated with different sentences or other expressions that share the same string.

Yet not all the inscriptions are clear. Most sound inscriptions are not clear[17] and do not unequivocally reflect one or the other string. They require some filtering in the course of which some of them are eliminated[18] and some are replaced by alternative inscriptions. This is represented by the *amplifier*. To present a suitable amplifier for a given natural language seems to be the joint task of linguists and psycholinguists. So far very little research has been done in this field.[19] Under the appropriate circumstances the production of an unclear inscription may be equivalent, in a sense, to the production of a clear inscription having been matched by the amplifier to the unclear inscription. For example, the inscription /this are the tree childs/ will be matched by such an amplifier to a set of clear inscriptions that contains /these are the three children/, /this is the third child/, etc. Whenever the inscription of any utterance is of this unclear type, it may be an instance of a sentence or of a non-sentential expression. The transition from the inscription of the utterance to the string of a sentential or non-sentential expression is performed by means of two functions, viz., the internal function of the language and the amplifier of the language. The amplifier matches the inscription of the utterance with a set of clear inscriptions. The internal function assigns to any one of these clear inscriptions a string. It is evident, therefore, that the unclear inscriptions may be associated with various sentences or non-sentential expressions or both. These expressions generally do not share the same string.

With the aid of these two functions it is possible to present the *simple instance function* of the language, by which sentences are matched to utterances, and the more general *instance function* of the language, which matches sentential and non-sentential expressions to utterances. In presenting such functions reference is made not only to the inscriptions of the utterances but also to their indices – $\langle p, t, s \rangle$. This field of research, which again is the province of linguists and psycholinguists, has hardly been touched upon.

It is quite clear that according to this outline of a theory of linguistic performance, the theory of linguistic competence is a subtheory thereof. The competence theory will supply our performance theory with everything concerning the various levels of representation of expressions. The internal function, the amplifier and the instance functions will associate the theoretical representations with the observational inscriptions and the intermediate utterances.

Bar-Ilan University, Ramat-Gan and The Hebrew University of Jerusalem.

NOTES

* This work was supported in part by the Air Force Office of Scientific Research, through the European Office of Aerospace Research, OAR under contract No. F 61052–68–C–0036 (with the Hebrew University of Jerusalem). I am indebted to Professor Y. Bar-Hillel for invaluable comments on a draft of this paper.
[1] In some circumstances these rules are related not to one natural language but to a family of natural languages that, for example, share the same alphabet. We shall not discuss these cases in the sequel.
[2] We shall not deal here with the related complex problems of intuition memory.
[3] *De Interpretatione*, 4, 16b26–9, according to I. M. Bocheński, *A History of Formal Logic* (translated by I. Thomas), University of Notre Dame Press, 1961, 10.11. A different version of the same answer reads: 'A sentence is defined voice significant by compact, of which any part separately possesses a signification as a word . . .' (O. F. Owen, 'Analysis of Aristotle's Organon', in: *The Organon*, George Bell and Sons, London, 1900, p. 643).
[4] L. H. Gray, *Foundations of Language*, Macmillan, New York, 1939, pp. 224–5.
[5] R. A. Jacobs and P. S. Rosenbaum, *English Transformational Grammar*, Blaisdell, Waltham, 1968, p. 6.
[6] Cf. *Aspects of the Theory of Syntax*, MIT Press, Cambridge, 1965, pp. 63, 195.
[7] Cf. *loc. cit.*, pp. 135–6, 162, and J. Lyons' review of Chomsky's book, *The Philosophical Quarterly*, **16** (1966), pp. 393–5.
[8] Cf. N. Chomsky, *loc. cit.* p. 222 (n. 2).
[9] *An Integrated Theory of Linguistic Descriptions*, MIT Press, Cambridge, 1964, pp. 24–5.
[10] That people can grasp what string of formatives has been uttered without understanding it, is well known to aphasiologists. Cf. E. Weigl and M. Bierwisch, 'Neuropsychology and Linguistics: Topics of Common Research', *Foundations of Language*, **6** (1970), 7–8.
[11] Elsewhere I argued that each *vc* is an ordered triple $\langle syns, sems, prgs \rangle$, where *syns* is a unique syntactic structure of the string *st*, *sems* is a unique semantic description of $\langle st, syns \rangle$, and *prgs* is a unique pragmatic description of $\langle st, syns, sems \rangle$.
[12] *Philosophical Investigations*, Basil Blackwell, Oxford, 1953, p. 5. It was suggested to me by Professor John Lyons (private communication) that sentences should be defined independently of semantic and pragmatic considerations, because otherwise, given the "indeterminacy of the boundary between meanings", it will be unclear when we have one or two sentences. Beyond the terminological issue involved in this remark, it raises the real problem of the possibility of a *complete* specification of a linguistic, meaningful, and useful individual, such as a sentence. Let us express our belief that such a specification is theoretically attainable, although it might be found that the specification of even one sentence requires the specification of a considerable part of the language under consideration.
[13] It should be clear that we do *not* claim that these four examples share the same degree of wellformedness. Neither do we claim that any of these examples should be assigned a degree of wellformedness that is just one step away from the degree of sentences that are maximally wellformed.
[14] It may be worthwhile to examine the following 'grammatical evolution' hypothesis:

From one stage to the next in the course of natural linguistic ontogenesis and phylogenesis the degree of wellformedness of any string of formatives *cum* a unique syntactic structure of it changes by no more than k, which is a low natural number. The absolute value of k depends on the general linguistic theory within which the hypothesis is formulated. Cf. J. Lyons, 'Existence, Location, Possession and Transitivity', in: *Logic, Methodology and Philosophy of Science, III* (ed. by B. Van Rootselaar and J. F. Staal) North-Holland, Amsterdam, 1968, p. 502.

[15] It has to be emphasized that F may not be defined for some of the elements of *INS*.

[16] The value of G_0 is a set of inscriptions, while F_0 is defined only for individual inscriptions. Hence, we naturally define '$F_0(G_0(ins))$' as the following set:

$$\{y \mid (Ex)(y = F_0(x) \text{ and } x \text{ belongs to } G_0(ins))\}.$$

[17] Cf. C. E. Osgood, 'Contextual Control in Sentence Understanding and Creating', in: *Speech, Language and Communication* (ed. by E. C. Carterette), California University Press, Los Angeles and Berkeley, 1966, p. 206, and L. L. Earl, V. B. Bhimani, and R. P. Mitchell, 'Statistics of Operationally Defined Homonyms of Elementary Words', *Mechanical Translation*, **10** (1967), 18–25.

[18] Recall our discussion of hollow utterances, above.

[19] Cf. C. E. Osgood, *loc. cit.*

HANS-HEINRICH LIEB

ON SUBDIVIDING SEMIOTIC

"Syntactics, semantics, pragmatics" – if the reader has ever heard of semiotic, he will immediately associate with it this triad of terms. It may be surprising that anybody should wish to discuss a distinction as well known as the subdivision they designate: one tends to speak unhesitatingly of a semantical investigation or a pragmatical one, so presumably the distinction is useful and well understood. But Professor Bar-Hillel, for one, cannot have shared that feeling when he organized the symposium that has given rise to the present essay: its very first session was devoted to a discussion of 'the validity of the syntactics-semantics-pragmatics trichotomy'. And indeed, judging by the discussion, apparently no one was fully at ease with the distinction; there even seemed to emerge a tendency to reject it altogether.[1]

Besides, there is more to subdividing semiotic than just drawing a distinction between three branches: Morris, who introduced the triad of syntactics, semantics, pragmatics, also distinguished 'pure semiotic' and 'descriptive semiotic' (Morris, 1938); Carnap adopted the terms "pure" and "descriptive" but used them in his own way (Carnap, 1942); and ever since, the relation between the trichotomy and the dichotomy has been far from clear. It should be useful to reopen the discussion.

Any attempt to distinguish branches of a scientific discipline will involve general assumptions on how a discipline and its branches are related, as well as points of view for distinguishing the branches of the given discipline. In Section I of this essay, I first outline the subdivision of semiotic presented in Morris (1938) and make explicit some of the general assumptions that seem to underlie that division; I then turn to the subdivision in Carnap (1942). In Section II, I begin by evaluating the points of view that the two authors present. (Both in Section I and Section II, I deliberately concentrate on the conception in Morris's and Carnap's work; modifications that have been or might be proposed are more easily evaluated when the original framework is clearly understood.) The 'pure-descriptive' dichotomy is discussed in greater detail, rather at the expense of the familiar trichotomy. Taking account of later modifications, I eventually propose a new sub-

Yehoshua Bar-Hillel (ed.), Pragmatics of Natural Languages, 94–119. All Rights Reserved.
Copyright © 1971 by D. Reidel Publishing Company, Dordrecht-Holland.

division of semiotic. In a concluding section, I discuss some general problems that are relevant to understanding what is involved in subdividing a discipline.

I. THE SYSTEM OF SEMIOTIC DISCIPLINES AND ITS STRUCTURE: THE VIEWS OF MORRIS AND CARNAP

1. Morris's Subdivision of Semiotic and Its Structure

1.1. *The subdivision.* In Morris (1938), "semiotic" is introduced as the name of a science ("the science of semiosis", 8); so are 'syntactics', 'semantics', and 'pragmatics' (52). The basic relation of the latter sciences to semiotic is variously indicated by the terms "component discipline" (52), "discipline (of)" (52), "component" (53), "subscience" (53), "subordinate science" (8), "subordinate branch" (8), "branch" (13). For my further presentation I choose "(is a) branch (of)" as a representative term.

At first sight the situation seems to be quite straightforward: Semiotic has the three branches syntactics, semantics, and pragmatics. This indeed is what Morris says (8). Nonetheless he goes on to introduce a second distinction, between what he calls pure semiotic and descriptive semiotic (9). These entities are presumably also sciences (Morris speaks of the 'subject matter' of descriptive semiotic, 57); but their relation to semiotic itself is never clarified: I do not find any instance where "branch" or one of its equivalents is used to relate them to semiotic, so it is uncertain whether they, too, may be regarded as branches of semiotic. On the other hand, they may have branches; in particular, pure semiotic has "the component branches of pure syntactics, pure semantics, and pure pragmatics" (9), and descriptive semiotic is to be divided analogously (9). This seems to suggest that pure syntactics, for instance, is also a branch of syntactics, but again I do not find any case where one of the relevant terms is used to relate a branch of pure or descriptive semiotic to one of the three branches of semiotic that Morris explicitly recognizes. (Rather, he speaks of pure and descriptive semantics as being different "aspects" of semantics, 21; similarly in the case of pragmatics, 30.)

There seems to be no basic tenet in Morris (1938) that would forbid us to apply the concept of branch also in the doubtful cases (beyond the fact that Morris occasionally speaks of 'the three' branches of semiotic), and I will indeed adopt this solution. Hence, descriptive and pure semiotic will be regarded as branches of semiotic, and each of their branches will also be considered a branch of the appropriate one among the three branches of semiotic recognized by Morris, e.g., pure syntactics will be a branch both of pure semiotic and of syntactics. On the other hand, neither descriptive semiotic nor pure semiotic can be a branch of any branch of semiotic, if essential features of Morris's account are to be retained. We thus arrive at the situation diagrammed in Figure 1 (where the line between two entries reads, from the bottom to the top, "is a branch of").

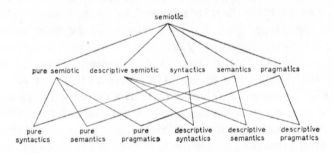

Figure 1.   The subdivision of semiotic according to Morris, 1938.

We wish to isolate general assumptions concerning the relations in any 'system of disciplines' that may be said to underlie Morris's account. For this purpose, we use the diagram to describe the structure of what it represents.

1.2. *Structure of the subdivision.* As a first basic fact we note that we are confronted with a two-place relation, which may be called ". . . is a branch of . . . on the basis of Figure 1", or simply "Branch-of". (The former expression is to remind the reader that we consider a relation just between the entities indicated in Figure 1.) Which properties may be attributed to Branch-of?

There is exactly one initial member of Branch-of (i.e., semiotic), and the field of the relation is obviously finite. Furthermore, on the basis of Morris (1938) we are justified in assuming that disciplines with different names in Figure 1 are different. Therefore, inspection of Figure 1 shows that Branch-of is asymmetric (hence, irreflexive). Extending Morris's account without modifying it in any substantial way, we may also assume that

Branch-of is transitive.[2] Being asymmetric and transitive, Branch-of is a strict partial ordering.

Figure 1 exhibits, relative to semiotic, two levels of branches such that no two elements of the same level are related by Branch-of. This should be formulated more clearly. Let n be a natural number $\neq 0$. By an *n-th branch of x* we understand any y such that the n-th power of Branch-of holds between y and x, and there is no integer $m > n$ such that the m-th power of Branch-of holds between y and x. The first part of the original statement can now be formulated as: Every branch of semiotic is either a first branch or a second branch of semiotic.[3] Given two first branches or two second branches, neither is related to the other by Branch-of: This follows from the definition of "n-th branch of x", and hence, need not be stated separately.

We are now in a position to take account of a second basic fact that can be read off the diagram: All the second branches of semiotic are 're-combinations' of first branches in the sense that each second branch is a branch of two first branches simultaneously; and if the set of first branches is partitioned into the sets {pure semiotic, descriptive semiotic}, {syntactics, semantics, pragmatics}, then the second branches can be characterized as follows: There is no second branch that is a branch of different elements of the same set, and for each pair consisting of an element of the first and an element of the second set there is a second branch of semiotic that is a common branch of the two elements.

Obviously, the two sets are of special importance. Let us call them *criteria* and further analyse their properties.

Each criterion has at least two elements. Furthermore, all elements of a criterion are first branches of the initial member of Branch-of (i.e., semiotic), hence, of some member of Branch-of.[4] Restating one of our previous findings we may now say that there are no two different elements of a criterion such that a first branch of the first and a first branch of the second are identical.[5] Finally, every second-place member of Branch-of is either an element of a criterion or a first branch of elements of different criteria, and any two elements of different criteria have a first branch in common.[6]

In describing the situation in Figure 1, we have isolated and characterized two basic entities, one a two-place relation (Branch-of), the other a set of sets of second-place members of that relation, a set whose elements we chose to call criteria.[7]

Generalizing from our findings, we may now formulate assumptions on any 'system of disciplines' that may be said to underlie Morris's account of the 'semiotic sciences'. (At a few points we deviate slightly from Morris in order to achieve greater generality, just as we have already omitted some statements that could have been made.)

1.3 *"System of disciplines" as a set-theoretical predicate.* Our presentation will take the form of an axiomatization within set theory. That is, we define "system of disciplines" as a set-theoretical predicate, where the definiens consists of axioms retaining as much as possible of our account of Morris's system. In this way, the general assumptions implicit in Morris's presentation can be stated explicitly.

We assume an axiomatic set theory such as the version in Suppes (1960). The following letters (with or without subscripts) are used as variables: "A", "B", ... for sets, "x", "y", "z" for sets or individuals; "m", "n" for natural numbers other than 0. [For the possible benefit of some readers the customary symbols may be explained: "$\in$" designates the element relation; "$\notin$" its negation; "$\subseteq$" set inclusion; "$\cap$" intersection of sets; "$\varnothing$" the empty set. "$x, y \in A$" is short for "$x \in A$ and $y \in A$", "$\langle x, y \rangle$" designates the ordered pair with x as its first and y as its second member. "$\{x: ...\}$" designates the set of all x such that ..., where the dots are to be replaced by the formulation of some condition.]

We first define an auxiliary term corresponding to "n-th branch of x":[8]

DEFINITION 1. If B is a binary relation, then $n \, B \, x = \{y: \langle y, x \rangle \in B^n$ and there is no $m > n$ such that $\langle y, x \rangle \in B^m\}$.[9]

The main definition can now be formulated:

DEFINITION 2. A is a *system of disciplines* if and only if there is a binary relation B and a set D such that $A = \langle B, D \rangle$ and:

AXIOM 1. The field of B is finite.

AXIOM 2. B is a strict partial ordering.

AXIOM 3. B has at most one initial member.[10]

AXIOM 4. $D \neq \varnothing$.

AXIOM 5. For every $C \in D$:

(a) If $C_1 \in D$ and $C \neq C_1$, then $C \cap C_1 = \varnothing$.

(b) There are different elements of C.

(c) There is no x, y, z such that $x \in C$, $y \neq z$, and $x \in 1 \, B \, y \cap 1 \, B \, z$.

(d) For some x, $C \subseteq 1 \, B \, x$.

(e) If $x, y \in C$ and $x \neq y$, then there is no z such that $\langle z, x \rangle, \langle z, y \rangle \in B$.

AXIOM 6. For every $x \in$ the range of B:
  (a) For some $C \in D$: $x \in C$ or for some $y \in C$, $\langle x, y \rangle \in B$.
  (b) If for every $C \in D$, $x \notin C$, then there is a y, z, and n such that:
    (a) $y \neq z$.
    (b) If x_1 is an initial member of B, then y, $z \in n \, B \, x_1$.
    (c) $x \in 1 \, B \, y \cap 1 \, B \, z$.

This definition goes beyond Morris's explicit formulations in the following respects: (a) Axiom 5c is introduced (cf. note 4). (b) 5d is stated for some x rather than for the initial member of B (cf. note 4). (c) 5e is not restricted to $1 \, B \, x$ and $1 \, B \, y$ (cf. note 5). (d) Axiom 6 does not require that all possible 'recombinations' of elements of different criteria should actually occur (cf. note 6), and it also covers the case of 'indirect recombinations' by means of branches of elements. Even so, Morris's system of semiotic sciences as represented in Figure 1 (where certain lines have to be added, cf. note 2), is a model for our theory, i.e., satisfies Definition 2. Thus, Definition 2 formulates general assumptions underlying Morris's account as represented in Figure 1. (In arriving at Figure 1 we applied "branch" in some cases where a corresponding formulation in Morris (1938) was not to be found.) [11]

1.4. *Application of the predicate.* Definition 2 provides a framework for future discussion. First, linguistics can be accommodated within this framework. Morris (1938) is not clear about the relation between linguistics and semiotic (except for stating that the former "clearly falls within" the latter (55)), but the following proposal can be defended: We introduce as a new criterion {linguistic semiotic, non-linguistic semiotic}, where linguistic semiotic = linguistics and where the second element might be replaced by several elements. The elements of the new criterion are considered as first branches of descriptive semiotic. [12] Linguistic syntactics, semantics, and pragmatics can be obtained by 'recombination'. We thus arrive at the situation diagrammed in Figure 2 (the 'pure' branches of semiotic have been omitted, since they are supposed not to combine with any of the new branches, and of the six third branches of semiotic only the three linguistic ones are given).

Obviously, the system of semiotic sciences (on the basis of Figure 2) again satisfies Definition 2. It also illustrates the increase in complexity that may result from addition of a single two-element criterion, thus emphasizing the general importance of criteria.

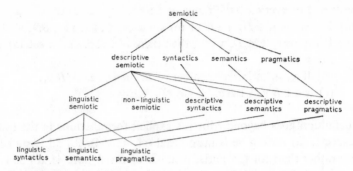

Figure 2. Linguistics and semiotic (Morris, 1938) (incomplete diagram).

Turning to Morris (1955) we find just one modification: Applied semiotic is introduced. This simply amounts to adding another element to the criterion {pure semiotic, descriptive semiotic}.[13]

We may now investigate Carnap's subdivision of semiotic. By describing its structure, we shall be able to decide whether it is a system of disciplines in the sense of Definition 2.

2. *Carnap's Subdivision of Semiotic and Its Structure*

Disregarding Carnap (1939) (the relevant passages of which are completely covered by his later book), we turn to Carnap (1942).

On p. 9, semiotic is identified with 'the science of language'.[14] Instead of Morris's "subscience" etc., Carnap uses "part" (3, 9 etc.; "branch" also occurs, 155). Semiotic 'consists of' the three parts, pragmatics, semantics, and (logical) syntax (9). The three parts are also called "fields", or "fields of investigation of languages" (9). The term "descriptive semiotic" occurs (9), but neither it nor "pure semiotic" is used when the terms "descriptive semantics (syntax)" and "pure semantics (syntax)" are introduced (11). Nor is "part" used in that passage to relate the four 'fields' (12) to any other 'part' of semiotic, and the same is true for the passage introducing "special descriptive semantics" and "general descriptive semantics" (11). However, in the case of descriptive and pure syntax Carnap remarks that "[we] divide these fields into two parts, *special* and *general syntax*" (12).[15]

Most gaps in this account can be easily filled within the general framework of Carnap (1942), in the following way: Special and general pure semantics are explicitly allowed for as 'parts' of pure semantics. Pure semiotic is introduced alongside with descriptive semiotic.[16] Pure syntax and semantics are considered as 'parts' of pure semiotic, descriptive syntax and semantics as 'parts' of descriptive semiotic, and pure and descriptive semiotic as 'parts' of semiotic (cf. 13: "the descriptive, empirical part of semiotic"). General syntax and semantics, with the appropriate 'parts', are explicitly recognized, and so are special syntax and special semantics (see also note 15). The former may be considered as 'parts' of general semiotic, the latter as 'parts' of special semiotic.[17] Finally, transitivity of 'part' seems to be implied by the very choice of the term, and there is nothing in Carnap (1942) to contradict the assumption of asymmetry.

One gap, however, must remain: Carnap does not seem to admit pure pragmatics.[18] This appears to be surprising, when "pure (semiotic)" and "pragmatics" are understood as in Morris (1938), but indeed both terms are understood differently in Morris (1938) and Carnap (1942).[19] Without analysing the difference here we may point out its consequences as contained in the following key passage, which assigns a place to linguistics within semiotic (13):

Linguistics, in the widest sense, is that branch of science which contains all empirical investigation concerning languages. It is the descriptive, empirical part of semiotic (of spoken or written languages); hence it consists of pragmatics, descriptive semantics, and descriptive syntax. But these three parts are not on the same level; *pragmatics is the basis for all of linguistics.*

Here the descriptive part of semiotic (of the science of language) is identified with linguistics, and pragmatics is considered as one of its 'parts'.[20] Therefore, since for Carnap 'pure' excludes 'descriptive', there is no pure pragmatics.

In the same passage Carnap goes on to remark that "descriptive semantics and syntax are, strictly speaking, parts of pragmatics" – which would be impossible in Morris's system. The following equation would seem to result: Linguistics = descriptive semiotic = pragmatics. However, we are confronted with an equivocation: "Pragmatics" in the passage previously quoted was used as defined on p. 9, as designating the field of investigations where *explicit* reference is made to the user of a language. "Pragmatics" in the new sense – "pragmatics*" – further includes investigations that (roughly) result from pragmatical ones in the former sense, when reference to the user is omitted (cf. 13). It is only for pragmatics* that the above equation holds.[21]

If our account is correct (allowing for deliberate filling-in of certain

gaps), then the subdivision of semiotic in Carnap 1942 can be represented
as in Figure 3. (The lines may be read as "is a part of"; 'transitivity lines'
– cf. note 2 – have to be added; different entries designate different entities; "descriptive semiotic" may be replaced by either "pragmatics*" or
"linguistics".) [22]

Inspection of the diagram leads to the following result: Let p be the
relation Part-of as represented in Figure 3. There is no set of sets of members of p such that the pair consisting of p and that set is a system of disciplines by Definition 2. For any such set would have to contain {prag-
matics}, which has only one element, in contradiction to Axiom 5b. If,

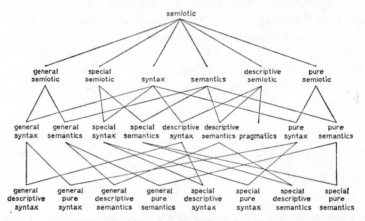

Figure 3.   The subdivision of semiotic according to Carnap, 1942.

however, 5b is replaced by "There is an element of C", then $\langle p, c \rangle$ satisfies the definition, where c = {{general semiotic, special semiotic}, {syn-
tax, semantics}, {pragmatics}, {descriptive semiotic, pure semiotic}}. (c
is the only set of this kind.)

We thus see that Carnap's treatment of pragmatics not only deviates
from Morris's treatment, it even forces us to liberalize one of the general
requirements (for any system of disciplines) that Morris apparently accepts. It seems to me that the overall effect of the liberalization is undesirable. Also, the set c, which we had to assume, has a questionable
property: Since syntax, semantics, and pragmatics are not elements of
the same element of c, the fact that they were distinguished on the basis
of a single point of view is not properly reflected.

So far we have not considered any of the points of view that are used by either Morris or Carnap for subdividing semiotic. The *points of view* underlying individual *criteria* will now be subjected to a critical examination.[23] We shall concentrate on the basis for {pure semiotic, descriptive semiotic} in Morris's and Carnap's subdivisions, considering only briefly the bases of the better-known trichotomies. (Our discussion will, however, involve a more extensive coverage of pragmatics.) Developments later than Carnap (1942) and Morris (1955) will be taken into account, but no comprehensive review is intended. Our critique will eventually lead to a proposal for a new subdivision of semiotic.

II. A CRITIQUE AND A NEW PROPOSAL

3. *"Pure" and "Descriptive": Morris vs. Carnap*

Comparing Figures 1 and 3, we find that Carnap introduces a criterion that apparently is not recognized by Morris: {general semiotic, special semiotic}. The underlying point of view can be inferred from the following passage (Carnap 1942, 11):

By *descriptive semantics* we mean the description and analysis of the semantical features either of some particular historically given language, e.g. French, or of all historically given languages in general. The first would be *special* descriptive semantics; the second, *general* descriptive semantics.

Generalizing from this, we arrive at a point of view that might be called: investigation of all (actual) languages vs. investigation of some (actual) language. Morris does not use a distinction 'all . . ., some . . .' in establishing his criteria. However, the point of view underlying his criterion {pure semiotic, descriptive semiotic} is different from Carnap's and appears to be half-way in between the points of view underlying Carnap's {pure semiotic, descriptive semiotic} on the one hand, and {general semiotic, special semiotic} on the other. Let us quote in full the passage from Carnap (1942, 11f), which directly continues the previous passage:

Thus, descriptive semantics describes facts; it is an empirical science. On the other hand, we may set up a system of semantical rules, whether in close connection with a [12] historically given language or freely invented; we call this a *semantical system*. The construction and analysis of semantical systems is called *pure semantics*. The rules of a semantical system S constitute, as we shall see, nothing else than a definition of certain semantical concepts with respect to S, e.g., 'designation in S' or 'true in S'. Pure semantics consists of definitions of this kind and their consequences; therefore, in contradistinction to descriptive semantics, it is entirely analytic and without factual content.

Since "pure syntax" is defined in an analogous way, the point of view underlying Carnap's {pure semiotic, descriptive semiotic} may be called: construction and analysis of syntactical and semantical systems vs. description and analysis of 'historically given' languages.[24]

Now compare Morris (1938, 8f):

> It is possible to attempt to systematize the entire set of terms and propositions dealing with signs. In principle, semiotic could [9] be presented as a deductive system, with undefined terms and primitive sentences which allow the deduction of other sentences as theorems. . . .
>
> Such a development [sc. a formalization of semiotic] remains . . . as a goal. Were it obtained it would constitute what might be called *pure semiotic*, with the component branches of pure syntactics, pure semantics, and pure pragmatics. Here would be elaborated in systematic form the metalanguage in which all sign situations would be discussed. The application of this language to concrete instances of signs might then be called *descriptive semiotic* (or syntactics, semantics, or pragmatics as the case may be).

Morris's point of view for {pure semiotic, descriptive semiotic} might be called: elaboration vs. application of the basic terminology of semiotic.

This is clearly different from the two points of view underlying Carnap's {general semiotic, special semiotic} and {pure semiotic, descriptive semiotic}, even if Carnap's basic restriction of semiotic (to a science of *languages*) is disregarded. There are, however, certain similarities. Just as pure semiotic according to Carnap is 'entirely analytic and without factual content', so Morris seems to envisage a pure semiotic allowing only for analytic sentences in some Carnapian sense. [25] On the other hand, the terms occurring in these analytic sentences are the basic terms of semiotic; therefore one might very well say that pure semiotic in Morris's sense is concerned with all *possible* signs, languages etc., just as Carnap's general semiotic would deal with all actual languages. Morris's wider conception of pure semiotic, which does not restrict itself to constructed languages, enables him to achieve, in a sense, what might be achieved by Carnap's 'general-special' distinction. (The latter applies, of course, solely within descriptive semiotic as Morris uses the term.)

For a comprehensive semiotic neither of Carnap's points of view appears to be as basic as Morris's distinction between pure and descriptive semiotic. Now in 1955 Carnap advocated what he called theoretical pragmatics (1956c, 248), a discipline not provided for in the system of Figure 3. At roughly the same time, Morris urged Carnap to recognize pure pragmatics (in Morris's sense), and it is clear from Carnap's answer that his theoretical pragmatics is very close to pure pragmatics as Morris proposed it.[26]

To avoid constant equivocation let us at this point replace "pure" and "descriptive" in the sense of Carnap (1942) by "of constructed languages" and "of (natural) languages"; "pure" and "descriptive" will now be used only in the sense of Morris.

Obviously, there are just two disciplines in Figure 3 that could be regarded as branches of pure semiotic: general syntax and general semantics of constructed languages. We might now add pure pragmatics of languages and pure pragmatics of constructed languages.[27] Of course, Figure 3 would have to be modified substantially. But what about pure syntactics and pure semantics of natural languages? If Figure 2 is correct then even Morris did not allow for pure branches of linguistics, at least in 1938.[28] Clearly, this is inadequate: If linguistics is to be reconstructed within semiotic, much of 'general linguistics' should reappear in pure semiotic.[29] Therefore, the two branches of pure syntactics and pure semantics of languages should be added.

These modifications do not yet solve all problems connected with the 'pure-descriptive' distinction.

4. *"Pure"* and *"Descriptive"*: The Problem of Analyticity

For both Morris and Carnap, the distinction between pure semiotic and descriptive semiotic is linked to the distinction between 'analytic' and 'synthetic': Apparently every sentence of pure semiotic is to be 'analytic', i.e. true or false either because of its form or because of 'meaning relations' that exist between the terms of semiotic. Since Carnap's account of analyticity is by far superior, I will restrict myself to discussing his position.

In 1963a, 861, Carnap remarks with reference to his paper 1956c:

I briefly indicated some concepts (belief, intension, assertion) which, together with related concepts, might serve as a basis for theoretical pragmatics. A study of the logical relations between concepts of this kind, relations that would be expressed by meaning postulates, would constitute a theory of pure pragmatics.

However, in 1956c, Carnap radically modified a previous attitude that had been basic even in 1956b. Making use of the framework published in Carnap 1956d he remarks (1956c, 248):

I think today that the basic concepts of pragmatics are best taken, not as behavioristically defined disposition concepts of the observation language, but as theoretical constructs in the theoretical language, introduced on the basis of postulates and connected with the observation language by rules of correspondence.

Indeed, this change seems to have prompted the expression "theoretical pragmatics". But now the concept of meaning postulate as developed in Carnap (1956a) no longer applies in connection with the 'basic concepts of pragmatics'.[30] Therefore, the 'logical relations' between the basic concepts cannot 'be expressed by meaning postulates' in the sense of Carnap (1956a), and if in the above quotation "meaning postulate" is to be understood in this way, theoretical pragmatics has been incorrectly characterized.

However, in 1963e Carnap develops his ingenious solution for applying the analytic-synthetic dichotomy also in connection with theoretical terms (§ D; cf. also Carnap (1966)). Consider, then, theories that develop 'basic concepts of pragmatics'. It might be proposed that theoretical pragmatics should be concerned with the 'logical relations' that hold between the 'theoretical terms' of such a theory, relations that are based on A-postulates ('meaning postulates') for the theoretical terms.[31] Now Carnap's method provides us only with a single A-postulate for all the theoretical terms at once, namely with the sentence $^{R}TC \rightarrow TC$. Here ^{R}TC is the so-called Ramsey-sentence of the theory, and TC is the conjunction of T and C, where T is the conjunction of the (theoretical) axioms of the theory (containing all the theoretical terms and no observation terms) and C is the conjunction of the 'correspondence rules' relating theoretical terms to observation terms. Obviously, TC must be known for establishing the A-postulate; once it is known, finding the A-postulate is a completely mechanical step.[32] Therefore, the fruitfulness of theoretical (i.e., pure) pragmatics should be greatly reduced if we exclude the task of theory construction itself and restrict the discipline to a study of the 'logical' relations holding between 'basic concepts', even if we admit the feasibility of this step.[33] Rather, pure pragmatics should be concerned with developing theories on certain basic problems of semiotic such as (perhaps) the problems of assertion, utterance, etc.; the 'logical aspects' of such theories would, of course, be taken into account.

A similar conclusion is possible for any branch of pure semiotic. I would therefore reject any interpretation of pure semiotic that restricts it to a study of 'logical' relations between 'basic concepts' of semiotic. As a point of view for distinguishing pure and descriptive semiotic, I propose instead that pure semiotic should develop theories on the basic problems of semiotic, descriptive semiotic being that part of semiotic where such theories will be presupposed.[34] Of course, this is only a vague indication. It is sufficient, though, to raise the following problem: How would the 'general-special' distinction relate to the new point of view for {pure semiotic, descriptive semiotic}? A recent proposal by Bar-Hillel is relevant here; by discussing it, we may also further elucidate our distinction between pure and descriptive semiotic.

5. *"Pure" and "General": Bar-Hillel's "Universal"*

In Bar-Hillel (1969, 9), the following suggestion is made for the semantics of natural languages:

> ... it might be useful to propose not to treat the terms "general semantics" and "universal semantics" as synonymous.... Whereas, I propose, *general* should be used to denote "accidental allness", *universal* should be reserved for "necessary allness". Whereas generality should therefore allow o ʲdegrees..., universality would be absolute. A given linguistic feature would be termed universal, rather than just general, not simply because the state of affairs was such and no totherwise, but rather because we would not want to call something a language unless it contained that feature, in other words, if the occurrence of that feature was necessitated by the very meaning of the term"language".

In any relevant theory containing "language", this would doubtless be a theoretical term.[35] Therefore, the distinction between universal and general again raises the problems previously discussed for pure semiotic. Assuming Carnap's A-postulate for theoretical terms (and to my knowledge, there is nothing more advanced), we cannot interpret "necessary allness" simply by "the very meaning of the term 'language'" – no such entity being at our disposal – but must refer to the complete interpreted theory TC: any change of the theory, that is, replacement either of one of the theoretical axioms in T or of a correspondence rule in C, results in a new A-postulate for the theoretical terms (since the A-postulate is the implication $^{R}TC \rightarrow TC$). I therefore suggest a change in Bar-Hillel's chain of "universal linguistic feature" – "we would not want to call something a language unless it contained that feature" – "the occurrence of that feature is necessitated by the very meaning of the term 'language'". The last two members should be replaced by "we would not want to call something a theory of language unless it allowed derivation of a theorem stating that every language has that feature", which is, of course, a requirement that the theory contain axioms, either in T or in C, with a certain property. Whether we keep any particular axiom in the theory is, however, up to us; it depends on a decision we choose to make (which is correctly expressed by the phrase "we would not want to"). On this conception, "universal linguistic feature" is relative to a decision of a certain person at a certain time to make certain demands concerning any theory of a certain type. On the other hand, "(n-degree) general linguistic feature" is relative only to a specific theory of that type. (Of course, whether anything is an n-degree general linguistic feature relative to that theory depends on the state of the world.)

Let us tentatively assume that this distinction between "universal linguistic feature" and "general linguistic feature" is acceptable. Then I would still maintain that it should not be used for setting up different disciplines, one dealing with universals, the other with the factual generality of features (as Bar-Hillel suggests in the case of linguistic semantics). "Universal linguistic feature" is relative to a decision concerning theories, and in principle any such decision can be revoked. Findings about the factual generality of features (relative to an appropriate theory) should be of central importance in considering or reconsidering a relevant decision, and systematic investigation into the generality of a feature should hardly ever occur unless material is needed for either proposing or defending a universality decision. Hence, whether we consider investigations into 'generality' or 'universality', it seems unwise to set up separate disciplines for the two kinds of study.

Generalizing from this result, I understand the pure-descriptive distinction to cover as 'pure' both 'universality' and 'generality'; and indeed, this is only another formulation for what the previous formulation was intended to convey ("pure semiotic should develop theories on the basic problems of semiotic").

I should like, however, to replace the terms "pure" and "descriptive" by "general" and "special". In this way, I hope to avoid the misleading suggestion that semiotic is to be divided into two branches, the first of which deals exclusively with what is 'analytic', all the rest being assigned to the second. Henceforth, I shall use the terms "general semiotic" and "special semiotic". General semiotic develops theories on the basic problems of semiotic, thus dealing with the complete domain (both actual and 'possible') of semiotic; special semiotic deals with the set of all 'parts' of the actual domain of semiotic (where the sense of "part" has to be specified).[36] Corresponding statements hold for the branches of either discipline; for instance, general linguistics develops theories on the basic problems of linguistics, and special linguistics deals with the set of 'parts' of the actual domain of linguistics.[37]

Obviously, "special" is not to be understood on the analogy of Carnap's "special" (which implies a restriction to individual languages, cf. above, Section 3): two branches of (a branch of) special semiotic may differ in comprehensiveness.

After these clarifications we may now formulate criteria for a subdivision of semiotic that tries to avoid the shortcomings of previous divisions.

6. A New Subdivision of Semiotic

6.1 *"General"*, *"special"*, *"applied"*; *"linguistic"*, *"non-linguistic"*. As my first *basic* or *first-level* criterion (consisting only of first branches of semiotic, cf. Definition 1) I propose a set containing at least general semiotic and special semiotic as now understood. I further include applied semiotic, on the basis of the hint in Morris (1946, 1955, 220).[38] I believe that the point of view underlying {general, semiotic, special semiotic} can be extended so as to justify the criterion {general semiotic, special semiotic, applied semiotic}, in some reasonable sense of "applied semiotic". However, I will leave this question open; the inclusion of applied semiotic should be considered as tentative.[39]

A second basic criterion is obtained by applying the point of view 'fundamental differences in subject matter': (natural) languages as subject matter vs. constructed languages as subject matter vs. . . . (where a finite number of terms are to be added).

In the light of recent developments in logic (Montague, e.g., 1970) it might be argued that 'natural languages as subject matter' and 'constructed languages as subject matter' should not be distinguished as parts of our point of view, but should be replaced by something like 'linguistic systems as subject matter', which would be quite contrary to the spirit of Carnap (1942). It is impossible to discuss this important and rather subtle point within the limits of the present paper. I shall tentatively assume that the distinction may be kept (at the present basic level where points of view for first-level criteria are considered). However, no substantial change in the general framework is required when the assumption is given up.

Besides languages and constructed languages as subject matter, we may consider communication systems used by animals other than man (cf. e.g., Sebeok (ed.), 1968). I will leave it undecided here how precisely the above formulation should be completed so that a point of view of maximal fruitfulness may be obtained. (Certainly none of the 'subject matters' should be 'contained' in any of the others.) However it is completed, the corresponding criterion could be stated in the following form: {linguistic semiotic, non-linguistic semiotic$_1$, ..., non-linguistic semiotic$_n$}, where linguistic semiotic = linguistics. We assume that linguistics is restricted to the study of natural languages; one of the non-linguistic semiotics, say semiotic$_1$, may then be identified with the study of constructed languages.

The elements of the new criterion may combine freely with the elements of the previous criterion to form common branches; thus, we allow for general/special/applied linguistics etc. We thus reject the treatment of linguistics in Figure 2 and apply the general-special distinction also to constructed languages, a move that is compatible with Carnap's introduction of theoretical pragmatics (see Section 3).[40]

6.2. *"Syntactics"*, *"semantics"*, *"pragmatics"*. As a third basic criterion we choose {syntactics, semantics, pragmatics}. I must here leave open what might be considered an adequate point of view for this criterion; justification of any proposal would require going much more deeply into the basic problems of semiotic than is feasible in the present context. However, some general points can be made.

In 1938, § 3, Morris analysed the 'sign-process' (semiosis) as a three-place relation, from which he "abstracted for study" (6) three kinds of two-place relations: between sign and interpreter, sign and 'designation' or 'object denoted', and between sign and sign, calling the 'study' of each kind pragmatics, semantics, and syntactics, respectively. His account is not very clear, and is inadequate for a number of reasons (such as failure to distinguish properly between 'sign-design' and 'sign-event', in spite of his § 13).

Carnap's point of view in (1942, 9) is very similar to Morris's for syntax ('syntactics' in Morris) and semantics but differs, as Carnap notes, for pragmatics: an investigation is assigned to pragmatics if it makes "explicit reference ... to the user of a language". This is inadequate for linguistics on the following grounds. In linguistics, statements such as "'blau' means Blue for Hans" and "'blau' means Blue in German" are closely related, and Carnap is fully aware of the fact that it is relations of abstractions that are relevant here. However, these relations have a degree of complexity that Carnap, not being a linguist, tends to underestimate.[41] They do not just consist in dropping explicit references to speakers. Indeed, the fact that at a certain point *explicit* reference may disappear should be, for the linguist, a fairly irrelevant aspect of a total analysis of the abstraction relations. Therefore, Carnap's definition of "pragmatics" is hardly fruitful for linguistics if taken literally. On the other hand, if we disregard "explicit" in the definiens, then linguistics as a whole becomes a part of pragmatics (there should always be implicit reference to speakers), and the part of linguistics that is not 'syntax' or 'semantics' becomes that convenient dump where the more important problems are left to rot.[42]

At present I believe that the distinction between syntactics, semantics and pragmatics should be kept in semiotic, even as a point of view for a first-level criterion. My two short analyses were meant to provide some background for the following general assumptions (whose formulation is admittedly vague): (1) Morris and Carnap are right in relating the distinction to fundamental aspects of communication. (2) For a fruitful formulation of the distinction, it is necessary to develop much more elaborate theories of communication than those assumed in Morris (1938) or Carnap (1942).[43] (3) If in a given formulation the distinction cannot be fruitfully applied in linguistics, it should be rejected in that formulation.

These three points do not specify a point of view for {syntactics, semantics, pragmatics}. We break off the discussion at this point, assuming that an adequate point of view for the criterion will again allow all elements to combine freely with all elements of the other two criteria. (Difficulties that Morris or Carnap encountered in admitting particular combinations should not reappear if the other two criteria are understood as above.)

I tentatively assume that no other basic criterion is required for a fruitful subdivision of semiotic.[44] Further criteria will of course be necessary at other 'levels', say, the level of second branches of semiotic. What kind of system results if the three criteria are taken as basic?

6.3. *Outline of the subdivision.* I propose a system of semiotic disciplines that is partially indicated in Figure 4. The basic relation may again be called Branch-of (on the basis of Figure 4). The only first-level criteria are the criteria discussed previously. Strictly for the purpose of illustration, a third-level criterion has been assumed: {$group_1$-linguistics, ..., $group_m$-linguistics}, where $group_i$ is a group of languages. (The underlying point of view might be: study of a 'maximal' set of genetically related languages. If "maximal" is suitably restricted, then, for some $i = 1$, ..., m, $group_i$-linguistics might be Indo-European linguistics.) To keep the complexity of the diagram within reasonable limits, only one element of the second and one of the third first-level criterion have been taken into account, just as a single element of the third-level criterion has been selected.

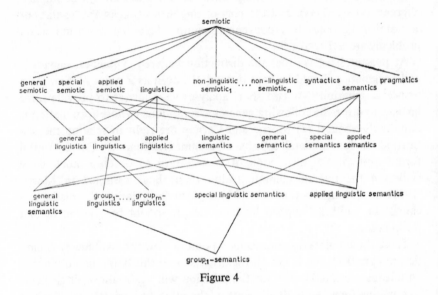

Figure 4

The subdivision, when completely specified, is supposed to be a system of disciplines in the sense of Definition 2. As a new feature, there are disciplines that are first branches of more than two disciplines, e.g., special linguistic semantics. This can be covered in the following way: If the set of elements of criteria of which a given discipline is a branch is properly contained in the set of elements of criteria of which a second discipline is a branch, then the second must be a branch of the first. (Therefore, special linguistic semantics must occupy the place it does.) For an explicit formulation, we first define, for any binary relation B and any set D: *the BD-set of* $x = \{y$: There is a $C \in D$ such that $y \in C$ and $\langle x, y \rangle \in B\}$. We now add the following axiom in Definition 2:

AXIOM 7. If the BD-set of x is a non-empty proper subset of the BD-set of y, then $\langle y, x \rangle \in B$.

My proposal for a system of semiotic disciplines is tentative. Still, I do believe that it begins to approach 'the true picture', that is, a fruitful reconstruction of the complex system of interrelations that are involved in the study of signs.

I readily admit that a number of important problems have not been mentioned. I should like to conclude this essay by pointing out three of them, indicating how they might be attacked.

7. *Three General Problems*

The first problem may be called the problem of parts. Throughout this essay a scientific discipline has been taken as an unanalysed entity, and only one kind of relation between disciplines was considered ('is a branch of'). This approach has been made explicit in Definition 2; correspondingly, the definition assigns no set-theoretical structure to the members of the basic relation B. Therefore, the following questions cannot be answered: May we assume that the basic relation is contained in some kind of 'part'-relation (as Carnap's use of "part" and the division terminology in general would suggest)? If so: How are we to interpret "part"? Is there a 'part' of a discipline that is not a branch of the discipline? May different elements of the same criterion have a common 'part'? These four questions together constitute the problem of parts.

An actual discipline may be considered as an abstract historical entity (similar in this respect to languages); as such, it would be subject to change. We are therefore confronted with the 'historicity problem': How may we account for the historical character of actual disciplines?

At various points of the essay we tacitly assumed that it makes sense to speak of a 'possible' discipline (which as such could be 'proposed'). But how this is to be understood is far from obvious. Therefore, the 'possibility problem' should be investigated: How are we to explicate the concept of a possible discipline?

Definition 2 represents an answer to some of the general problems that are involved in subdividing semiotic. The three new problems should also be solved in an explicit form since the solutions will affect our whole attitude towards the 'possibility', the 'value' etc. of subdividing semiotic, and also towards specific divisions.

Concerning the problem of parts I have reached the conclusion that the 'branch'-relation should indeed be contained in a 'part'-relation, but that for the latter nothing as simple as 'is an element of' or 'is a subset of' will do. I propose to proceed as follows. As a first approximation, let us consider an *investigation* during a time interval as a certain ordered sixtuple consisting of six sets: the investigators, the objects of study, the aims of study, the problems to be solved, the methods, and the (formulated) results, all relativized to the interval. *A stationary discipline* is an ordered sixtuple obtained in the following way from a maximal set of investigations satisfying certain similarity conditions: The first member is the union of the first members of the investigations, and so on. An n-tuple of sets is called a *part* of another, if the i-th member of the first is a subset of the i-th member of the second, for $i = 1, \ldots, n$. We now stipulate for stationary disciplines that, if one is a branch of the other, then it is a part of the other.

This answers (in a preliminary way) the first two questions of the parts problem for stationary disciplines. Concerning the third question let me just remark that Carnap and Morris presuppose different answers.[45] As for the last question, it should indeed be required that elements of *different* criteria have common parts; we now see that this need not present a logical problem.[46] In the case of different elements of the same criterion neither Morris nor Carnap seems to allow for 'overlapping', but this need not be adopted as a general requirement.[47]

We might now construct an *historical discipline* out of appropriate stationary disciplines, e.g., identify it with a sequence of these disciplines on the basis of a temporal relation (note that the underlying investigations are all relative to time); the stationary disciplines would form the *stages* of the historical discipline. The problem of parts could now be solved also for historical disciplines. Moreover, we would have a basis for tackling the historicity problem.

To repeat, this is not meant as a solution for the two problems, but as an argument that a solution may be achieved by proceeding in a certain way. Quite likely, analysis beyond a certain point would require an intensional logic (to deal with the 'aims' and 'problems to be solved'). This seems fairly certain in the case of the possibility problem. All I can offer at present concerning this problem is a suggestion: Possible disciplines should be constructed in the same way as actual ones, but taking sets of 'possible individuals' as first members of investigations and modifying the other members accordingly. The logical problems involved might then be tackled by using the intensional systems that Montague and his colleagues have been developing over the past few years (cf., for instance, Montague, to appear).

I hope that in this concluding section some of the general objections to my subdivision of semiotic have been countered; and I believe that the following claim is defensible: Certain results that have been obtained in the present essay are relevant not only for semiotic but for a better understanding of scientific study in general.

Dept. of Linguistics, University of British Columbia.

BIBLIOGRAPHY

Bar-Hillel, Y.: 1969, "Universal Semantics and Philosophy of Language: Quandaries and Prospects", in: J. Puhvel (ed.), *Substance and Structure of Language*, Berkeley and Los Angeles, pp. 1–21 [reprinted as Chapter 15 in Bar-Hillel, Y., 1970, *Aspects of Language*, Jerusalem–Amsterdam].

Carnap, R.: 1939, *Foundations of Logic and Mathematics*, Chicago (= *International Encyclopedia of Unified Science*, I, 3).

Carnap, R.: 1942, *Introduction to Semantics*, in: R. Carnap, *Introduction to Semantics and Formalization of Logic*, two volumes in one, Cambridge, Mass., 3rd pr. 1968. (First edn. of vol. I, 1942).

Carnap, R.: 1956, *Meaning and Necessity. A Study in Semantics and Modal Logic*, Chicago–London, 2nd edn.

Carnap, R.: 1956a, "Meaning postulates", in: Carnap 1956, pp. 222–9, (= App. B). (First publ. 1952.)

Carnap, R.: 1956b, "Meaning and Synonymy in Natural Languages", in: Carnap 1956, 233–47, (= App. D). (First publ. 1955.)

Carnap, R.: 1956c, "On Some Concepts of Pragmatics", in: Carnap 1956, 248–50, (= App. E.) (First publ. 1955.)

Carnap, R.: 1956d, "The Methodological Character of Theoretical Concepts", in: H. Feigl, M. Scriven (eds.), *Minnesota Studies in the Philosophy of Science*, I, Minneapolis, pp. 38–78.

Carnap, R.: 1958, *Introduction to Symbolic Logic and Its Applications*, New York.

Carnap, R.: 1963a, "Charles Morris on Pragmatism and Logical Empiricism", in: P. A. Schilpp (ed.) 1963, pp. 860–2.

Carnap, R.: 1963b, "My Conception of Semantics", in: P. A. Schilpp (ed.) 1963, pp. 900–5.

Carnap, R.: 1963c, "W. V. O. Quine on Logical Truth", in: P. A. Schilpp (ed.) 1963, pp. 915–22.

Carnap, R.: 1963d, "E. W. Beth on Constructed Language Systems", in: P. A. Schilpp (ed.) 1963, pp. 927–33.

Carnap, R.: 1963e, "Carl G. Hempel on Scientific Theories", in: P. A. Schilpp (ed.) 1963, pp. 958–66.

Carnap, R.: 1966, M. Gardner (ed.), *Philosophical Foundations of Physics*, New York–London.

Lieb, H.: 1969, "On Explicating "Language" for Linguistics", *Semiotica* 1, 167–84.

Lieb, H.: 1970, *Sprachstadium und Sprachsystem. Umrisse einer Sprachtheorie*, Stuttgart.

Martin, R. M.: 1959, *Toward a Systematic Pragmatics*, Amsterdam (*Studies in Logic and the Foundations of Mathematics*).

Montague, R.: 1970, "English as a Formal Language", in: *Linguaggi nella società e nella tecnica*, [Proceedings of a conference held in Milan, Oct. 14–17, 1968], Edizioni di Comunità, Milano (= *Saggi di cultura contemporanea* 87), pp. 189–223.

Montague, R.: 1970a, "Pragmatics and Intensional Logic", *Synthese* **22**, 68–94.
Morris, C. W.: 1938, *Foundations of the Theory of Signs*, Chicago (= *International Encyclopedia of Unified Science*, I, 2).
Morris, C. W.: 1955, *Signs, Language and Behavior*, New York. (1st edn. 1946.)
Morris, C. W.: 1963, "Pragmatism and Logical Empiricism", in: P. A. Schilpp (ed.), 1963, pp. 87–98.
Schilpp, P. A. (ed.): 1963, *The Philosophy of Rudolf Carnap*, La Salle, Ill., (= *The Library of Living Philosophers*, 11).
Sebeok, T. A. (ed.): 1968, *Animal Communication: Techniques of Study and Results of Research*, Bloomington.
Sebeok, T. A.: 1969, "Semiotics and Ethology", in: T. A. Sebeok and A. Ramsay (eds.), *Approaches to Animal Communication*, The Hague–Paris, pp. 200–231.
Suppes, P.: 1960, *Axiomatic Set Theory*, Princeton, N.J.

NOTES

[1] Already in the case of Morris there is a complete shift of emphasis between Morris (1938) and Morris (1955): Whereas the distinction is basic in the former book, it is introduced in the latter only on p. 217, and Morris goes on to remark that "The present study has deliberately preferred to emphasize the unity of semiotic rather than break each problem into its pragmatical, semantical, and syntactical components" (219).

[2] This amounts to drawing an additional single line between any two entries in Figure 1 that are connected via a third entry. It means that any branch of a branch of semiotic is a branch of semiotic; thus, we must again modify statements on 'the three' branches of semiotic in Morris (1938).

[3] The first power of Branch-of is Branch-of itself, the second power is the relation Branch-of-a-Branch-of.

[4] In a formulation not restricted to the situation of Figure 1, we may wish to choose the second, weaker condition, thus allowing for 'criteria' consisting of first branches of a non-initial member of the basic relation. In this case we may further wish to require that no element of a 'criterion' is a first branch of more than one member of the basic relation, which of course is trivially true in the situation of Figure 1.

[5] When there are branches other than first ones, it seems reasonable to generalize this statement to arbitrary branches. (It does not seem that Morris would allow for pure semiotic and descriptive semiotic to have a common branch, either.)

[6] In a more general formulation it may be unwise to require that all possible 'recombinations' of elements of different criteria should actually occur; we might wish, then, not to include an equivalent of the second part of the above statement.

[7] Either 'criterion' may be thought of as the result of applying what would ordinarily be called a criterion (for subdividing a given discipline). Although our choice of the term was motivated by this fact, criteria in the second sense which are relevant to Morris's subdivision of semiotic will be discussed only in Section II. To avoid confusion, I will then use "point of view" instead of "criterion" (in the second sense).

[8] The constant "Branch-of" is replaced by the variable "B", just as in Definition 2 the variable "D" replaces the expression "the set of criteria".

[9] Here B^n is the n-th power of B. ($B^1 = B$; $B^2 = B/B = \{\langle x, y \rangle$: There is a z such that $\langle x, z \rangle, \langle z, y \rangle \in B$; $B^3 = B^2/B$; etc.). – $n\, B\, x$ is the set of members of B that are, so to speak, 'n B-steps away' from the member x of B, where n is the greatest appropriate number.

[10] Existence of at least one initial member follows from Axioms 2, 4, 5b, and 5d.

[11] Stated more formally, the following relation holds between Definition 2 and the system represented in Figure 1. Let us define "the system of semiotic sciences (on the basis of Figure 1)" by "$\langle b, d \rangle$", where "b" and "d" are to be defined as below. Then $\langle b, d \rangle$ is a system of disciplines, where $b = \{\langle$pure semiotic, semiotic$\rangle$, $\langle$pure syntactics, pure semiotic$\rangle$, ...$\}$ (23 pairs), and $d = \{\{$pure semiotic, descriptive semiotic$\}$, $\{$syntactics, semantics, pragmatics$\}\}$.

[12] The examples that Morris lists on p. 21 for descriptive semantics seem to indicate that linguistics as a whole must be subsumed under descriptive semiotic. (Cf. also Morris, 1955, p. 219, and pp. 220–3.) Otherwise, we might introduce the elements of the new criterion as additional first branches of semiotic.

[13] The question of 'recombinations' involving the new element remains open. Due to the change of emphasis noted above (note 1), Morris (1955) is rather non-committal about the relation corresponding to Branch-of in Section 1.2 ("pragmatics is that portion of semiotic . . .", "the subdivisions of semiotic", 219).

[14] This is different from Morris's conception, as was pointed out by Morris himself in 1955, 218. However, in the informal summaries of Chapter A and § 4, Carnap (1942) calls semiotic "the theory of signs and languages" and "the general theory of signs and languages", respectively.

[15] Carnap's formulation is unclear and should probably be replaced by a reformulation such as: Syntax is divided into descriptive and pure syntax and into special and general syntax; descriptive syntax is divided into two parts, special descriptive syntax and general descriptive syntax, and pure syntax likewise. Later on in the book, the terms "general/special syntax/semantics" tend to be used instead of "general/special pure syntax/pure semantics" (e.g., § 38a).

[16] "Pure semiotic" occurs in the index.

[17] These two terms are not used in Carnap (1942). Still, this classification can be defended on the ground that Carnap allows for applying the 'general-special' distinction to each of the four 'fields', pure/descriptive syntax/semantics. As far as our formal apparatus (Definition 2) is concerned, this fact could be accounted for without assuming any new 'parts' of semiotic.

[18] This was criticized already in Morris (1955, 279, fn. B). (Morris's reference is to Carnap (1939)). Cf. also Martin (1959, 3f).

[19] This is acknowledged in Carnap (1942, 9) for "pragmatics", but not realized in Morris (1955, 279, fn. B) for "pure (semiotic)". In the discussion between Carnap (1963a) and Morris (1963), Carnap seems to be moving to Morris's interpretation. That Morris and Carnap have different conceptions of "pure" is recognized in Martin (1959, 7). For further discussion see below, Section 3.

[20] In the above quotation I understand "(of spoken or written languages)" as "that part which deals with spoken or written natural languages". Any other interpretation seems to create serious difficulties.

[21] In Carnap (1956b, 233), the term "pragmatics" corresponds to "pragmatics*": "the empirical investigation of historically given *natural languages*" (233); descriptive semantics is again included in pragmatics as a part (233), although the term is apparently used in a wider sense than in Carnap (1942).

[22] 'Immediate combinations' of general (special) semiotic and pure (descriptive) semiotic are not included; such an extension would be possible without invalidating the following results.

[23] In speaking about subdivisions of a discipline, I use "criterion" for a set of disciplines that functions more or less like a set in D in Definition 2; by "point of view" I refer to a set of properties used by a given author to single out disciplines that might form a criterion.

[24] "Historically given language" should refer to natural languages although Carnap is not

completely clear on this point (but cf. our note 21). I understand the first part of the above formulation in the sense of "construction and analysis of 'quasi-languages' specified by syntactical or semantical systems". Such systems, according to Carnap (1942), consist of rules formulated in a metalanguage (where the 'quasi-language' is the object language); a 'language system' is a special kind of semantical system (1942, 23). "Quasi-language" (my term) is meant to refer either to a language, or a calculus, or an interpreted language, or an interpreted calculus, in the sense of Carnap (1958, § 26b). From now on, I will speak simply of *constructed languages* in all these cases (a term also used by Carnap in 1963d), without implying that 'constructed' and 'natural' languages are languages in the same sense.

25 This is very clear in Morris (1955, 219), where the distinction between pure and descriptive semiotic is drawn as follows: "This distinction simply marks the difference between the formative discourse of semiotic and its designative discourse, that is, the difference between semiotic as logic and semiotic as scientific discourse. Semiotic, as a language to talk scientifically about signs, will have its own formative ascriptors (such as 'Every sign has an interpretant') and such ascriptors belong to logic...." (An ascriptor is, roughly, a sentence.)

26 Cf. Morris (1963); Carnap (1963a, 861f) (cf. 861 for the date of Morris (1963)).

27 A relevant work in the second field is Martin (1959), which is already referred to in Carnap (1963a, 862, fn. 2).

28 For justification of Figure 2, see above, note 12.

29 It would mean an artificial restriction to exclude the basic terms of linguistics from the terms that are the concern of pure semiotic.

30 In 1963e, 964, Carnap remarks: "The explanation given here [sc. in 1956a] is . . . directly applicable only to descriptive constants whose meanings are completely known, thus in language L only to the O-terms", where the O-terms are the terms of the observational part of L. (That is, the explanation is not directly applicable to the theoretical terms.) It is true, in 1956a the concept of meaning postulate is extended to cover the case of disposition terms introduced by 'reduction sentences'; in 1963e, 'pure disposition terms' are taken as theoretical terms (958, fn. 38); but in 1956c the 'basic concepts of pragmatics' do not seem to be considered as disposition terms anyway.

31 I am not sure whether Carnap's proposal for 'theoretical semantics' (1963b, § V) should be interpreted in this way.

32 This is quite different from establishing meaning postulates in the old sense, as would still be done for the observation terms: Such postulates, if they are not declared meaning postulates by fiat (cf. Carnap's answer to Quine, Carnap 1963c, 918f), may only be introduced for terms whose meanings are completely known (cf. Carnap's remark quoted in note 30). Thus, they presuppose that knowledge; they do not require knowledge of any theory formulated in the given language (other than might be relevant for a complete determination of the meanings).

33 We should still have disregarded the many objections that have been raised against Carnap's insistence on a sharp boundary-line between the analytic and the synthetic.– We have been considering axiomatic theories of the form TC. Our argument remains valid when theories of other forms are allowed: (a) If we take the theory to be the conjunction of the Ramsey-sentence and the A-postulate for theoretical terms, TC must still be known. (b) If we replace T by a definition of a set-theoretical predicate (where the definiens corresponds to T), then it is not clear how Carnap's method applies. (c) If we replace TC by an 'informal' theory (allowing for such a thing), then Carnap's method does not apply.

34 Any theory in pure semiotic should be an interpreted theory, or at least be interpretable if supplemented by other (interpreted) theories, which may well belong to descriptive semiotic.

[35] Cf. for instance the attempt in Lieb (1969).

[36] This formulation is still fairly vague. (Note that the 'domain' of a discipline need not be identified with the 'objects studied' as introduced below in Section 7.)

[37] If the actual domain of linguistics is identified with the set of actual languages, then the set of 'parts' might be the set of sets of actual languages.

[38] Analogously, Sebeok distinguishes between pure, descriptive, and applied 'zoosemi-otics' (1969).

[39] Note that applied semiotic cannot have any branches in common either with general or with special semiotic, if it is included and Definition 2 is accepted. (Thus, there will be no applied general linguistics, applied general semantics, or applied Indo-European linguistics, whereas – on the conception to be developed – applied linguistics and applied semantics are possible.) As an alternative, one might consider modifying Axiom 5b and establish {applied semiotic} as a separate criterion.

[40] We even allow for the applied study of constructed languages. This may be quite advantageous if we decide to include artificial languages among the constructed languages (thus broadening our use of the latter term), rather than treat them separately or include them among the natural languages.

[41] A large part of Lieb (1970) is devoted to studying these relations, still in a preliminary way.

[42] Which, of course, has been the fault of the linguist. As I tried to show above (Section 2), Carnap indeed tends to ignore "explicit", thus replacing pragmatics by pragmatics*. It may be pointed out that his descriptive syntax and semantics, i.e., syntactics and semantics of natural languages, are not very fruitful for linguistics, either, if understood on the basis of his general definition for syntax, semantics, and pragmatics (9). In linguistics, it should be at least possible that a 'semantical' statement explicitly refers to speakers (such as the first of our two previous examples), and a 'syntactical' one to 'meaning' or speaker or both. (Carnap himself points to differences between his 'logical syntax' and syntax as understood, at his time, in linguistics: 1942, 239.)

[43] Much has been done in the meantime, but applications to our problem seems to have been rare. (Cf., however, Sebeok 1969.)

[44] A linguist might suggest that another basic criterion should result from the 'syn-chrony-diachrony' distinction; however, after my work in Lieb (1970), I should hesitate to accept this proposal.

[45] Morris is quite emphatic about semiotic being more than its 'three' branches taken together (1938, § 14), whereas Carnap states that semiotic 'consists of' syntax, semantics, and pragmatics (1942, 9).

[46] We previously noted a curious indeterminacy in Morris (analogously, in Carnap) concerning the status of pure and descriptive semiotic as branches of semiotic alongside with syntactics etc. If there was doubt about the logical aspect, it could have been resolved.

[47] Confronted with the problem of how to deal with studies treating the *relations* between 'syntactical systems' and 'semantical systems', Carnap does not assign them to pure syntax and semantics simultaneously, but sets up a new 'field' for the study of 'systems' and their interrelations (1942, 14), an *ad hoc* solution, which remains unrelated to his general framework. (The problematic position of pragmatics has been discussed above, cf. Section 2.) Morris's insistence that semiotic is more than its three branches is also motivated by the problems of 'interrelations'.

ROBERT L. MARTIN

SOME THOUGHTS ON THE FORMAL APPROACH TO THE PHILOSOPHY OF LANGUAGE

I

This essay is offered in the spirit of interdisciplinary goodwill that prevailed during the Jerusalem meetings. It is not intended for specialists in the formal approach, though it will certainly stand in need of their corrections and comments; it is addressed rather to others who study language and philosophical problems concerning language – linguists, psycholinguists, 'ordinary-language' philosophers, etc. I am prompted to express the thoughts that follow, first of all, because the non-specialist already has available to him some general accounts of the nature of the formal approach that claim to show its ultimate fruitlessness for the study of *natural* language.[1] I think these accounts are fundamentally wrong, and I hope to show this. I am motivated, secondly, by the belief that some recent developments in the formal approach could be extremely suggestive to those who adopt other approaches. Much of what has been written on these developments is difficult to follow, and I propose to say something about some of them later in reasonably non-technical language.

In more detail, the plan of the paper is as follows. In Section II I will discuss an elaborate but, so I shall argue, misguided critique of the formal approach – that found in Katz [14]. My main quarrel with Katz in this section is that most of what he has criticized is not central to the formal approach; therefore, in Section III, I will mention some genuinely important elements in the development of this approach. In Section IV I will consider first what I take to be Katz's most serious criticism of the formal approach; this will lead to a consideration of the principal argument in Strawson [28] against the "constructionists". Section V contains the brief discussion of three recent developments that I mentioned above – (1) a model-theoretic treatment of meaning (or intension); (2) the construction of a pragmatic language; (3) the semantical investigation of non-bivalent formal languages.

Yehoshua Bar-Hillel (ed.), *Pragmatics of Natural Languages, 120–144. All Rights Reserved.*
Copyright © 1971 by D. Reidel Publishing Company, Dordrecht-Holland.

II

I should begin by saying a few words about what it is that I mean to defend. The formal approach,[2] as I understand it, has its roots in the work of Frege, Russell and Whitehead, Hilbert, Carnap, and Tarski. It flourishes today in the work of, for example, Montague, Hintikka, Scott, Kaplan, Kripke, and van Fraassen (I mention just a few, practically at random). The distinguishing characteristic of the formal approach is its use of formal (constructed) languages, or perhaps, more generally, its reliance on the notations and techniques of mathematical logic.

I want to argue that most of Katz's detailed critique of this approach in [14] is irrelevant, because it ignores everyone except Carnap and the Vienna Circle. Of course it must be shown that Katz means to criticize the entire formal approach, and not only Carnap and others of the Vienna Circle. This is established, I think, when Katz identifies what he calls logical empiricism, along with ordinary-language philosophy, as "the two dominant movements in twentieth century philosophy to concern themselves with language" (p. 16). He speaks, in connection with both, of the "sadly mistaken" expectation "that they are able to offer some philosophically relevant account of language" (p. 16). Two pages later he identifies the logical empiricists as "those philosophers who followed Carnap, Schlick, and Reichenbach, among others". As "others" the reader must include at least Frege, Russell, Hilbert, and especially Tarski. If this is not intended by Katz then he is simply wrong to call logical empiricism one of the two dominant movements; surely the Polish school, for example, contributed as much to whatever one opposes to ordinary-language philosophy as did the Viennese. And surely Katz means to include the people I have mentioned; he speaks of each in the course of his subsequent remarks.

But if Katz is speaking generally about the formal approach, then he should not dwell as he does on the difficulties of Carnap's antimetaphysics programme. This aspect of the formal approach was not generally accepted even in its heyday, and has not survived in more recent developments. I will summarize Katz's treatment briefly, so the reader can see precisely the narrowness of its scope relative to the generality of the claim based on it.

Katz says that the logical empiricists saw three major uses to which then recent advances in mathematical logic and metamathematics could be put.

The first, having to do with logical truth, Katz assigns to the philosophy of mathematics; the second, having to do with a verifiability criterion, Katz assigns to the philosophy of science; only the third, strangely enough, does Katz take as central to the philosophy of language: it is "the attempt to construct an ideal, artificial language whose principles of sentence formation and semantic interpretation would exclude metaphysical statements as violations of proper linguistic relations"[3] (p. 21). First Katz criticizes the logical empiricists for failing to examine natural language to see how much of the elimination of metaphysics was left unaccomplished by its own rules. "Theirs was", he writes (p. 24), "a wholly a priori decision about natural languages."[4]

Katz next describes Carnap's distinction between the material and the formal mode, and his view that metaphysical statements are "pseudo-object sentences" for which there are no syntactical translations. He criticizes Carnap for supplying us with no criteria for distinguishing these metaphysical statements from the pseudo-object statements, which do have syntactical translations. He summarizes his objections to this early phase of Carnap's work roughly as follows: (1) Carnap's reliance on syntactical methods makes adequate translations of pseudo-object sentences (even those he wants to be translated) impossible; he needs semantical concepts such as synonymy; (2) Carnap's principle of tolerance makes impossible a motivated rejection of formal frameworks into which the metaphysical statements *could* be translated.

Promising to return to point (2) later, Katz next considers Carnap's subsequent endorsement of a semantical approach. He describes some of the machinery of Carnap [6] and then dismisses the entire approach as inadequate, because of a "basic criticism" of it (p. 47). The criticism is that sense (meaning) must be distinguished from reference, and that Carnap's designational semantics treats only reference. Katz then objects to Carnap's device of *meaning postulates* and *semantical rules* for the theory of meaning: (1) again, the principle of tolerance rules out using the meaning postulates and semantical rules as part of an ideal language that has convincing *philosophical* use (i.e., that rules *against* some things); (2) the meaning postulates and semantical rules are vacuous, as pointed out in Quine [24], because they tell only which expressions to attribute, say, analyticity to; they do not explain *what* we are attributing. Katz expounds this objection, carrying it over at some length, against Carnap's discussion of pragmatic operational definitions of concepts such as *analytic* and *synonymous*. Katz concludes that "the last of Carnap's attempts to offer an acceptable theory of an ideal language ends in failure too" (p. 61). He closes his critique of the formal approach by claiming that its failure rests on *two*, not clearly differentiated, conceptions of an artificial language. It is here that Katz raises a question of general importance to the whole of the formal approach; we will return to it later.

I hope it is clear now that the burden of Katz's attack on the logical empiricists is aimed at the way(s) in which they sought to construct an 'ideal' language that would contain philosophically justified rules to bar the formation of metaphysical statements. I do not wish to deny that there was, for a certain period of time, some serious interest in constructing such a language; nor do I wish to deny that this interest provided the motivation for some work of continuing significance in the formal approach. But the antimetaphysics programme of the Vienna Circle is *not* a central part of the formal approach. To show this it is sufficient to point out that the antimetaphysics programme has not survived: the people who use formal techniques today are simply not occupied in trying to find ways to discredit metaphysics.[5] But even without looking to recent work one can see that the Vienna Circle's concern with the elimination of metaphysics through the construction of an ideal language was by no means the central or characteristic concern of the formal approach. I shall support this by saying a few words about the Polish school.

As we have seen, the crucial weapon in the Vienna Circle's antimetaphysics campaign was the reduction of so-called pseudo-object sentences (i.e., sentences that are apparently, but not actually, about objects in the universe of discourse of the language) to syntactic sentences in the metalanguage. In a paper [18] published in 1936, Łukasiewicz wrote: "I have strong and unyielding objections to the way in which Carnap attempts to reduce objective questions to linguistic ones ... Carnap's consideration of this matter I regard as hazardous philosophical speculation which will pass away as all similar speculations have done" (trans. in Skolimowski [27], pp. 73, 74). The same year at the Congress of Scientific Philosophy held in Paris, Ajdukiewicz delivered a paper in which he said: "In Poland there are no close followers of the Vienna Circle; I personally do not know any Polish philosopher who would accept as his own the 'subject matter' theses of the Vienna Circle" (Ajdukiewicz [1]; this remark translated in Skolimowski [27], p. 76).

Of course the point is not that the Polish philosophers defended the kinds of metaphysical statements that the Vienna Circle opposed. It seems that Łukasiewicz, Ajdukiewicz, Tarski, and others felt that metaphysical nonsense would simply fall victim to scientific method and high standards of rigour. It was characteristic of the Polish philosophers to attack specific philosophical problems according to a highly sophisticated and self-conscious methodology: notable examples are Ajdukiewicz' work on meaning and Tarski's work on truth. Sweeping reductionist programmes such as Carnap's were not in favour.[6] This situation is also characteristic of current work in the formal approach.

III

So far my remarks have been mainly negative. Before we turn to more substantive criticisms of the formal approach, it may be well to mention some genuinely important elements in its development. I will speak briefly of the contributions of Frege and Tarski.

Frege's goal was to show that mathematics is derivable from the principles of logic, and the points I wish to make are directly linked to this. To begin with, Frege's objections to natural language (for example, that not every name has exactly one referent, that expressions with the same sense may yet differ with respect to emotional colouring, etc.[7]) were relative to his own needs. He saw the difference between natural language and a perfected, symbolic notation as indicating a difference in function, not a defect in the former. If one was to *prove*, contrary to Kant's view, that reasoning in mathematics is purely analytic, then it seemed obvious that one needed a notation in which the most minute progressions of thought were rendered explicit and unambiguous. Frege required further that the *theory* in which the deductions were to be carried out meet high standards of rigour. The conditions he set down are still accepted in their essentials as defining the notion of a *formal theory* (for example, all undefined symbols must be listed, the concept of well-formed formula must be explained solely by reference to the shapes of the symbols involved, all formulas asserted without proof must be listed as axioms, etc.). The point I wish to emphasize is that although one can speak of Frege's intermediate goal as the development of an "ideal" language, it is "ideal" only in the sense of being very well fitted to the task of providing a precise account of the logical foundations of mathematics.

Despite the apparent crisis in foundational studies caused by Russell's

discovery of paradox in Cantorian set theory, the remarkable achievements of Frege and of Russell and Whitehead made it clear that the study
of mathematical reasoning is in large part nothing else but the study
of logical reasoning itself. Since this reasoning is carried out not only
in thought but also in (natural) languages, their "ideal" languages
for the study of the foundations of mathematics were also in a sense
"ideal" for the study of the logic imbedded in the rules of natural
languages.

The semantic paradoxes played an important role in the development
of the formal approach, especially through Tarski's investigation (see
Tarski [29]) of the concept of truth. A rough analogy can be drawn between the role of the set-theoretical paradoxes in stimulating work in
logical syntax, and the role of the semantic paradoxes in connection with
semantics. I shall not rehearse here the familiar story of the separation of
the semantic from the logical paradoxes, and of the simplification of the
theory of types that left the former in search of a solution (see, for example, Kneale and Kneale [17], pp. 652–65). Both sets of paradoxes seem
to have shaken confidence in the trustworthiness of intuitive, informal
methods in their respective domains. The semantic paradoxes provided
the impetus for the development of semantical theory and underscored
the importance of using the most precise techniques available. Until
Tarski's work on truth the concepts of semantics were viewed by most
analytic philosophers (outside Poland, at least) with considerable suspicion, as perhaps not susceptible to clear-headed treatment.[8] Tarski
established the respectability of the field. The introduction of semantical
considerations brought us from the study of syntactical systems to the
study of languages.

Unfortunately, certain of Tarski's remarks were influential in suggesting
the existence of an uncrossable gulf between natural and formal languages.
I refer specifically to his comments on semantic closure and on the consistency of natural languages (in Tarski [29] and [30]).[9] After deriving the
Liar paradox in [29], Tarski offers the opinion that natural languages
do not contain the restrictions necessary to bar the derivation (p. 158).
He concludes that no formally adequate definition of 'true' is possible for
a natural language, and he turns his attention in the rest of [29] to formal
languages, in which restrictions of expressivity are in force. Tarski
speaks again in [30] of conditions under which the semantic paradoxes
may be derived. A language L with the following properties is said to be

semantically closed: (1) L contains some way of referring to its own expressions; (2) L contains semantical predicates, such as 'is true in L', which apply to expressions of L itself, in accordance with the conditions of material adequacy for the predicates.[10] Any semantically closed language that abides by the classical laws of logic is demonstrably inconsistent. On the one hand, Tarski's further remarks suggest that he believes that natural languages are semantically closed. He remarks in [29] that it seems a characteristic feature of a natural language that it have a certain universality. "But it is presumably just this universality of everyday language that is the primary source of all semantical antinomies. . . . These antinomies seem to provide a proof that every language that is universal in the above sense, and for which the normal laws of logic hold, must be inconsistent" (Tarski [29], p. 164). But on the other hand Tarski notes in [30] that it is simply not clear what is meant by saying that a natural language is inconsistent. A formal language is inconsistent if two of its well-formed sentences, one the negation of the other, are both derivable according to the axioms and/or rules of inference of the language. For natural languages, says Tarski, we have no precise characterization of the notion of a well-formed sentence, not to mention a precise characterization of the notion of a derivation.

Tarski's remarks on this subject seem to me to combine an important insight into a problematic feature of natural language (its apparent universality – the fact that it contains its own metalanguage) with an eagerness (I judge it a matter of taste on his part) to get on with the study of intrinsically interesting formal languages. Unfortunately his remarks had the effect I mentioned above, of making it appear that the positive results of his investigation, and indeed of the tradition that his work generated, have *no bearing on natural language*. I will try to show very briefly why this conclusion is unjustified.

In the first place, Tarski's remarks show at most that an adequate definition of truth is impossible for a natural language *taken as a whole*. Any one of the successively more comprehensive formal languages for which his investigation has positive results may be taken as a formalization of a segment of natural language, and the concept of truth thus explicated may be regarded as the concept of truth applicable to sentences of that segment. (I am assuming that sense can be made of the notion of a formal language being a formalization of a segment of natural language; more on this later.)

A second, and similar, position is suggested by Tarski in [29]; he writes:

Whoever wishes, in spite of all difficulties, to pursue the semantics of colloquial language with the help of exact methods will be driven first to undertake the thankless task of a reform of this language. He will find it necessary to define its structure, to overcome the ambiguity of the terms which occur in it, and finally *to split the language into a series of languages of greater and greater extent, each of which stands in the same relation to the next in which a formalized language stands to its metalanguage* (p. 267, emphasis added).

A large number of philosophers have adopted the view that a natural language really is an infinitely extended hierarchy of sublanguages.[11] This is the familiar levels-of-language view, based on the use-mention distinction, which is often cited in orthodox solutions to the semantic paradoxes. Each "higher" sublanguage contains the syntactic and semantic predicates applying to expressions of the sublanguage one level lower. Here Tarski's results are seen as applicable not to a segment of natural language, but rather to the whole of natural language, one level at a time. Each level is restricted, but the whole, through its infinite upward-extendability, is thought to have lost nothing of importance under this conception.

A third, quite different, view, is based on the opinion that natural languages, even without a hierarchical conception, are not semantically closed. The second condition of semantic closure was that the semantic predicates of L, which apply to expressions of L, do so in accord with the conditions of material adequacy. We know the condition of material adequacy that Tarski set down for the truth predicate: it requires that every instance of the semantical schema be true. With this understood it is no longer clear that natural languages are semantically closed. It seems reasonable, to begin with, to say that natural languages are *not* bivalent (every sentence true or false). Not all grammatical sentences, and not even all sentences of the "right" grammatical kind, are either true or false – one thinks of performative utterances, category mistakes, and sentences with non-referring singular terms, for example. Once this is noted it seems reasonable to look for an explanation under which the paradoxical sentences are placed in the same company. But now consider an instantiation of the schema T by a truth-valueless sentence S. It is surely not clear that the instantiation is true in English, since it contains, on the right side, a truth-valueless part. To put the matter simply, Tarski's condition of material adequacy seems appropriate only for bivalent languages: in non-bivalent languages we can expect truth-valueless instances of the schema. But if we use a restricted condition of material adequacy in our definition of semantic closure, then it is no longer clear that the paradoxes are derivable in semantically closed languages, since the schema may not be applicable to the paradoxical sentences. This leaves open the possibility of a variety of solutions to the paradoxes in natural language, and thus the possibility of the consistent formalization of the semantics of natural language, without relying on levels.

IV

I turn now to a consideration of the final portion of Katz's discussion of the formal approach, in which he raises some questions that are indeed important. Katz speaks in the last pages of his critique of the existence of conflicting conceptions of a formal language. On the one hand he describes a conception of an ideal language, providing precise rules and specifications where natural language lacks these, for the purpose of avoiding metaphysics. On the other hand he describes a conception of a formal language as a *theory*, in the form of an idealization, about the structure of natural language. Carnap's comment on this conception in [7], quoted also by Katz, is very suggestive:

The direct analysis of (natural languages), which has been prevalent hitherto, must inevitably fail, just as a physicist would be frustrated were he from the outset to attempt to relate his laws to natural things – trees, stones, and so on. In the first place, the physicist relates his laws to the simplest of constructed forms: to a thin straight lever, to a simple pendulum, to punctiform masses, etc. Then, with the help of the laws relating to these constructed forms he is later in a position to analyze into suitable elements the complicated behavior of real bodies. . . . One more comparison: the complicated configurations of mountain chains, rivers, frontiers and the like are most easily represented and investigated by the help of geographical co-ordinates – or, in other words, by constructed lines not given in nature (p. 8).

Katz says that the two conceptions are incompatible: "One conception assumes, as does any scientific investigation, that there exists regularity and structure to be described, while the other assumes it is lacking" (p. 66). But surely this is wrong. Just because a formal language contains rules and specifications that natural language is thought to lack, it by no means follows that natural language is taken to be "so vague, irregular, and amorphous that there are no philosophically significant facts . . . to be faithful to" (p. 66). Only according to a caricature of this conception is *every* rule and specification "made up" without regard to natural language. It is more plausible to think it necessary to *add* rules and specifications and to sharpen up distinctions where only fuzzy ones exist in natural language;

the basic layout may well be dictated by the facts of natural language, and even the additions may be suggested by the facts.

Not only are these two conceptions not incompatible, they may even be ultimately indistinguishable. Quine has emphasized in [25], pp. 157–61, that the impulse to add further specifications, to introduce newly devised distinctions, and generally to clarify, plays a familiar and essential role in natural language communication. It turns out that for fixed purposes it is convenient to keep certain regimentations in force. This is entirely within the spirit of natural language, and provides us with a discourse that will be improved, if not quite ideal, for these purposes. Quine's point has to do primarily with notation, and not with the investigation of the structure of the language whose sentences are written in this notation, but the point may be extended. For such an investigation the "scientific" conception of the formal language is appropriate, and the adding of specifications and new distinctions etc., may simply be taken as a feature of the ultimate object of the investigation, not the result of a different conception of the formal language.

In any case, the second or "scientific idealization" conception is obviously of primary interest for the use of formal languages in the study of natural language. Katz claims that the formal languages actually developed by Carnap and his followers cannot satisfactorily fit this conception. He complains, first of all, that Carnapian formal languages, unlike successful idealizations in physics, are under "no strict empirical controls that determine their adequacy". He continues: "A scientist who proposes an idealization must demonstrate that it predicts accurately within a reasonable margin of error and that the closer the actual conditions approximate the ideal, the smaller this margin of error becomes" (p. 64).

Without denying that there are significant differences between idealizations in physics and idealizations in the study of language, one can see, in case after case, that Katz is wrong about the latter. Rules of interpretation associate sentences of the natural language with sentences of the formal language; then, once axioms and/or rules of inference are supplied, the correct derivations of the formal language may be regarded as predictions that particular inferences in natural language are sound ones; theorems of the formal language may be regarded as predictions that certain sentences of the natural language are valid ones (truths of logic); further, certain claims about the axioms and rules of inference (completeness claims) may be regarded as predictions that if a certain natural language inference is a logically sound one, then the associated formal language inference is in accordance with the rules. This is a very simple-minded answer to Katz's objection; still, if it is not a satisfactory answer then I have failed to understand the objection. I grant that it is not always obvious from the practice of logicians that such predictions are intended, but I think it is often obvious. Systems are criticized and sometimes abandoned because they yield peculiar results (inconsistency is the limiting case of this); new directions are explored because of the unwelcomeness of certain of the predictions of familiar systems. A good example of this is the investigation (see Anderson and Belnap [2]) of the system E of entailment. If Anderson and Belnap did not regard formal languages as models of the logic of natural languages, they might not have been concerned with the fact that in classical formal languages any sentence whatsoever is a consequence of any contradiction. Taken as providing a multitude of predictions about logical correctness in natural languages (to the effect that, for example, the sentence 'Richard Nixon sells used cars' is a logical consequence of the two sentences, 'Grapefruit contains vitamin C' and 'Grapefruit does not contain vitamin C') the classical formal language seemed to Anderson and Belnap to be shown defective by the *facts*. They argue that it is indeed a fact about English, and especially about the meaning of the word 'consequence', that the pair of sentences listed above does *not* have the other sentence as a consequence. So they set out to produce a formal language which, among other things, does not predict that such an inference is sound.[12]

I would like to comment also on Katz's remark that in genuine scientific idealizations one can show that "the closer the actual conditions approximate the ideal, the smaller the margin of error becomes" (p. 64). There are certainly cases in natural language argumentation where the inference from p to $p \vee q$ seems unacceptable ("You'll get the raise" said the employer to his employee. Then the employee to his co-worker: "The boss implied that either I'll get the raise or he'll shut down the factory."). There is some reason to think that such deviations from what the "theory" (classical sentence logic) predicts can be accounted for by explicating certain pragmatic rules that may be in force in natural language argumentation, for example, in our case, a rule to the effect that one should not draw conclusions in which information is lost.[13] Now to extend the example: perhaps we can imagine a case in which all parties know the truth of p, but in which it is useful, for the sake of demonstrating some remote conclusion, to draw the intermediate inference, $p \lor q$.[14] If we *can* imagine such a case, then we have a simple example of the phenomenon Katz mentions: we have a case where actual conditions are closer to the ideal, and the theory's predictions are more accurate.

In a second objection, Katz argues that even if we allow that formal languages yield predictions, these predictions are "quite empty" when contrasted with those of physical theories. For in the latter the predictions spring from a "tightly integrated system upon which the coherence of the predictions and explanations offered by the theory is based" (p. 64). For his example from formal languages Katz chooses the list of sentences labelled "analytic" or the list of pairs of expressions listed as "synony-mous" in a formal language equipped with meaning postulates. One can call these lists predictions, says Katz, that the associated natural language expressions are analytic (or synonymous), but such predictions rest on no network of principles. Again I wonder if I have understood Katz's objec-tion; if I have, it shows at most that certain predictions drawn from formal languages are theoretically empty. One need only consider the results of the interworking of the logic of the formal language with the meaning postu-lates to find interpreted theorems that can be taken as predictions, and which will indeed rest on a theoretical substructure. In the case of the Tarskian definition of truth one sees the adequacy of the definition by confirming its "predictions" that all instances of the semantical schema are true. This is an especially good case in point, for the predictions seems trivial ('Snow is white' is true if and only if snow is white); however, the predictions follow from a complicated network of principles that relate such theoretical notions as *satisfaction, open-formula, denotation* etc., and which has considerable explanatory power.

Strawson, in [28] arrives at a conception of formal languages quite like the one we are considering:

Let me state a little more fully the position the constructionist is now assumed to occupy. . . .[15] He offers his system as an object of contemplation which has the following features: first, it is intrinsically clear, in that its key concepts are related in precise and determinate ways (which the system exhibits) . . . ., and second, at least some of the key concepts of the system are, in important respects, very close to the ordinary concepts which are to be clarified. . . . The system as a whole then appears as a precise and rigid structure, to which our ordinary conceptual equipment is a loose and untidy approxima-tion (p. 511).

The "naturalist" alternative, Strawson has told us earlier in the essay, describes "the complex patterns of logical behaviour which the concepts of daily life exhibit." The naturalist describes "the actual conduct of actual words" (p. 503).

Strawson notes, quite justly, that on this conception of a formal language it is still possible for the argument between the constructionist and the naturalist to end in deadlock. The constructionist may simply insist that the mastery of such a system is both necessary and sufficient for *real* understanding of the concepts involved. The naturalist may insist with equal vigour that "since, *ex hypothesi*, the ordinary concepts to be examined do not behave in the well regulated way in which the model concepts of the system are made to behave, there can be no real understanding of the former except such as may be gained by a detailed consideration of the way they do behave . . ." (p. 512).

The way beyond the deadlock is, as Strawson says, to look at what philosophical problems are like – "for the claim to clarify will seem empty, unless the results achieved have some bearing on the typical philosophical problems and difficulties which arise concerning the concepts to be clarified" (p. 512). In the very next sentence Strawson characterizes philosophical puzzlement in a way that leads, apparently, in a very few steps, to the conclusion that the naturalist method has, at the very least, a natural priority over the constructionist method. Here is his argument:

Now these problems and difficulties (it will be admitted) have their roots in ordinary, unconstructed concepts, in the elusive, deceptive modes of functioning of unformalised linguistic expressions. It is precisely the purpose of the reconstruction (we are now supposing) to solve or dispel problems and difficulties so rooted. But . . . if the clear mode of functioning of the constructed concepts is to cast light on problems and difficulties rooted in the unclear mode of functioning of the unconstructed concepts, then precisely the ways in which the constructed concepts are connected with and depart from the unconstructed concepts must be plainly shown. And how can *this* result be achieved without accurately describing the modes of functioning of the unconstructed concepts. . . . (This) *by itself* (may) achieve the sought-for resolution of the problems and difficulties . . . (p. 512).

Briefly then, Strawson argues: (1) the formal approach provides models that ignore many details of the entangled geography of ordinary concepts; (2) philosophical problems arise characteristically in the entanglements that the model ignores; hence, (3) the formal approach must at least be supplemented by naturalist investigations to be of philosophical value, and, given (2), the construction of a model may be unnecessary. Actually Strawson's conclusion seems milder than his argument warrants (if it is correct). If he is right both about the locus of philosophical perplexity and about the limitations of constructed models, then naturalist investigations *must* be the principal source of philosophical enlightenment. My objection is to this stronger conclusion.

Let me begin by granting (1) of Strawson's argument; this asserts nothing more than that the formal languages of the constructionist are idealizations, as are any scientific models. I take it to be basic in the methodology of theory construction that what *actually happens* (in whatever domain) is almost always to be seen as the result of interaction between theoretically irrelevant circumstances and the laws that the theory states. We have alluded to this point before in suggesting a difference between pragmatic rules governing 'or' and the operation of 'or' as "predicted" by classical logic. Essentially the same point can be made in terms of the competence-performance distinction. Not all features of the behaviour of some unconstructed concept are likely to be relevant for philosophical purposes; that is, there will be features of the performance of a competent speaker, involving his use of this concept, that we shall choose to view not as part of his competence, but as imposed by factors from which the theory abstracted[16], e.g., matters of style. The constructionists' formal models will abstract from whatever is not significant for the philosophical problem under consideration.

It is premise (2) of Strawson's argument that I wish to reject. I think much of its plausibility is removed by our consideration of (1); it is tempting to say simply that it is analytic of a well-made formal model, constructed for the solution of a particular problem, and that the model does not ignore *any* features that are significant with respect to the problem of the logical behaviour of the relevant concepts. Of course this alone will not do – perhaps there are no such models of natural language – but it suggests an important point. If an objection is made to any particular formal treatment of a philosophical problem on the ground that it ignores crucial features of the unconstructed concepts, this objection does not constitute a criticism of the formal approach. It is entirely within the spirit *and practice* of this approach to introduce new complexities into our formalisms on the basis of arguments to the effect that such complexities play a role in the philosophical problem under consideration. Of course *these* arguments are usually informal, but this does not show that the "real" work is the naturalists'. For it is characteristically not clear either what complexities need to be added, or what their significance is, until after considerable formal work has been done.

If at this point, despite our emphasis on the on-going character of the formal approach, the naturalist still wishes to argue that philosophical problems have their roots outside the purview of the constructionist, then he must claim that there is something inherently unformalizable about the philosophically important functioning of the unconstructed concepts. He might sensibly mean by this, I suppose, that a model that was faithful to *enough* of the important details would be too complex to retain the advantages of the familiar models. The question now is whether modes of functioning that are *this* elusive are really the source of deep and persistent philosophical problems. It seems to me that they are certainly not, but I am not sure how to argue this; I will mention just one example to support my view. The semantic paradoxes raise questions about the workings of such concepts as truth, reference, well-formedness, proposition, etc. For practically every ordinary way of employing these concepts there are suitable formulations of the paradoxes; this suggests that the problem has to do with the most obvious features of the behaviour of these concepts – not with the "elusive modes of functioning" that vary from formulation to formulation.

v

Model theory looms large in the recent history of the formal approach. A model is a kind of interpretation for the syntax of a formal language, and one speaks of sentences of a language being true or false relative to, or in, a model; then semantic concepts such as validity and logical consequence may be defined in terms of truth "in" a model.[17] The Löwenheim-Skolem theorem and the proof of completeness for first order logic are two familiar results in model theory. Generally speaking, the field has moved in two directions. On the one hand model theory has been shown to have intrinsic mathematical interest and numerous mathematical applications;[18] on the other hand model theory has been seen to have illuminating applications to the philosophy of language. There are of course those who work within the formal approach and do not make use of model-theoretic techniques. But the developments I have chosen to describe are model-theoretic in character; they are offered merely as *examples* of recent developments of philosophical interest.

1. It is possible to state very simply and directly the conception of meaning that has found some favour within the formal approach,[19] and I will do this in a moment. However, it should be kept in mind that the usefulness of this conception can only be fairly judged when it is examined at work with the rest of the machinery of model theory. To provide a basis for this kind of evaluation would require a presentation far beyond the scope of this essay, and available elsewhere.[20]

With this disclaimer understood, we proceed. The reader is probably familiar with the "possible worlds" locution of model-theoretic semantics. A model for the language of sentential modal logic contains a set of objects called possible worlds, with a relation of relative possibility defined on this set (so that one may speak of one world as possible relative to another). Now truth is relativized not only to a model but to a possible world in a model. For an ordinary sentence it is enough to require that it be true in the specially designated possible world called the *actual* world; however, for sentences such as $\ulcorner \Box \phi \urcorner$ (which we read: $\ulcorner$it is necessary that $\phi \urcorner$) we require that the sentence ϕ be true in every world that is possible relative to the actual world; for $\ulcorner \Diamond \phi \urcorner$ we require that ϕ be true in some world possible relative to the actual world.

Suppose we turn now to modal predicate logic. We need, in addition to the set W of possible worlds, and the relation of relative possibility defined on W, a domain of objects as universe of discourse. There are various possibilities here. A single domain D can be chosen to provide objects for all the possible worlds, so that worlds other than the actual are understood as containing the same objects as does the actual world, but having different properties and standing in different relations. Or a function Q can be included in each model that assigns some subset D_i of D to each possible world w_i in W. Thus each possible world has its own domain; we allow for the idea that certain objects may not exist in certain possible worlds. And beyond the specification of possible worlds and their domains, we must specify, for each possible world, the extension of each non-logical term in that possible world. If we were simply to make one assignment – a denotation to each individual constant and a set of ordered n-tuples to each n-place predicate – then it is clear that every sentence would have the same truth value in every possible world. Since we conceive of objects as having different properties in different possible worlds, we must supply the predicates with (possibly) different extensions in different possible worlds.

Thus we arrive at the idea of including in each model of the language a function F that assigns to non-logical terms yet another function – this one having the set of all possible worlds as domain and either elements or sets of elements of D as range.[21] To take the case of predicates: a model includes a function that associates with each n-place predicate a function that takes a possible world as argument and has, as value, the extension of that predicate for that possible world. The same function assigns to each individual constant a function from possible worlds into elements of D, and finally, the functions assigns to each sentence of the language a function from possible worlds into the set of truth-values, true and false.[22]

Let us return to the case of predicates, and think for the moment only of 1-place predicates. The function F of each model assigns to each such predicate c a function F_c; *it is this function F_c that we may regard as the meaning of the predicate.* For F_c takes us from the specification of a possible situation – moment of time, or whatever (the abstract notion of possible world has many intuitive realizations) to the specification of an extension for c in that situation. Similarly, if c is a term, then F_c is taken to be the meaning of c, for it tells us the denotation of c in every possible world. And if c is a sentence, the F_c may be regarded as the proposition expressed by c; it gives the truth-value of c in every possible world.

Is there any plausibility to this conception of meaning? Does it seem to be an idealization of any important sense of the word 'meaning'? I expect the reader to grant for the time being that it is a very *useful* notion in model theory, and appears to yield elegant treatments of many important problems in intensional logic; but the question is whether the conception is at all intuitive. I think the answer must be affirmative. Note the attractiveness, to begin with, of thinking of meaning as a rule or function, not as an object of some kind. And in this case the rule in question governs the *use* of the expression; for example, with a predicate the notion of extension underlies the notion of correct use (application).

How do I find out whether a person knows the meaning of an English predicate? I do not in general require him to produce a definition – the test lies simply in whether he uses the predicate correctly in various situations. But how can we express the knowledge he has that enables him to apply the predicate correctly? The most direct way is to say that he has somehow internalized a rule or function that hooks up possible situations with sets containing exactly those objects to which the predicate correctly applies. It would be irrelevant to look for cases where it is allowable that a person should not respond with either application or refusal when a situation is described: there are many explanations of this compatible with this conception of meaning (note, for example, that we assume that the function operates on *adequately described* possible worlds).

Another way to check this conception is to consider the familiar way of showing the distinction between the extension and intension (meaning) of predicates. We cannot identify the extension of a predicate with its meaning because two predicates may have the same extension ('rational animal' and 'featherless biped') but differ in meaning. But what are our grounds for asserting this difference? One simple answer is: we can easily *imagine* a situation, though there may be no actual one, where we should predicate 'rational animal' of a thing, but refuse to predicate 'featherless biped' of the same thing; we can easily think of a world inhabited by rational, feathered creatures. Again what is appealed to as *meaning* is something like a matching of possible worlds with correct predications.

One more thought-experiment: imagine a person supplied with a function of the kind we are considering. He knows in every possible situation whether to apply or withhold the predicate in question. What more could we require before we grant that he knows the meaning of the predicate? In fact, we want to say he knows more than we should require. But the difference between the performance that we regard as adequate to demon-strate knowledge of the meaning, and what the theory states as the com-petence of one who knows the meaning, can perhaps be explained in terms of factors that are not significant for the theory.

The view of propositions as functions from possible worlds into truth-values is, if anything, more intuitive. Surely it is sufficient, in knowing the meaning of a sentence, to be able to say whether the sentence is true in any arbitrarily chosen situation – how else could we have this information? And again we justify treating the condition as not only sufficient but also necessary by appealing to the notion of theoretical idealization. Similarly for singular terms: that a person affirms that Nixon is President of the United States does not show that he understands the sense, as opposed to the current reference, of the description; we regard his grasp of the sense as an ability to refer correctly with it in a wide variety of circumstances.

2. It has long been noted by critics of the formal approach that the formal languages so far studied abstract entirely from questions of prag-matics – that is, from questions which involve the context of language *use* as well as its syntax and semantics. I think that many of these critics, and even many practitioners of the formal approach, assumed that serious attempts to deal with questions of pragmatics would require the adoption of a framework at least as different from the model-theoretic one used for semantics as that for semantics differed from the syntactical methods employed earlier.

Recent work of Montague, Scott[23] and others suggests quite emphatically that the complaints about pragmatics can to some extent be met, and that the assumption that went with these complaints was misguided. Specifically, they have shown that significant questions in pragmatics can be treated in a natural manner within the basic framework of semantics.

Before proceeding we must distinguish two very different enterprises, both of which may be called pragmatics. The first introduces pragmatical considerations into the construction of a formal language; the second involves the construction of a *theory* that has as its subject matter the relationships between a language, *its* subject matter, and the users of the language. The distinction, then, is between a (formal) *pragmatic language* and a *theory of pragmatics*. Of course the latter may be a formal theory, i.e., itself formulated in a formal language; interesting complications are introduced if the formal language in which the theory is formulated is also taken (at least in part) to be the language whose relation to its users is under investigation.[24]

Formal pragmatic languages are given their point by the fact that the determination of the meaning and truth-value of many natural language sentences depends on the circumstances surrounding their production.[25] What was lacking until recently was a formal language in which certain symbols are made to play the roles of, for example, demonstrative pronouns, future tense operators ('it will be the case that . . .') etc., and in the semantics of which an explication is given of the bearing of such symbols on the truth-conditions for the sentences that contain them.[26] One such explication is provided in the pragmatic language described in Montague [21].

The basic idea of this explication is obtained as a generalization of the notion of a set of possible worlds. Given a model for a formal language L, we speak now not of the truth-value of each sentence of L with respect to each possible world, but instead of the truth-value of each sentence of L with respect to (or "at") each element of a set of *points of reference*. Each point of reference i (let I be the set of such points) is taken to have as much complexity as we require for an intended interpretation; we include in each point of reference whatever items are required to determine the truth-values of sentences that we wish to treat. For example, if we think of I as the set of contexts relevant to the truth-value of the formal counterpart of 'He is there', then each i will be an ordered pair whose first element is a person and whose second element is a place. 'He is there' may be true at one point of reference and false at another. One of the advantages of this arrangement is that it has so many familiar conceptions as special cases. In the case of modal logic we can think of the set of all worlds possible with respect to the actual as, in a sense, part of the context of an utterance of the sentence $\ulcorner$It is necessarily the case that $\phi\urcorner$. Just as we must have specified at least a person and a place to determine the truth-value of 'He is there', so we must have specified the possible worlds to determine the truth-value of such a modal statement. In the case of tense logic we may let the points of reference be moments of time and impose an ordering on the set. Suppose we have a sentence such as $\ulcorner F\phi\urcorner$ (read: $\ulcorner$It will be the case that $\phi\urcorner$: we take $\ulcorner F\phi\urcorner$ to be true at a point of reference (time of utterance) i_j if and only if ϕ is true at some point of reference i_k, where $k > j$. In related ways Montague illustrates that a wide variety of formal treatments are obtained as special cases by imposing restrictions on the definition of model, and in particular by varying the features of the set of points of reference.

The upshot is that we can now regard our "scientific model" as representing a far larger segment of natural language than was possible before. We can now speak precisely about logical relations between sentences containing indexical terms, including tensed verbs; most importantly, the "theory" of these sentences is introduced as a natural extension of a well-developed general theory.

3. If one thinks of the treatment of meaning as a deepening of the formal approach, and of the developments in pragmatics as a broadening of its scope, then perhaps we may regard the investigation of non-bivalent languages as an addition of flexibility.

There was a time when philosophers barred undesirable sentences from formal languages through rules of syntax; we have now the increasingly well-studied alternative of allowing such sentences into the language as well-formed, with semantical ways of denying them truth-value.[27] There are some fairly obvious intuitive advantages to this. It is, to begin with, quite plain that natural languages contain grammatically correct sentences that are, either always or on certain occasions of utterance,

neither true nor false. (One could argue that two-valued semantics constitute a theoretical idealization of the kind I have been defending; indeed
this is correct, but it does not rule out investigations of a slightly less
idealized character.) And apart from the desirability of constructing a
model that is more faithful to natural language, it should be noted that
the study of non-bivalent formal languages brings the formal approach
into a better relationship with both linguistics and the theory of speech
acts. To say that the sentence 'The set of cows is not itself a cow' is, with
respect to a consistent formal language, *not* a sentence (i.e., it has no formal
counterpart among the sentences of the formal language), is to place a
barrier between oneself and linguistics. On the other hand, to devise a
semantical treatment that explains the truth-valuelessness of, for example,
'Virtue is triangular',[28] is to invite and facilitate a comparison of this
treatment with, for example, the Katz-Fodor treatment of "anomalous"
sentences in [15]. And to allow that a sentence may be true on one occasion
of utterance (i.e., at one point of reference), false on another, and neither
true nor false on yet another – as one would with a non-bivalent pragmatic language – suggests the utterance-statement distinction that is
crucial to the theory of speech-acts (a statement is produced when a
sentence is true or false). One can even imagine the treatment of other
speech-acts, such as questions, commands, promises etc., within this formal
framework, perhaps supplemented by parameters other than truth and
falsity.

Another important notion from the domain of ordinary-language
philosophy has a natural treatment within non-bivalent formal languages,
and has in fact come in for detailed investigation within this framework.
I refer to the Frege-Strawson notion of *presupposition*, according to which,
if A presupposes B, then A lacks truth-value if B is false. Van Fraassen
has formalized the semantics of presupposition (see van Fraassen [32]) and
applied the notion not only to the problem of non-referring singular terms
(see his [31]), but also to the Liar paradox (see his [33]).

One important factor in the development of non-bivalent formal languages was the distinction, emphasized and clarified in van Fraassen [31],
between the principle of bivalence and the principle of excluded middle.
The latter says that every sentence of the form $p \vee \neg p$ is true; the former
says that every sentence is either true or false Van Fraassen developed a
technique, and a rationale to go with it, according to which one can retain
the validity of all the valid sentences of classical logic and still give up the

principle of bivalence; for example, $p \lor \neg p$ will be true under all interpretations, even where p is neither true nor false. This *supervaluation* technique, as it is called, is well explained elsewhere (see, for example, van Fraassen [31]), and I shall not dwell on it here.

The three developments I have mentioned are only some of the many ideas being explored within the formal approach today; and of course there is no unanimous feeling, even within this approach, that any of the results I have referred to constitute definitive solutions to the problems considered.[29]

Livingston College, Rutgers University

BIBLIOGRAPHY

[1] Ajdukiewicz, K.: 1936, "Der logistische Antirationalismus in Polen', *Actes du 8ᵉ Congrès International de Philosophie*, Paris.
[2] Anderson, A. and Belnap, N.: 1962, 'The Pure Calculus of Entailment', *Journal of Symbolic Logic* **27**.
[3] Bar-Hillel, Y.: 1954, 'Indexical Expressions', *Mind* **63**.
[4] Bar-Hillel, Y.: 1970, *Aspects of Language*, Amsterdam and Jerusalem.
[5] Carnap, R.: 1959, 'The Elimination of Metaphysics through the Logical Analysis of Language' in A. Ayer (ed.), *Logical Positivism*, Glencoe, Ill.
[6] Carnap, R.: 1942, *Introduction to Semantics*, Cambridge, Mass.
[7] Carnap, R.: 1937, *Logical Syntax of Language*, London and New York.
[8] Carnap, R.: 1963, 'Reply to Strawson' in P. A. Schillp (ed.), *The Philosophy of Rudolf Carnap*, LaSalle, Illinois and London.
[9] Caton, C.: 1967, 'Artificial and Natural Languages' in P. Edwards (ed.), *The Encyclopedia of Philosophy*, New York and London.
[10] Davidson, D.: 1969, 'On Saying That' in D. Davidson and J. Hintikka (eds.), *Words and Objections: Essays on the Work of W. V. Quine*, Dordrecht.
[11] Grice, H. P.: 1967, 'The Causal Theory of Perception' in *Proceedings of the Aristotelian Society*, Suppl. Vol. 35.
[12] Henkin, L.: 1967, 'Systems, Formal and Models of Formal Systems' in P. Edwards (ed.), *The Encyclopedia of Philosophy*, New York and London.
[13] Hintikka, J.: 1969, 'Epistemic Logic and the Methods of Philosophical Analysis', in J. Hintikka, *Models for Modalities*, Dordrecht.
[14] Katz, J.: 1966, *Philosophy of Language*, New York and London.
[15] Katz, J. and Fodor, J.: 1969, 'The Structure of a Semantic Theory' in J. Fodor and J. Katz (eds.), *The Structure of Language*, Englewood Cliffs, N.J.
[16] Katz, J. and Fodor, J.: 1962, 'What's Wrong with the Philosophy of Language', *Inquiry* **5**.
[17] Kneale, M. and Kneale, W.: 1962, *The Development of Logic*, Oxford.
[18] Łukasiewicz, J.: 1961, 'Logistyka i filosofia' reprinted in a volume of Łukasiewicz' selected papers, *Z zagadnien logiki i filozofii. Pisma Wybrane*, Warsaw.
[19] Martin, R. L. (ed.): 1970, *The Paradox of the Liar*, New Haven and London.
[20] Montague, R.: 1969, 'On the Nature of Certain Philosophical Entities', *The Monist* **53**.

[21] Montague, R.: 1968, 'Pragmatics' in R. Klibansky (ed.), *Contemporary Philosophy*, vol. 1, Milan.

[22] Mostowski, A.: 'Thirty Years of Foundational Studies: Lectures on the Development of Mathematical Logic and the Study of the Foundations of Mathematics in 1930–1964', *Acta Philosophica Fennica*, Fasc. 17 (1965); Oxford, 1966.

[23] Popper, K.: 1963, *Conjectures and Refutations*, London.

[24] Quine, W. V.: 'Two Dogmas of Empiricism', *Philosophical Review* 60 (1951), reprinted in Quine, *From a Logical Point of View*, Cambridge, Mass., 1953 and 1961.

[25] Quine, W. V.: 1960, *Word and Object*, New York.

[26] Scott, D.: 1970, 'Advice on Modal Logic' in K. Lambert (ed.), *Philosophical Problems in Logic: Some Recent Developments*, Dordrecht.

[27] Skolimowski, H.: 1967, *Polish Analytical Philosophy: A Survey and a Comparison with British Analytical Philosophy*, New York.

[28] Strawson, P. F.: 1963, 'Carnap's Views on Constructed Systems versus Natural Languages in Analytic Philosophy' in P. A. Schillp (ed.), *The Philosophy of Rudolf Carnap*, LaSalle, Illinois and London.

[29] Tarski, A.: 1956, 'The Concept of Truth in Formalized Languages' in *Logic, Semantics, Metamathematics: Papers from 1923 to 1938*, Oxford. This English translation of Tarski's paper contains a full bibliographical note on earlier versions and translations.

[30] Tarski, A.: 1944, 'The Semantic Conception of Truth and the Foundations of Semantics' in *Philosophy and Phenomenological Research* 4.

[31] van Fraassen, B.: 1966, 'Singular Terms, Truth-Value Gaps, and Free Logic,' *Journal of Philosophy* 63.

[32] van Fraassen, B.: 1969, 'Presupposition, Supervaluations, and Free Logic' in K. Lambert (ed.), *The Logical Way of Doing Things*, New Haven.

[33] van Fraassen, B.: 1970, 'Truth and Paradoxical Consequences' in R. L. Martin (ed.), *The Paradox of the Liar*, New Haven and London.

[34] Walker, J.: 1965, *A Study of Frege*, Oxford.

NOTES

[1] I have in mind such essays as Katz and Fodor [15], and the first part of Chapter 3 of Katz [14]. Strawson [28] has provided a less extreme criticism of what he calls the constructionist method. A kind of limiting case of what I have in mind is Caton [9]. Caton lists two uses to which artificial languages have been put: the formalization of particular theories, and as "ideal" languages; he nowhere even mentions the study of artificial languages as a way of studying natural language.

[2] Many terms have been used: pure semantics, logical semantics, scientific semantics, metamathematical semantics, etc. All of these terms, though not in all cases their authors, suggest that pragmatics will be ignored; recent developments belie this. 'Formal semiotic' might do, but suggests more a finished theory than a way of attacking problems.

[3] Several pages later Katz acknowledges: "this antimetaphysical motivation was not the only one that provided an incentive to develop a theory of logical syntax. Carnap also wished to provide a syntactic analysis of concepts in formal deductive logic such as provability, derivability from premises, etc. But", concludes Katz, "the *philosophical* motive was dominant" (p. 28, emphasis added). The confusions in the quoted passage and in the rest of the paragraph that contains it are manifold. First of all, we note that Katz implicitly identifies the "antimetaphysical" with the "philosophical" motivation, and opposes it to the desire to do such things as give a syntactic analysis of provability. But surely Carnap's philosophical motivation went beyond the antimetaphysics programme; indeed the passage that Katz cites to support his view that the

"philosophical" motive was dominant contains not a word about the elimination of metaphysics, but presents the far more basic Carnapian position that all philosophical problems are linguistic in character. Then in the same passage Carnap draws the natural conclusion that the study of these problems should be carried out in a precise metalanguage. Given that at this stage a precise metalanguage was, for Carnap, a syntactical metalanguage, and given the central importance in philosophy of notions such as provability, it follows that such things as the syntactic analysis of provability were of primary philosophical importance to Carnap.

4 For historical reasons, which Katz himself explains later (having to do with the remarkable early successes of the Hilbert School in treating a number of important logical notions in purely syntactic terms), Carnap was looking only for *syntactic* conventions that might rule out objectionable sentences. Katz blurs this point at the crucial place in his argument by saying, falsely, that Carnap, in [5], held "that there are no *semantic* conventions to which the meaninglessness of 'Caesar is a prime number' and similar cases can be referred . . ." (pp. 21, 22, emphasis added). Carnap does not mention semantic conventions anywhere in the paper; his view accords with most present-day thinking, including Katz's elsewhere, that natural language has no such *syntactic* conventions. He is to be criticized, if at all, for restricting his purview to the syntactical, not for making a "wholly a priori decision about natural languages".

5 A closely related positivistic coin that has lost currency is the warning never to use non-formal languages for serious work in science or philosophy.

6 A possible exception, Łukasiewicz' "new philosophy" (announced in 1927) carried with it standards of rigor so high that Łukasiewicz denied, as late as 1946, that its construction was as yet even possible. See Skolimowski [27], pp. 69, 71.

7 For discussion and references see Walker [34].

8 See, for example, Popper [23], p. 223, and Tarski's own remarks in [29], p. 252.

9 In this connection see Bar-Hillel [4].

10 For example, a materially adequate definition of 'is true in L' is one which has as consequences all sentences formed from the schema T:

X is a true sentence of L if and only if p

by replacing the letter 'X' with the name of some sentence of L, and replacing the letter 'p' with the sentence itself or with a translation of the sentence into the metalanguage in which the definition is framed.

11 This view is not quite the same as Tarski's. He speaks of *reforming* natural language, whereas the language-level view is rather a kind of *theory* about natural language.

12 In several places in the last paragraph I have ignored a distinction that was unnecessary for the point I wished to make, but which is otherwise quite important: the distinction between a formal language and a system of logic for that language. A *formal language* is given when its syntax and semantics are given. The syntax specifies the symbols used in the language and picks out strings of these symbols that are to count as well-formed. The semantics sets down principles of interpretation – it does not give one interpretation of the language, though it may specify a "standard" – interpretation – and defines the notion of truth under an interpretation as well as such other notions as satisfiability, logical consequence, and logical validity. By a *system of logic for a formal language* is understood a syntactic specification of certain of the well-formed sentences as *axioms*, of certain strings of well-formed sentences as *derivations*, and of certain well-formed sentences as *theorems*. The logic is *sound* with respect to the language if, whenever a sentence A is derivable from a set of sentences S, A is also a (semantically defined) consequence of S; the logic is *complete* with respect to the language if, whenever A is a consequence of S, A is derivable from S.

13 See, for example, Grice [11].

[14] On the other hand we could decide that classical logic ought to be amended on this point. I think other examples could be found then where circumstances which we choose to regard as extraneous to the theory can be held accountable for deviations from what the theory predicts.

[15] Strawson arrives at this assumption by a series of moves of the form: if x is what the constructionists have in mind, then the issue between them and the "naturalists" is a trivial one. Carnap has much to say against several of these moves (see Carnap [8]),but there is no indication that he objects to the conception that Strawson describes here.

[16] See Hintikka's illuminating discussion of the same point in [13]. Near the end of the article he suggests "that the difference between an approach to the logic of ordinary language in terms of my 'explanatory models' and an approach to it in terms of 'what we ordinarily say' or in other paradigmatic terms is to a large extent a difference between a genuine theory of the meaning of the words and expressions involved and a mere description of the raw data of the language" (pp. 14, 15).

[17] For an excellent presentation of model theory that does not presuppose mathematical background, see Henkin [12].

[18] For a brief account, see Mostowski [22], Lecture 13.

[19] See Montague [20] for notes on the origin of this conception.

[20] See, for example, Montague [20].

[21] As Montague points out in [20], we do not want to limit the extension of a predicate P in a possible world w_i to elements that belong to *its* domain, D_i; for consider the predicate 'is thought about', which may be true in w_i of an object that does not exist in w_i.

[22] By thinking of sentences as 0-place predicates we eliminate the need for a separate treatment of sentences. According to the pattern, a 0-place predicate is assigned, for each possible world, some set of 0-tuples. But there is only one 0-tuple (the empty sequence), so there are only two *sets* of 0-tuples: the empty set Λ and the unit set of Λ. Thus there are only two values for our function when it has a 0-place predicate as argument; we may conveniently identify Λ with 0 (falsity) and its unit set with 1 (truth). See Montague [20].

[23] See especially Montague [21] and Scott [26].

[24] I have in mind here D. Harrah's work on "standard formal messages" as a basis for a theory of pragmatics; see his contribution to this volume.

[25] See Bar-Hillel [3].

[26] Another word on the relationship of meaning to truth: as Davidson has written in [10], "a satisfactory theory of meaning for a language must . . . give an explicit account of the truth-conditions of every sentence, and this can be done by giving a theory that satisfies Tarski's criteria; nothing less should count as showing how the meaning of every sentence depends on its structure . . ." (p. 159).

[27] See, for example, the papers of van Fraassen, Herzberger, Kearns, Skyrms, Pollock, and Martin in Martin [19].

[28] R. H. Thomason has developed such an account, forthcoming in the *Journal of Philosophical Logic*.

[29] The support of the Research Council of Rutgers University made possible my attendance at the Symposium. This paper was written during a visiting semester, Fall, 1970, at the National Taiwan University (Department of Philosophy), supported in part by the National Science Council of the Republic of China. I read an earlier version there, and gratefully acknowledge the helpful comments and suggestions I received as a result, especially from Prof. R. Suter.

CHAIM PERELMAN

THE NEW RHETORIC

I began working on what I now call the new rhetoric with only a vague idea
of what it was about, with no intention to become a rhetorician.[1] As a
logician, I was interested in the study of reasoning, especially reasoning
about values. I wanted to develop a logic of value judgments.

The problem puzzled me. Given that a value judgment cannot appear in
the conclusion of an argument unless there is a value judgment in at least
one of the premises, and assuming an empiricist theory of knowledge,
how do we obtain underived value judgments? How do we validate them,
especially when controversial? They are not based on self-evidence, intention, or experience. Should we invoke revelation? Or say that they are
but the expression of our wishes and emotions, thus purely subjective and
irrational? Or could we find some rational method of tackling them?

I searched for answers to these questions, but the literature did not
satisfy me. There had been studies on instrumental value judgments, that
is, of value judgments that help us appraise the means, given the ends, as
for example in Ed. Goblot, *La logique des jugements de valeur* (1927). But
how should we evaluate these ends if not as means to further ends? That
problem had been evaded.

To find an answer I chose to follow Gottleb Frege, who studied the laws
of formal logic by analysing the reasoning of mathematicians. I began to
analyse reasonings concerning the good and the bad, the just and the preferable, as they are found in the writings of philosophers, politicians,
lawyers, and preachers. After years of such analytical work, jointly with
Mrs. L. Olbrechts-Tyteca, we understood that, when people criticize and
justify opinions or choices, they argue, give reasons *pro* and *con*, engage in
controversy. The theory of argumentation, thus rediscovered, had been
thoroughly studied by the Greek philosophers, under the name of dialectical reasoning: Aristotle devoted to it his *Topics*, his *Rhetoric*, and his
treatise *On Sophistical Refutations*, but it was almost completely forgotten
and ignored by modern logicians.

Dialectical reasoning, as opposed to the analytic reasoning of formal
logic, is a discourse addressed to an audience; this audience may be a

Yehoshua Bar-Hillel (ed.), Pragmatics of Natural Languages, 145–149.
All Rights Reserved. Copyright © 1971 by D. Reidel Publishing Company, Dordrecht-Holland.

special one, made up of many people, one interlocutor, or the subject him-self when he deliberates; or it may be universal, the ideal audience we address when we appeal to reason, be it God's perfect mind or the good sense shared by the community of men.

The point of a dialectical discourse is to convince the audience. To that end the speaker (or writer) must adapt himself to his audience. To per-suade, he must start from premises accepted by his listeners (or readers). If he does not and assumes erroneously that the audience agrees with his premise, his argument is a faulty one, known as *petitio principii*, begging the question. A good example of *petitio principii* is the speech of Antiphon on the murder of Herodes: "I would have you know that I am much more deserving of your pity than of punishment. Punishment is indeed the due of the guilty, while pity is the due of those who are the subject of an unjust accusation."[2]

Antiphon begs the question when, pleading before his judges, he implies that he is the object of an unjust accusation. The judges, of course, cannot agree before deciding on the case.

Begging the question is not an error in formal logic, where the principle of identity (if p, then p), being a tautology, is always true. The *petitio principii* is not a logical error, but a mistaken argumentation. By ignoring the theory of argumentation, the logicians got a confused view of the *petitio principii*, as becomes evident by consulting, e.g., the recent American *Encyclopedia of Philosophy*. *Begging the question* is listed there with the fallacies (under 11°), that is, "arguments which seem to be valid but really are not" (Vol. 5, p. 64). But somewhere else we read: "An argument that begs the question, that uses the conclusion as one of the premises, is always formally valid. A conclusion cannot fail to follow from a set of premises that includes it. This is also a fallacy only in the extended sense that such an argument gives no support to its conclusion" (Vol. 3, p. 177). But how can one say both that an argument is formally valid and that it only *seems* to be valid? If it is a fallacy, it must be from a perspective different from that of formal validity. This perspective is that of argumentation, related not to truth but to assent.

There is another difference of paramount importance between argument and formal proof. The standard logical calculi are formulated in artificial languages in which any one sign has one, and only one, meaning; in natural languages the same word often has different meanings. Some utterances would not even make sense if it were not for the ambiguity of the words. For example: "children are children". If we respect the speaker, we give him credit for saying something worth saying.[3] If he states a seeming tautology (A is A) or contradiction (A is not A), we assume that the intended meaning is more interesting.

Some years ago relatives of mine were awaiting their son at the railroad station after years of separation. When he stepped from the train, his mother saw tears in her husband's eyes and said: "Now I see that not only is a mother a mother, but that a father is a father."

If the mother needed this special event to conclude that a father is a father, her conclusion must be more than a truism.

It is in the same light that we can understand some seeming contradictions, such as Heraclitus' "We step and do not step in the same river". This makes sense only if the word "same" has two different meanings.

Just as formal logic can result from the analysis of mathematical reasoning, the theory of argumentation can be developed from the study of legal reasoning. This illuminates the differences between a formal system, in which conclusions are formally deduced from premises, and a legal system where decisions must be justified. In a formal system conformity to given rules is of paramount importance: when no rule enables us to deduce a proposition or its negation, or if both a proposition and its negation can be deduced, then the system is either incomplete or inconsistent, and there is no remedy for this within the system. But a judge *has* to settle the case before him and cannot invoke a gap or an antinomy in the law. If the normal procedures of interpretation and deduction do not lead to a decision, he must nevertheless search for a reasonable solution of the case. He will, to that end, use some non-formal procedure, such as reasoning by analogy or stretching the meaning of certain words.

In daily life, we all encounter situations where, like the judge, we must make a decision and cannot postpone it indefinitely. Most such decisions are not the product of constraining reasoning, and may thus be controversial. This is why the logic of choice, the logic of practical reasoning, is also the logic of controversy.[4] Whereas a formal proof is correct or incorrect, valid or invalid, an argumentation is strong or weak; arguments may be relevant or irrelevant, more or less convincing, but are never conclusive as are formally correct deductions.

In our treatise on argumentation, *The New Rhetoric*, we analysed some ninety different types of arguments (see the list on pp. 550–2). In a number of them, the form of presentation is an integral part of the content: most figures of speech for example are but abridged and efficacious arguments.

Many problems are specific to argumentation and completely foreign to formal logic, such as the question of the burden of proof in law or ethics. Through legal presumptions, one of the parties in a court of law is given an advantage, namely that it is incumbent upon the other party to prove its case in order to win. Similarly, in the field of ethics, those who conform to accepted norms are presumed to have been normally right unless shown otherwise.

The new rhetoric does not aim at displacing or replacing formal logic, but at adding to it a field of reasoning that, up to now, has escaped all efforts at rationalization, namely, practical reasoning. Its domain is the study of critical thought, reasonable choice, and justified behaviour. It applies whenever action is linked to rationality.

We may formalize some of the arguments used in practical reasoning.[5] Attempts have been made to develop programmes leading to the best decision on the basis of 'decision-functions'. This is done as a strategy towards pre-chosen ends referred to as 'the best solution'. But in the choice of these ends, we must use reasons that are themselves not amenable to formal treatment.

When we formalize an informal argument, we must eliminate ambiguities, define terms and state assumptions based on that which we consider relevant and reasonable. There will always remain some elements irreducible to a formal computation. Decision about those fundamental elements are preliminary to any operation. They have to be kept out of philosophical inquiry as purely emotional and subjective, unless we enlarge our concept of the reasonable and include considerations beyond the formal ones.

Analysis of the varieties of non-formal reasoning yields a tool for better evaluating philosophies like existentialism or pragmatism, and those that involve dialectical methods, as these all stress the importance of human existence, human action, and human history.

The University of Brussels

NOTES

[1] See for more details: 'The new rhetoric, a theory of practical reasoning' in *The Great Ideas Today, 1970*, Encyclopaedia Britannica, 1970, pp. 273–312.

[2] See Perelman, Ch. and Olbrechts-Tyteca, L.: 1969, *The New Rhetoric–A Treatise on Argumentation*, Notre Dame University Press, p. 113.
[3] See Perelman, Ch.: The new rhetoric, a theory of practical reasoning, p. 291.
[4] See Giuliani, A.: 1966, *La controversia, contributo alla logica giuridica*, Pavia.
[5] See Perelman, Ch.: 1968, 'Le raisonnement pratique' in R. Klibansky (ed.), *Contemporary Philosophy*, Florence, La Nuova Italia, Vol. 1, pp. 168–76.

I. M. SCHLESINGER

ON LINGUISTIC COMPETENCE*

Competence is one of the central concepts in the theorizing of the transformational school. The term has been introduced by Chomsky, who uses it mainly to characterize those issues that are the proper concern of grammar, while relegating other issues concerning speech behaviour to performance. The competence-performance distinction has become part of the stock-in-trade of transformationalists, and is employed by them extensively in handling phenomena that are occasionally cited by their critics as militating against their theories. These phenomena, so the transformationalists reply, do not concern competence – i.e., the native speaker's knowledge of the language – but performance, which is the way the speaker-hearer makes use of this knowledge.

In view of the frequency with which the twin terms "competence" and "performance" appear in liguistic writings it is all the more surprising that neither Chomsky nor other linguists of his school have ever presented a formal definition of the terms. Chomsky only explains them in passing in a most casual manner, as when he writes upon first using the term in his *Aspects* (1965, p. 4): "We thus make a fundamental distinction between *competence* (the speaker-hearer's knowledge of his language) and *performance* (the actual use of language in concrete situations)." Other passages in which he uses these terms yield little or nothing beyond this explication.

Further clarification of these terms seems important if one is to evaluate the theoretical issues in which they seem to play a central role. In his systematic treatise on language, Lieb (1970) examines the term "competence", concludes that its meaning is unclear, and therefore decides not to use it in his own system. In the present paper the competence concept is further examined.

I. THE "IDEALIZED SPEAKER"

In attempting to clarify the meaning of "competence", we shall take as our first clue an expression that tends to crop up in conjunction with this

Yehoshua Bar-Hillel (ed.), Pragmatics of Natural Languages, 150–172.
All Rights Reserved. Copyright © 1971 by D. Reidel Publishing Company, Dordrecht-Holland.

term. Occasionally, Chomsky speaks of the competence of the "ideal" or "idealized" speaker (e.g., 1965, p. 24). What is meant by these modifiers is not made explicit by Chomsky. We therefore turn to Katz (1966), who explicitly discusses the concept of idealization.

The purpose of a grammar, according to Katz (1966, p. 115), is to describe "the tacit knowledge of an ideal speaker" rather than what any actual speaker knows about his language. An actual speaker may have failed to acquire a certain rule for some reason or another, and this failure may make itself felt in his use of language. The resulting deviations are no concern of linguistics. "Competence of the idealized speaker", according to this interpretation, is the knowledge of the (perhaps non-existent) speaker who has learned his language to perfection, mastering all its rules.

In distinction from the competence of this idealized speaker, there is the competence of the individual speaker, which, unlike the former, is not a high-level abstraction but a psychological construct. It is this notion of competence that some writers have in mind when they discuss the competence of the child, or of a child at a certain age. Note that the above distinction shows some parallels with that between language and idiolect. Instead of "competence of the ideal speaker", it would be preferable to use the term *competence of the speaker community*, or *communal competence* for short. This would then have to be distinguished from *individual competence*. The latter is one of the concerns of developmental psycholinguistics, whereas the former seems to be what linguists talk about.

While the distinction between individual and communal competence is well motivated, there is no evidence that it is this that Chomsky had in mind when speaking about the "ideal speaker-listener". The first time this expression occurs in his *Aspects* is right on the first page: "Linguistic theory is concerned primarily with an ideal speaker-listener, . . .", and in the following it is made clear that the idealization is meant to exclude ". . . false starts, deviations from rules, changes of plan in mid-course . . .", and all those psychological factors that are no concern of linguistics, but belong to the study of performance.[1]

When Chomsky thereafter (1965, p. 24) speaks of a grammar describing the "competence of the idealized native speaker", he presumably just intends to remind us that performance factors like those mentioned previously are no concern of grammar. Note that if this is the correct interpretation of the phrase, it actually represents a pleonasm: the expression "idealized" is redundant, because competence is by definition distinct from those psychological factors it interacts with in performance. Katz (1966, p. 117) seems to have overlooked this when he says that "... linguistics studies the competence of ideally fluent speakers ..." and goes on to explain at length that "ideal" is intended to exclude performance factors. All this goes to show that it would perhaps be wiser not to use the term "ideal" in this connection at all, as Bar-Hillel (1967, p. 529) has suggested.

II. COMPETENCE AND KNOWLEDGE OF THE LANGUAGE

Several criticisms have been made of the concept of competence, and these may serve to show what competence is not. For Chomsky the objective of grammar is to formalize competence. Now, it has been argued, many things the speaker-hearer knows about his language, and which are thus by definition part of his competence, are not handled by a generative grammar. Phenomena that must be based on a tacit knowledge of the rules of use of language include the following:

(1) tendencies for hesitations to appear before certain words in a sentence and for certain words to be repeated after hesitations (see Matthews, 1967);

(2) varying transition probabilities between words and utterances (Hockett, 1968, p. 39; in referring to these, Hockett does not criticize Chomsky's notion of competence);

(3) relations between sentences, which *inter alia* make some sequences of sentences unacceptable (see Matthews, 1967);

(4) a host of socio-cultural factors determining, among others, not what is acceptable grammatically but what is deemed appropriate in a given situation (Hymes, in press).

None of these factors are dealt with by existing grammars, although they all reflect what the speaker knows about his language. Unless it is claimed that the grammar will have to handle all these phenomena (and I do not believe that many linguists would want to embrace such a view), there seem to be two possible courses open: (a) it might be claimed that the notion of competence covers more than is dealt with by grammar, i.e. that the grammar formalizes only a part of the speaker-hearer's competence; (b) alternatively, one might refine the definition of competence so that it includes only that part of the speaker-hearer's knowledge that is dealt with by a grammar. The second alternative seems to be more in line with the use of "competence" in the current literature. That it is a perfectly reasonable restriction of the term may be shown by an analogy with a quite different field, such as arithmetic. Arithmetical performance is governed largely by a knowledge of the rules of arithmetic, but it is also influenced by other kinds of knowledge: how to write digits, how to organize problems on a page, and even how to hold a pencil or pen. Now the latter types of knowledge clearly are not what one would want to call knowledge of arithmetic or competence in arithmetic. In the same way one may exclude (1)–(4) from linguistic competence. The latter may be summarized, by what seems to be the consensus of transformationalists, under the following headings:

(5) well-formedness of sentences;
(6) structural descriptions assigned to sentences;

and related to this, both of the following:

(7) detection of syntactic ambiguities in sentences;
(8) meaning relations between sentences;

and finally

(9) disambiguation of sentences by means of semantic relations reflected by them.

While it is defensible not to use the term "competence" for the areas of knowledge in (1)–(4), the tendency of calling these areas "performance" is not. Dumping everything not considered competence into one waste basket category labelled "performance" leaves the latter term without useful meaning. Instead, it is advisable to introduce additional terms, such as "communicative competence" (Hymes, in press) for the knowledge of social and cultural norms and the resultant expectancies. The term *grammatical competence* may serve as a reminder that not just a "knowledge of the rules of the language" but knowledge of rules of a special kind as described in (5)–(9) is referred to. Following the suggestion made in Section I, we then have *individual grammatical competence,* and what the linguist apparently tries to describe by grammar: *communal grammatical competence.* In the following I shall often use "competence" as short for "communal grammatical competence".

III. THE STUDY OF COMPETENCE AND PERFORMANCE

In the light of the preceding discussion we can now examine a methodological proposition made by transformationalists. It has been claimed repeatedly, and with varying degrees of decisiveness, that the study of competence is prior to that of performance and that the latter must be based on the former (e.g., Chomsky, 1965, p. 10; Postal, 1964; Weksel, 1965). We shall call this claim here for convenience the *priority hypothesis*. Since by "competence" linguists refer to what we have called "communal grammatical competence", the meaning of "performance" in the priority hypothesis has to be restricted to those aspects of performance related to communal grammatical competence. The hypothesis thus claims that a performance model that abstracts from non-grammatical aspects of language behaviour can be constructed only after a model of communal grammatical competence has been developed. Now, by the same logic, a parallel claim could be made concerning the construction of another model of language behaviour that abstracts from grammatical factors and explains, for instance, conformity to social norms of outputs like "yes", "no", and holophrastic utterances. Such a model, so the claim would go, must await the construction of a model of "communicative competence". But does not the study of "communicative competence" presuppose a knowledge of socio-cultural norms, and should not therefore the study of socio-cultural aspects of language use be postponed till after a sociological theory has been constructed?

This kind of argumentation can of course not be taken seriously. It only shows the futility of prescribing summarily what must be studied first and what should be studied only later (see Bar-Hillel, 1967, p. 535, on this point). In fact, I am not aware of similar claims being made regarding priorities in any other field. So far no one has seriously suggested that a psychological theory of creativity must await the construction of a theory of art, or that an economic theory is prior to a theory of decision-making. Even the most rudimentary knowledge of economics and art might serve as a basis for the construction of psychological theories dealing with economic behaviour and artistic creativity or art appreciation. These theories may of course have to be revised, and even discarded, as knowledge in the former disciplines increases. The endeavours of theorists in two related fields, say economics and decision-making, may converge: economic theory may provide valuable insights into regularities in decision-making, and decision theory will eventually contribute to economic theory. Returning to the "priority hypothesis", we find that the impetus given to the psychological study of grammar by advances in generative grammar is well known to have been great in the past, and it is only to be hoped that the former will continue to be goaded by the latter. At the same time a stimulating influence in the reverse direction is likely to make itself felt (see Schlesinger, 1967). This seems to be the normal way related disciplines develop, but the "priority hypothesis" disregards this possibility.

But there is another dictum by Chomsky that, if accepted, seems at first sight to add force to the "priority hypothesis". Any performance model will ". . . incorporate, as a basic component, the generative grammar that expresses the speaker-hearer's knowledge of the language" (1965, p. 9). The trouble with this pronouncement is that it is not clear what it means. It might be construed to make the very strong claim that a performance model must contain the same constructs and rules as the competence model, in addition to being subject to other psychological laws. It would be wrong to attribute this view to Chomsky, who expressly dissociates himself from the ". . . absurdity of regarding the system of generative rules as a point-by-point model for the actual construction of a sentence by a speaker" (1965, pp. 139–40).

Another interpretation of "incorporating a grammar" constitutes a much weaker claim than the above. It assumes some kind of parallelism between the grammar and grammatical performance, such that "for each grammatical operation there is a corresponding decoding operation" (Fodor and Garrett, 1967a), or else, encoding operation. This assumption entails a perfect or almost perfect correlation between grammatical and psychological complexity of sentences, and has engendered a considerable number of psycholinguistic experiments, many of them with strikingly negative effects (e.g., Fodor and Garrett, 1967a, 1967b; Schlesinger, 1968). It is therefore rejected by Fodor and Garrett (1967a) in favour of the still weaker claim ". . . that the grammar constrains only the output . . ." of the grammatical performance model. (Fodor and Garrett deal with the decoding mechanism, but the same holds true for the encoding mechanism.) In other words, the linguistic behaviour described by the grammatical performance model must accord with the sentences generated and the structural descriptions assigned to them by the grammar. On this interpretation, the fact that a performance model "incorporates a grammar" does not support the priority hypothesis.

IV. JUDGMENTS OF ACCEPTABILITY AND KNOWLEDGE OF THE LANGUAGE

Linguistic competence is the native speaker-hearer's knowledge of his language. The term "knowledge" here is in need of clarification. At least two meanings can be assigned to it. In everyday parlance, "knowledge" often implies awareness. But the term can also be used to refer to a person's abilities, which underlie his performance and which he is not necessarily aware of or knows how to formulate. Thus, in saying that one "knows" how to walk or how to drive a car, nothing is thereby implied about awareness of how one walks or drives. (A caterpillar, for instance, may be said to know how to walk without implying awareness on its part.) To investigate the former kind of knowledge, which I shall call here "$knowledge_1$", one often appeals to a person's reports of what he knows, whereas "knowledge" conceived as underlying ability, "$knowledge_2$", is a theoretical construct and need not necessarily be accessible to introspection and, still less, to verbal report. It might seem, then, that a person's $knowledge_1$ is that part of his $knowledge_2$ of which he has become aware. However, the matter is not as simple as this, as will become evident further on.

In the following, I shall try to examine whether in characterizing competence as "the speaker-hearer's knowledge", $knowledge_1$ or $knowledge_2$ is referred to. To do so, some data will be presented about the speaker-hearer's $knowledge_1$ of his language, which henceforth will be called "K1" for short. It will be shown that these data about K1 are not formally describable by present-day generative grammars. Hence K1 is not to be identified with the competence of which these grammars are a model.

In investigating K1, one poses to the native speaker certain questions concerning utterances of sentences of his language. Not all answers to such questions may be considered reliable, of course. Care must be taken that the question is properly understood, that the respondent answers truthfully, and that he is careful enough in formulating the results of his introspection; in short, the task of obtaining data about K1 is beset by all the difficulties attendant on the use of experimental techniques in general. Chomsky (1965, pp. 21–4) enlarges on some of these, and concludes: "It may be necessary to guide and draw out the speaker's intuition in perhaps fairly subtle ways. . . ". The methodological dangers of such "guiding" of the informant are too evident to need dwelling upon. It must be conceded, though, that posing certain questions to a native speaker is not a foolproof technique for obtaining insight into his K1. The linguist will have to make allowance for known flaws and biases of his instrument, just as a man looking at a landscape through a window-pane will shift his viewpoint so as to avoid, as far as possible, distortions due to flaws and imperfections of the glass.

The data about K1 to be considered in the following were obtained from judgments of acceptability. Several writers have argued that some judgments of acceptability of centre-embedded (self-embedded) sentences contradict the teachings of transformationalists. Both Lehrer (1968) and Reich (1969) claim (a) that strings in which more than two sentences are embedded one within another are unacceptable to native speakers; and (b) that this fact should be represented in the grammar. Transformationalists would argue that even if (a) were true, (b) would not follow (for reasons that will become clear further on).[2] Actually, (a) is not true. Some writers occasionally embed one parenthetic clause within another and, though the result may sound somewhat strange and cumbersome, it certainly will not be judged unacceptable. (William Faulkner is one writer in whose work I have observed this construction, though only rarely, but it can also be found in less poetic writings.) In an experimental situation such sentences are also usually judged to be well-formed (Schlesinger, 1968, pp. 114–15). While it is true that sentences with higher degrees of centre-embedding will often be judged unacceptable, the question *which* degree of centre-embedding constitutes the limit of acceptability has no simple answer: the limit will depend on a number of factors, as will become evident in the following. Since no fixed limit exists, it has been argued, there is no motivation for the grammar to block recursive centre-embedding.

However, one consistent trend in speakers' judgments of acceptability shows up with a variety of linguistic materials: acceptability is not an all-or-none affair but a matter of degree. To well-formed sentences a speaker will often assign different degrees of acceptability. To substantiate this, I shall quote experimental findings as well as observations stemming from the judgments of a non-native speaker, namely myself, which I trust will agree with those of the readers, pertaining to grammatical sentences.

1. The degree of centre-embedding affects the degree of judged well-formedness. Other things being equal, the greater the degree of centre-embedding the less wellformed will the sentence be judged to be. In an experiment in which from 2 to 5 sentences embedded one within the other were presented such an effect was found, although it was not a very consistent one (Schlesinger 1968, pp. 114–15). Blumenthal (1966) found that all of 10 Harvard-Radcliffe undergraduates who were shown centre-embedded sentences (in each of which four sentences were embedded one within the other) judged them as not being well-formed. Marks (1968) presented subjects with self-embedded sentences and asked them to assign numbers according to "how ungrammatical each sentence seemed to be" (the exact wording of the instructions is not reported by Marks). He found the estimated degree of ungrammaticalness to rise with the number of self-embeddings.

2. Not only the degree of centre-embedding, but also the length of the centre-embedded clause will affect judgments of well-formedness. In the following sequence, each successive sentence will be judged less acceptable than the former:

> The gossip, who spread the tale that John, who lives next-door, loves Mary, is an old fool.
>
> The gossip, who spread the tale that John, who used to live quietly next-door to the chimney sweeper, loves Mary, is an old fool.
>
> The gossip, who spread the tale that John, who for the past thirty-two years generally managed to live a quiet life next-door to the not too well-to-do chimney sweeper James Tallman, loves Mary, is an old fool.

(It is realized that according to recent grammatical descriptions the longer sentences above contain more applications of recursive rules than the preceding ones, but the number of centre-embedded parenthetical clauses is the same.)

3. The same is true of discontinuous constituents. Consider:

> I called the man up.
>
> I called the man who read the book up.
>
> I called the man who read the book that was left lying on the table up.

4. Centre-embedded sentences are less likely to be judged well-formed in the absence of semantic cues than when such semantic cues are present. Compare the following two sentences:

> This is the boy, that the man, whom the lady, which our friend saw, knows, hit.
> This is the hole, that the rat, which our cat, whom the dog bit, caught, made.

The first sentence was found to be much harder to understand than the second one (Schlesinger 1968, pp. 129–43). This finding, though not unexpected, is not related to anything a grammar says about these two sentences. Both have the same syntactic structure. Now, if the amount of semantic constraint is gradually varied, the judged degree of well-formedness may be expected to vary with it. In respect to well-formedness the following sentence falls intuitively between the above two:

> This is the hole, that the man, whom the lady, which our friend saw, knows, made.

and the following sentence looks even better, though it does perhaps not seem quite as well-formed as the one above, which does not refer to people, but only to dogs and cats:

> This is the hole, that the man, whom the dog, which our friend saw, bit, made.

5. When relative pronouns are removed from centre-embedded sentences like the one above, utterances of these sentences become more difficult; this was shown in an experiment by Fodor and Garrett (1967a). Consider now the native speaker's intuition regarding well-formedness of sentences as relative pronouns are added one by one:

> The manager, the designer, the typist, the receptionist encourages, interests, consults, phoned the producer.
> The manager, the designer, the typist, whom the receptionist encourages, interests, consults, phoned the producer.
> The manager, the designer, whom the typist, whom the receptionist encourages, interests, consults, phoned the producer.

The manager, whom the designer, whom the typist, whom the receptionist encourages, interests, consults, phoned the producer.

(The last sentence was used in Blumenthal's (1966) experiment mentioned above.) According to present-day generative grammar all four sentences are grammatical, but judged well-formedness will increase gradually from the first sentence to the last.

The fact about K1 brought to light by the above observations is that grammatical sentences may be of varying degrees of acceptability. Present-day generative grammar *by itself* does not account for these differences between sentences. It must be concluded, therefore, that the competence that generative grammar is said to formalize is not identical with K1. In the next section we shall see with which kind of knowledge competence is to be identified.

V. WHICH KNOWLEDGE DOES A GRAMMAR FORMALIZE?

Judgments of acceptability usually covary with difficulty of comprehension. From the examples discussed in the preceding section it appears that the greater the difficulty experienced by the hearer in processing an utterance of a sentence, the less acceptable he will judge the sentence to be. There is also some experimental evidence for this connection between difficulty of comprehension and acceptability (Schlesinger 1968, pp. 114–118, 133–4). The difficulty may be due to such performance factors as memory limitations (see Miller and Chomsky, 1963, for a discussion of the difficulty of processing self-embedded sentences). It appears that to the extent that the speaker who is called upon to judge the well-formedness of a sentence experiences difficulties of processing, he will tend to assign to it a low degree of acceptability.[3] As Bever (1970) says in discussing the judged unacceptability of some sentences with discontinuous constituents (see Section IV: "I called the man . . . up"), ". . . there is a general perceptual strategy . . . which can be used to explain the unacceptability [of such sentences] on behavioral grounds, and thus explain why it is simultaneously grammatical and unacceptable."

It follows that while a grammar *in isolation* cannot explain judgments of acceptability of the kind discussed above, the latter can be explained by a grammar *in conjunction with certain psychological considerations*. Judgments of grammaticality, then, are just like any other linguistic performance, such as decoding and encoding of utterances, in that they are not accounted for by a grammar alone, but only by a grammar in interaction with psychological principles.

This brings us to the question posed in the heading of this section. As stated, a grammar does not describe K1, the linguistic knowledge$_1$ which the native speaker is aware of and which he can verbalize in his judgments. Instead, the competence formalized by the grammar must be taken to be knowledge$_2$ of some aspects of the language, namely (5)–(9) in Section II, which in interaction with certain psychological factors accounts for performance. I shall call this knowledge "K2". K2 is a theoretical construct underlying both encoding and decoding performance and judgments of grammaticality which reflect K1.

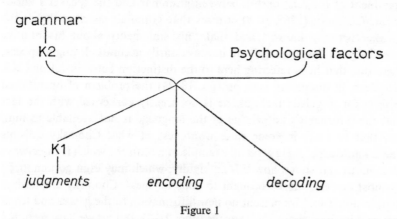

Figure 1

The results of the discussion so far can be summarized by the above diagram. The italicized terms in the bottom line refer to observables. The diagram makes salient the fact that a grammar is only a component in an overall theory that explains empirical data.

Competence, then, is that knowledge of the language which is put to use by the speaker in his linguistic performance and which he is not necessarily aware of. It should be noted that, viewed this way, the competence-performance distinction is one that psychologists have long since been familiar with under a different name: the learning-performance distinction. Perhaps linguists are right in eschewing the term "learning" in discussing this distinction in their field, because they do not want to commit themselves to the view that learning accounts for the development of grammar in a child. On the other hand, "learning" has the advantage of the absence of any connotations of awareness, at least for the psychologist, whereas competence defined loosely as "knowledge of the language" might be misconstrued as K1.

Note that K1 is not simply that part of K2 which comes to a person's awareness. Judgments of grammaticality reveal that a speaker knows$_1$ that certain sentences are less acceptable than others, whereas according to the grammar that formalizes K2 these sentences do not differ in grammaticality. K2 can only be retrieved by clearing the psychological debris from K1, by abstracting from it everything that can be accounted for by decoding difficulties due to memory limitations and other psychological determinants.

The latter point should be borne in mind in examining Chomsky's treatment of the relationship between grammar and the speaker's knowledge. Chomsky (1965, p. 8) stresses that grammar specifies "what the speaker actually knows" and that "his statements about his intuitive knowledge of the language" are not necessarily accurate. It might appear, therefore, that he is referring here to the distinction between K1 and K2. However, in discussing later on (pp. 18–24) the problem of operational criteria for linguistic theories, he is apparently concerned with the fact that the informant's knowledge of the language is not available to him, i.e., that he lacks in some cases awareness of what Chomsky calls his "tacit knowledge".[4] He gives an example of a sentence which is three-ways ambiguous and shows how this ambiguity, which may even go unnoticed by most hearers, can be brought to consciousness. Chomsky emphasizes that, in doing so, "we present no new information to the hearer and teach him nothing new about his language" (pp. 21–2). But, as we have seen, K2 is a theoretical construct that does not presuppose awareness. It is quite possible, therefore, that there are elements of K2 that the native speaker would never become aware of. It is the linguist, not the native speaker, who must retrieve K2, and he does this by extrapolating from his data so as to construct a theory that accounts for them.

The knowledge$_2$ of a recursive rule of centre-embedding is presumably an instance of K2, which is irretrievable for the native speaker's consciousness. In this connection I have heard the following argument. When an informant judges a multiply-embedded sentence as unacceptable, he can be made to conceive that the rule that permits embedding of one sentence within another also permits a third sentence to be embedded within the embedded sentence, and so on, up to any degree of centre-embedding. Thus, the informant can be made to see that the multiply-embedded sentence is really perfectly well-formed. According to this argument, the principle of recursiveness would be retrievable in the above sense. The argument takes Chomsky's line of turning "tacit knowledge" into knowledge the informant is fully aware of. But in this particular case, the "guiding and drawing out" of linguistic intuition, advocated by Chomsky (1965, p. 24), seems to have been carried too far. The linguist can of course convince the informant that if a rule like centre-embedding is applied once it must also be permissible to reapply it recursively, and once the informant admits this, he must accept the consequences and revise his former judgment of unacceptability. But the recursiveness principle is not shown thereby to belong to the informant's intuitive knowledge of the language; contrary to the procedure described by Chomsky, the linguist here has taught the informant something new about his language. It must therefore be concluded that while the recursiveness principle may be shown by theoretical considerations to belong to K2, it definitely is not part of K1. It has not been shown that the informant can be made aware that he operates on this principle: he might have only been seduced into accepting a recursiveness rule.

Let us now take another look at the "priority hypothesis". If competence is K2, the claim that the study of competence must precede the study of performance, if taken literally, does not make sense. A theory of K2 can be constructed only on the basis of performance data such as production and comprehension of utterances and judgments of their acceptability. The most plausible reading of the "priority hypothesis" is that before studying the use of language in speaking and listening one should study competence, i.e., K2, via native speakers' reports on K1. This advice seems to be of rather doubtful value since, as we have seen, a theory of K2 must be arrived at, *inter alia*, by taking into account how the process of comprehension affects judgments of acceptability. Construction of a grammar thus must take into account our present knowledge of psychological factors operative in comprehension, rudimentary as this may be.

The examination of "competence" has shown a number of points in which the term is in need of clarification. Competence has been defined as the idealized speaker's knowledge, and I have tried to show what is meant by "idealized" (Section I), what is the "knowledge" referred to in the definition (Section II), and finally, what kind of knowledge (K1 or K2) is represented by competence. Writers of the transformationalist school have not treated these points explicitly, and thus much room has been left for misunderstanding.[5]

This raises the question whether the time may not have arisen to dispense with the term "competence" altogether. Historically, the competence-performance distinction had an important part to play in pointing out certain misunderstandings of the objectives of a grammar. But in view of the confusion lurking in the use of these terms, it may now be advisable to refer instead explicitly to the place of grammar in an overall theory of language, namely as a component that in interaction with certain psychological principles accounts for linguistic performance such as encoding, decoding, and judgments of acceptability. To be more precise, it is knowledge of the grammar that interacts with these principles (Bar-Hillel, personal communication), but then it should be made explicit that knowledge$_2$ is meant. The term "competence" is not made use of in the above statement, and indeed it does not seem necessary any more. Note that by using the expression "knowledge$_2$ of the grammar" (or a more felicitous term not involving subscripts) all the questions raised by a definition involving "idealized speaker" and "knowledge of the language" no longer arise.

VI. THE QUESTION POSED BY QUESTION MARKS

In Section IV it has been shown that well-formedness is a matter of degree in the judgment of native speakers. The position taken so far has been that these judgments are evidence of the informant's K1, that the facts about K2 are different, and that the operation of factors such as memory limitations serve to explain the discrepancy between K1 and K2.

Now, there seem to be further examples for which no explanation suggests itself in terms of psychological principles. I am referring here to the ever-increasing number of sentences appearing in the linguistic literature that are preceded by a question mark. Some vagueness attends the use of this symbol, and possibly it is not even used in the same way by all writers. The question mark may be used to indicate that the writer has not quite made up his mind as to whether the sentence is grammatical or not (in the latter case it should rather be prefixed by an asterisk), or to indicate that the sentence is grammatical if understood in a certain way, given a certain context. On the other hand, prefixing a question mark to a sentence may express the feeling on the part of the linguist that, although the sentence is grammatical, there is something wrong with it, without its being clear what exactly is wrong. In the following I shall proceed on the assumption that this is indeed what the question mark is often meant to indicate. What this shows is that sentences that according to current conceptions of grammar are considered fully grammatical differ among themselves along a dimension of what one might call, for want of a better name, "questionability". (A new term seems to be needed here, since the term "degree of grammaticality" is reserved for distinguishing between sentences that are not fully grammatical, and the term "degree of acceptability" pertains to judgments assumed to be influenced by performance factors.) The possibility cannot be ruled out that these are grammatical but unacceptable sentences of the kind discussed above, and that a psychological explanation of their questionability will eventually be forthcoming. In fact, Bever (1970) has presented an impressive array of explanations, based on "perceptual strategies", of the questionability of a considerable number of sentences. But in view of the still more impressive variety of question-marked sentences, a sample of which will be given below, one begins to wonder.

It seems at least doubtful whether the questionability of the following sentences (presented here together with their fully acceptable counterparts) is due to memory limitations or to any perceptual strategy.

> Henry is a distant cousin.
> ? Henry is a crooked cousin.

> The girls in this dorm are all pretty.
> ? The girls in this dorm are all pretty ones.

> The addresses in this volume are mostly interesting.
> ? The addresses in this volume are mostly interesting ones.

The above examples are from a paper by Bolinger (1967a). Those that follow appear in another article by the same author (Bolinger, 1967b). Interestingly, Bolinger uses either one or two question marks to distinguish between lesser and greater degrees of what I call "questionability".

> I believe the rain is falling.
> ? I believe the rain to be falling.
> I believe the word has already come.
> ?? I believe word to have already come.

I believe the man to be honest.
? I believe George to be ready.
? I believe the lights to be on.

The prosecution believes Smith to be a member of that gang.
? The prosecution believes Smith to be a salesman at that store.

I believe the report to have been proved beyond a doubt.
? I believe the report to have been held up by a telegraph strike.
? I believe the report to have been disproved.

I believe John to be telling the truth.
? I believe John to be telling a lie.

We believe that man to be sane.
? We believe that man to be demented.

? I know John to be the guy you are looking for.
I know the facts to be true.

Why should sentences in which "believe" and "know" combine with certain structures be questionable? The reason cannot be simply a semantic one, because synonymous sentences with different structures are fully acceptable, and yet, on the other hand, semantic factors seem to play a role, because in other sentences the same structures may be combined with "believe" and "know" without resulting in "questionable" sentences.

Here now are some further examples by another linguist (Bresnan, 1969), who also finds it necessary to distinguish between different degrees of "questionability".

He used a breast stroke in swimming the Hellespont.
? He uses special racing shoes in running.

Seymour finally managed to open the door with his penknife.
? Seymour finally managed to use his penknife to open the door.

Seymour rapidly sliced the salami with a knife.
?? Seymour rapidly used a knife to slice the salami.

Seymour used a knife to slice the salami.
Seymour used a knife in slicing the salami.

She dressed nicely to please her mother.
? She dressed nicely in pleasing her mother.

The above examples seem to show that not only ungrammatical sentences can be ordered with respect to the degree to which they depart from full grammaticalness: a similar differentiation is indicated for sentences currently regarded as fully grammatical. This raises the question whether this is a fact about K2 or about K1. To repeat, if it could be shown how an interaction between K2 and psychological factors might result in the linguist's judgment that leads him to put a question mark before these sentences, there would be good reason to ascribe his intuition on this point to his K1. However, since no explanation along these lines appears to be in sight, further investigation into "questionable" sentences may lead to the conclusion that the above differentiation of sentences pertains to K2. Consequently, the grammar which formalizes K2 may have to be reconstructed to accommodate this phenomenon. In the following, I shall suggest one way in which this could be done.

The approach to be outlined here is essentially similar to Chomsky's (1961) suggestion for describing degrees of grammaticalness, except that the full ordering assumed by Chomsky to exist for semi-grammatical sentences is not assumed here (see Bar-Hillel, 1967, pp. 539–40 on this point). It calls for treating "questionable" sentences in the same manner as semi-grammatical sentences, which may be an advantage, since it is not clear whether there is any definite boundary line between these two types of strings. It is proposed, then, that the generative grammar comprises a set of subgrammars, differing from each other in the restrictions they retain. The subgrammar containing all restrictions, G_0, generates all sentences that are fully grammatical and not questionable in any way. Next, there is a set of subgrammars G_1 each of which has one restriction less than G_0. For each G_1 there is a set of subgrammars G_2, each of which relinquishes one of the restrictions in its related G_1. The set of subgrammars is thus (at least) partially ordered. Each subgrammar G_i generates a set of sentences S_i. Every set of sentences generated by a subgrammar has S_0, generated by G_0, as its subset, and in general, S_n has some of the sets S_{n-1} as its subsets. The degree of "questionability" of what are currently regarded fully grammatical sentences as well as the degree of grammaticality of a sentence can now both be defined in the same way, namely in terms of the *least inclusive* set of sentences to which the sentence belongs. Conceivably, it will also be possible to explain some facts about metaphorical usage by specifying subgrammars in which certain restrictions are relinquished.

In Section IV a number of cases were discussed in which fully grammatical sentences differ in degree of acceptability, and the question was discussed whether this was a fact about K1 or about K2. This issue can be settled only on the basis of methodical considerations pertaining to the overall theory of language behaviour, which comprises grammatical and psychological components. Such considerations led to the proposal that judgments of acceptability reflect K1. Now, in the light of the present suggestion concerning the format of grammar, it may not be uneconomical to regard certain facts about acceptability as reflecting K2 and to take account of them within the grammar. While the conceptual apparatus of "classical" generative grammar does not provide a means of limiting the number of applications of a recursive rule, it would be feasible to enable the grammar to do this by introducing rules sensitive to the history of their derivation. Let subgrammar G_i permit only one centre-embedding and subgrammar G_{i+1} differ from it in that it permits a second centre-embedding within the first one, and so on for additional centre-embeddings. The degree of acceptability will then be paralleled by the number of centre-embeddings permitted by various subgrammars, G_i, G_{i+1}, etc. To avoid an infinite series of subgrammars one could introduce a G_j $(j > i)$ permitting any degree of centre-embedding.

No point-by-point correspondence between this set of subgrammars and judgments of acceptability is to be expected. It is conceivable, for instance, that a sentence with four centre-embeddings will be judged as being of the same degree of acceptability as a similar sentence of five centre-embeddings. Such a result would be due to certain behavioural principles that make these sentences indistinguishable in regard to acceptability. According to this version of a grammar – just as according to the version discussed in Section V – K2 (which is explicated by a grammar) accounts for performance only in interaction with psychological factors. The same holds of course also for the degree of difficulty in decoding and encoding centre-embedded sentences, which presumably will increase monotonously but not linearly with the number of centre-embeddings, because it will be affected by certain psychological determinants. Moreover, a number of pragmatic factors (e.g., the plausibility of the statement made by uttering a sentence) may also be expected to influence judgments of acceptability and difficulty in decoding and encoding, and these too are not taken care of by the grammar.

The suggestion sketched here in its outline of a grammar containing a set of subgrammars may be applied not only in dealing with different degrees of centre-embedding, but also with other factors which were shown in Section IV to affect judgments of acceptability. Consider, for example, the absence or presence of relative pronouns introducing a centre-embedded clause. Let G_n be a subgrammar permitting n centre-embeddings and containing the restriction that each of the centre-embedded clauses must begin with a relative pronoun, and G_{n+1} a subgrammar permitting the same number of centre-embeddings, but waiving this pronoun restriction for one of the centre-embedded clauses; similarly, there will be a G_{n+2} for two, a G_{n+3} for three clauses, and so on. Suppose now, that for each number of centre-embeddings there is such a set of subgrammars differing from each other in the number of embedded clauses that may appear in the sentence without being introduced by a relative pronoun. We shall then have a partially ordered set of subgrammars. Presented with a sentence containing a given combination of these two factors the number of centre-embeddings and the number of pronoun restrictions that have been waived – the native speaker will know₂ which subgrammars can generate the sentence. But, as mentioned, his judgment of acceptability of the sentence, which reflects his K1, will be influenced also by additional factors.

The above system of subgrammars appears to be highly complex; but it should be clear that it is really no more complex than a fully articulated explanation of judgments of acceptability in terms of behavioural principles. The proposed organization of a grammar that constitutes a hierarchy of subgrammars seems to be needed independently to account for "questionable" sentences. What has been suggested now is to remove some of the burden of explanation from the psychologist's shoulders and put it onto the linguist's; as we have seen, the psychologist is still left with his hands full to deal with judgments of acceptability. One might ask why the linguist should worry about problems that the psychologist is well enough equipped to deal with. However, this is not a valid criterion for deciding what a grammar should treat of. Remember that according to the transformationalist school of thought a grammar is concerned with such "mental" phenomena as the speaker's intuitions about relations between sentences (see (8) in Section II), and this task is not assigned to the psychologist, although he might well be capable of explaining such relations by referring to pragmatic factors. As stated, the decision as to what does and what does not belong to a grammar must be based on criteria like parsimony and elegance, which are commonly referred to in evaluating a theory. No such evaluation of the present proposal will be attempted here (and in view of its undeveloped state such an evaluation would be premature in any case). There is only one point to which I would like to draw attention. By describing acceptability phenomena within a grammar, the number of issues on which K2 contradicts K1 is diminished. This may be a minor bonus, since intuitively it seems somewhat forced to postulate too much discrepancy between what one is aware of knowing (K1) and what one "really" knows (K2). But of course, such an "ordinary-language" approach to theoretical constructs should not weigh too heavily in the balance when alternative ways of constructing a theory are evaluated.

Hebrew University and
The Israel Institute of Applied Social Research

BIBLIOGRAPHY

Bar-Hillel, Y.: 1967, Review of J. A. Fodor and J. J. Katz, *The Structure of Language: Readings in the Philosophy of Language. Language* 43, 526–50. Reprinted in Bar-Hillel, Y.: 1970, *Aspects of Language*, Magnes Press, Jerusalem, and North-Holland, Amsterdam.
Bever, T. G.: 1970, 'The Cognitive Basis for Linguistic Structures', in J. R. Hayes (ed.), *Cognition and the Development of Language*, Wiley, New York, pp. 279–352.
Blumenthal, A. L.: 'Observations with Self-Embedded Sentences', *Psychonomic Science* 6, 453–4.
Bolinger, D.: 1967, 'Adjectives in English: Attribution and Predication', *Lingua* 18, 1–34.
Bresnan, J. W.: 1969, 'On Instrumental Adverbs and the Concept of Deep Structure', *Quarterly Progress Report*, 92, Research Labor. Electronics, MIT.
Chomsky, N.: 1961, 'Some Methodological Remarks on Generative Grammar', *Word* 17, 219–39.
Chomsky, N.: 1965, *Aspects of the Theory of Syntax*, MIT Press, Cambridge, Mass.
Chomsky, N.: 1968, *Language and Mind*, Harcourt, Brace and World, New York.
Fodor, J. A. and Garrett, M.: 1967a, 'Some Syntactic Determinants of Sentential Complexity', *Perception and Psychophysics* 2, 289–96.
Fodor, J. A. and Garrett, M.: 1967b, 'Some Reflections on Competence and Performance', in: J. Lyons and R. J. Wales (eds.), *Psycholinguistics Papers*, Edinburgh University Press, Edinburgh.
Hockett, C. F.: 1968, *The State of the Art*, Mouton, The Hague.
Hymes, D.: 1971, 'On Communicative Competence', in E. Ingram and R. Huxley (eds.), *Studies in Language Acquisition: Methods and Models*, Academic Press, London (in press).
Katz, J. J.: 1966, *The Philosophy of Language*, Harper and Row, New York.
Lehrer, A.: 1968, 'Competence, Grammaticality and Sentence Complexity', *The Philosophical Forum* 1, 85–89.

Lieb, H. H.: 1970, *Sprachstadium und Sprachsystem*, W. Kohlhammer, Stuttgart.
Marks, L. E.: 1968, 'Scaling of Grammaticalness of Self-Embedded English Sentences', *Journal of Verbal Learning and Verbal Behavior* 7, 965–7.
Matthews, P. H.: 1967, Review of N. Chomsky, *Aspects of the Theory of Syntax*, *Journal of Linguistics* 3, 119–52.
Miller, G. A. and Chomsky, N.: 1963, 'Finitary Models of Language Users', Part II, in R. D. Luce, R. Bush, and E. Galanter (eds.), *Handbook of Mathematical Psychology*, Vol. 2, Wiley, New York, pp. 419–91.
Postal, P. M.: 1964, 'Underlying and Superficial Linguistic Structure', *Harvard Educational Review* 34, 246–66.
Reich, P. A.: 1969, 'The Finiteness of Natural Language', *Language* 45, 831–43.
Schlesinger, I. M.: 1968, *Sentence Structure and the Reading Process*, Mouton, The Hague.
Schlesinger, I. M.: 1967, 'A Note on the Relationship between Psychological and Linguistic Theories', *Foundations of Language* 3, 397–402.
Stolz, W. S.: 1967, 'A Study of Ability to Decode Grammatically Novel Sentences', *Journal of Verbal Learning and Verbal Behavior* 6, 867–73.
Weksel, W.: 1965, Review of U. Bellugi and R. Brown (eds.), *The Acquisition of Language* (Monographs of the Society for Research in Child Development, 29, 1964), *Language* 41, 692–709.

NOTES

* I am indebted to Y. Bar-Hillel for his critical comments on a draft of this paper, some of which led to a radical revision of my treatment of the issues in Sections IV and V.

[1] See also Hockett's (1968, p. 39) summary of Chomsky's views: "A convenient device for barring from consideration linguistically irrelevant factors in performance is to imagine 'an ideal speaker-listener'"; and Katz (1966, p. 115), who after presenting the first interpretation of "ideal" quoted above, continues, "But the idealization goes even further than that," and discusses abstractions from psychological factors.

[2] It has often been pointed out that acceptability should not be confused with grammaticality. Without going into the argument further here, it should be noted that it is unlikely that experimental subjects can be induced to make this distinction. It is immaterial whether they are told to judge the "acceptability", "well-formedness", or "grammaticality" of sentences; all these terms will be taken by them to mean the same (i.e., whether the sentence is what in everyday terms one might call "good English"). See also Schlesinger (1968, p. 125).

[3] A further complication is introduced by some findings of Stolz (1967). His subjects listened to multiply-embedded sentences such as:

> The chef that the waiter that the busboy appreciated teased admired good musicians.

and were instructed to write down the component sentences. Although they were given ample time for this (in order to alleviate stresses on processing), half of the subjects failed in the task. Two of them consistently assigned the same wrong structure to the sentences. This parallels Blumenthal's (1966) finding that in about 75% of the multiply-embedded sentences rewritten by his subjects the relative pronouns were interpreted as referring to the first noun of the sentence (for the above sentence this would result, e.g., in: "The chef that the waiter appreciated and that the busboy teased . . . ."). One possibility considered by Stolz is that recursiveness is not part of the subject's competence. In view of the fact that some multiply-embedded structures seem to be perfectly comprehensible (see Section IV above), this would have to be qualified to apply only to sentences of a certain structure.

[4] Chomsky (1965, pp. 18–19) seems to identify linguistic intuition with tacit knowledge, and he stresses that verbal reports do not invariably describe linguistic intuition correctly. By contrast, Bever (1970) seems to identify linguistic intuition with the speaker's account thereof.

[5] Among those who have tried at length to clarify the concepts of competence, performance, and linguistic intuition are Fodor and Garrett (1967b) and Bever (1970).

HELMUT SCHNELLE

LANGUAGE COMMUNICATION WITH CHILDREN –
TOWARD A THEORY OF LANGUAGE USE

I. METHODOLOGICAL ABSTRACTION IN LINGUISTIC THEORY

What is the task of linguistic theory? A common answer to this question is: the description of the pairings of sound and meaning of words, sentences and texts in a language, and the explanation of how the complex system of pairings of a language can be learned by a child on the basis of its always limited exposure to stretches of sounds in the community using that language. It is usually understood that a fruitful and sufficiently complete solution of this problem is only possible on the basis of a fairly radical theoretical abstraction. In particular one has to *abstract* – as is usually argued – from the questions regarding the nature of the actual psycho-physiological *mechanisms* embodying the pairings as well as from the global constraints stemming from perceptual, operational, and cognitive *procedures and strategies* realizing the pairings in the organism.

Though it is acknowledged that the context of use of a certain utterance of language may influence the assignment of meaning to sound in the actual use, it is held that the linguist can and must *abstract from the context.* One of the strongest arguments given is that a sufficiently complete description of contextual influence requires encyclopedic description unattainable at present.

Finally, one abstracts from the essentially *communicative nature* of language use. For the purpose of certain structural problems (such as pronominalization and certain problems depending on deixis) one would even be willing to take account of the communicative framework formed by speaker, hearer, time and place of uttering and – in languages where this has structural consequences – of the relative or absolute social status of people. But these are rather external aspects of the communicative nature of language use. The internal aspects can only be represented when potential differences in language competence and knowledge, experiences, aims, plans etc. of the partners of communication are not only taken account of by theoretical description (instead of postulating a homogeneous set of ideal speaker–hearers), but when there is acknowledgment

Yehoshua Bar-Hillel (ed.), Pragmatics of Natural Languages, 173–193.
All Rights Reserved. Copyright © 1971 by D. Reidel Publishing Company, Dordrecht-Holland.

and description of how the partners take account of their respective differences.

All of these abstractions have been criticized recently – in some cases quite convincingly. From a philosophical point of view, the importance of taking account of the essentially communicative nature of language use has been stressed against the more abstract approaches based on formalizing the notions of truth and grammaticality (or some additional syntactic and semantic notions) by Strawson (1970). I tried to do the same in (1967) with respect to structural linguistic approaches. The problematic neglect of the role of procedures and strategies even in the very process of the abstraction of linguistic structure has been argued very vigorously by Bever (1970a, b). An adequate description of mechanisms has been attempted in stratificational grammars by Lamb (1966) and others (among these the present author in earlier work along similar lines (Schnelle, 1964a, b)). In this case, however, one is forced to acknowledge that we still lack much information; it is too early to attempt a reconstruction. In the present article I want to question the neglect of context in the theoretical description of language by showing that, at least for restricted language systems, to aim at a full description of the contextual influence is not utopian at all. But even for research on fully developed languages at least the form and types of contextual influences should be explicated in order to show what has been abstracted from. It is no longer possible to be satisfied with the mere terminological distinctions between linguistic – non-linguistic, langue-parole, competence-performance etc. In order to comply with these requirements we should begin by unpacking the extremely condensed phrase "pairing of sound and meaning". This unpacking may result in statements like the following (relative to a given group of people using a certain language):

Whenever a speaker X *produces a noise* of shape p at some time t, then – given the context type i – he may be taken to *utter* thereby *a well-formed expression* q (of language L) and – depending on the properties of wellformedness SD(q) and the given context type j – he may be taken to express thereby a speech act complex s, comprising

(a) a propositional content (including reference, predication, quantifying, modalizing, causally connecting, etc.)

(b) the implicates of the propositional content

(c) the communicative force he intends to establish over the communicative relation between him, the addressee(s), the audience, etc.

as well as to *signalize* his *choice of communicative effectivity* r (including indication of topic, focus, presupposition, and other more typically rhetoric factors) appropriate to the given communicative relation and context j.

It is to be understood that within context type j the information in focus of awareness is stratified as to what the speaker himself perceives, does, knows, plans, wants, infers and what he assumes that the addressee, or the audience, perceives, does, knows, etc., or what he assumes that the addressee (resp. the wider audience) assumes concerning the speaker (the audience, the hearer) or – in more complicated cases – what the speaker assumes that the addressee assumes that the speaker assumes. . . . It is this system of assumptions that is representative of the essentially communicative nature of language use. The usual abstraction takes the following direction: It enumerates the elementary entities of each level (p, q, r, s), assigns to them the relevant properties on each level and interrelates the descriptions of a given entity (phoneme, word, sentence) on the various levels as well as fully and partially equivalent[1] different entities. In the endeavour to reduce the necessary basic information one even tries to find out whether the information on one level (phonetic, syntactic, semantic) is sufficient to determine or to derive systematically the information on all other levels, defining thereby a phonetic or syntactic or semantic basis for all theoretical statements about a language. In spite of the recent very heated debates between generative semanticists and others I do not consider this to be a very crucial question. However, the usual assumption of all schools of structuralism is that one may and should abstract – in the definition of the structures on each level as well as for their mapping – from the context of use (i and j).

II. THE STUDY OF RESTRICTED LANGUAGES

As already indicated above, the argument that a consideration of context would require encyclopedic knowledge is conclusive only for fully developed languages; it is not so for certain restricted languages. I therefore propose to study appropriate restricted-languages.[2] Linguists tend to stress the priority of research into the fully developed system because otherwise, they say, one would lack criteria for evaluating restricted systems and one would not get a sufficiently clear idea of the sense in which the restricted system is restricted. The argument would be sound if it were possible at present to obtain a complete and adequate description of language use in its fully developed variety. But this is not the case. The alternatives are, on the one hand, descriptions of radical abstractions and subsections (phonology, parts of syntax and even smaller parts of semantics) of language systems with very tenuous correlation to processes and conditions of language use, and, on the other, adequate descriptions of the regularities of such processes and conditions, leaving the relation to the fully developed system unspecified. Neither of these approaches may derive evaluation criteria with respect to the alternative, though it is possible to use within the latter approach, as we shall do, methods developed in treating the former.

In searching for fruitful examples of restricted natural languages two directions promise to be particularly important: (a) the forms of natural language uses to be found in various stages of the ontogenetic and phylogenetic development of languages; (b) the forms of languages developed for specific purposes including in particular constructed languages developed for use in scientific discourse or in communication with the computer. I think that a description of early stages of language development in *all* of its aspects will prove most rewarding in particular in the fields of (1) analysis of children languages, (2) analysis of animal "languages", and (3) philosophical analysis of the necessary conditions for possible acquisition processes for natural languages. From the point of view of the linguistics of natural languages it is obviously the first field that is the most interesting. I will be concerned with this in the present article and refer to the literature for the other two fields.[3] In research on children's languages one expects to find any degree of complexity, depending on the stage of development. This seems to be corroborated by the facts, to a certain extent at least.[4]

However, the intertwining of language development with other psychological factors becomes extremely intricate when a fully adequate description is attempted. This seems to complicate our task. Fortunately, however, there are closely related systems that are almost ideal candidates for our description, namely languages and regularities of adults in their communication with children as well as the models of language understanding and processing, which they implicitly or explicitly assume to underly the behaviour of children. We shall therefore turn to the description of language communication as it might be presupposed by an intelligent but not psychologically trained adult communicating with a, say, two-year old child.

There cannot be any doubt that – at least for very young children – the assumptions and models adults cherish with respect to their children are descriptively inadequate and usually overinterpreted. On the other hand, they are obviously not practically inadequate since communication usually proceeds quite effectively on the basis of these assumptions.

An adequate representation of the communication process between an adult and a child will have to describe the possibly quite different processes in these partners of communication. As far as literature and personal information from competent psycholinguists shows, empirical research has been applied only to one of these partners, namely the child. With respect to the adult it is assumed that the description of his fully developed language competence will take account of all that is relevant also in his communication with the child. However, it is quite obvious, at least to me, that, considering all factors determining language communication, phonetic, syntactic and semantic competence as well as relevant context of knowledge, experience etc., presupposed to exist in the partner, the adult drastically reduces his assumptions when communicating with a child. He restricts himself to a subsystem of the system put to use with a normal adult, and assumes that, at least in principle, the child shares this subsystem with him, apart from minor modifications and imperfections of performance. He may sometimes be inclined to adapt even to these modifications, to fall for instance into a kind of baby talk. But baby talk is surely a minor aspect in the descriptions of adult assumptions and adaptations to children. I propose that psycholinguistic research should be conducted on these assumptions of the adult communicating with children.

At present, because of the lack of such research, I shall have to rely mainly on my own competence and experience with children and explicate my own assumptions confronting and controlling them as much as possible with the help of data and analyses of psycholinguistic research on children's language. Particularly fruitful for my present purpose have been the careful study of data and analyses by Bloom (1970).

Before turning to the details of the description, I shall present a brief outline of the form the theory should acquire. The explanation of the basic regularities should be presented by a theory P of the phonetic shape of utterances, a theory Q of the syntactic conditions of wellformedness of expressions, a theory S of the semantic form of speech acts, and a theory R of factors of communicative effectivity together with two theories stating how – under given conditions of context i and j – phonetic shape and syntactic conditions of wellformedness, on the one hand, and syntactic conditions and forms of possible speech acts and communicative effectivity factors, on the other hand, are interrelated among each other or determine each other (see Figure 1).

In its standard form the complete theory should be built up from sub-theories of the following form: For each level (phonetic, syntactic, seman-tic), the corresponding subtheory should enumerate the terms denoting the

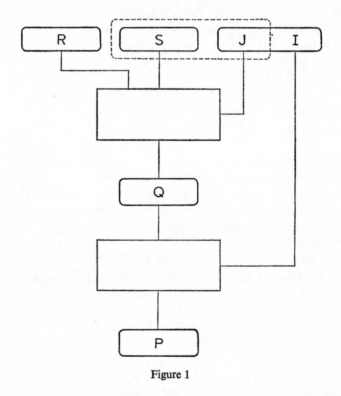

Figure 1

entities of that level (where the formation of the terms represents the combinatorial structure of the entities denoted, i.e., their formation from primitive or basic entities) as well as statements assigning properties and relations that are true of the entities according to the theory. Moreover, we should have a theory enumerating the possible contexts i and j together with their relevant properties and relations. However, as some reflection shows, the set of possible semantic contents and the set of possible contexts j (or components of contexts) are practically the same: Any aspect that can become a relevant context can, in another speech act, become expressed itself. Therefore the description of possible semantic contents and of possible contexts j is the same. For contexts i we will possibly have to add certain kinds of peripheral context information such as surrounding noise level.

On each level one might wish to have rules of inference showing which statements (or statement complexes) may be derived from others. Moreover, there should be rules by which statements on different levels about the same entity (the phonetic shape, the syntactic form and function, and the semantic representation of a word or sentence) may be paired.[5]

III. THE FRAMEWORK FOR THE REPRESENTATION OF SEMANTICS AND CONTEXT

I shall assume – as already indicated – that the system of semantic representations of a language (potentially expressed or functioning as a part of context) takes the form of a set of statements (and possibly statement forms) appropriately partitioned and systematically interrelated. The statements should be represented by wellformed expressions of a semantic metalanguage. A possible framework for such a metalanguage should be developed – at the present state of theoretical semantics for natural languages – along the lines indicated by pragmatic languages[6] or interpreted languages for modal logic.[7] It may be hoped that in the description of adult languages for small children no essential further development of the framework for semantic representation will be necessary, except for the clarification of the still controversial issues. I shall now try to present a tentative outline of such a system. The set of possible *particular entities* (individuals) will be conceived of as the union of sets of entities of the following categories:

A-subjects (animated or actor subjects) such as identified or identifiable persons, dolls, and animals. The normal expressions denoting these entities may syntactically take the function of subjects of sentences in deep-structure analysis of early child language.[8] *M-Objects* (objects that may be acted upon or with by the child; manipulatable objects) such as food, instruments used for eating, toys, dresses, objects used for cleaning (of the body, or of the environment, E-objects or M-objects), objects used for transporting and keeping things and – the special category – pictures and books (i.e., objects with symbolic or iconic function used to look at). The normal expressions used to refer to E-objects usually take the function of predicate-objects in deep-structure analysis.[9] *E-objects* (objects at, on, under, in . . . which A-subjects and M-objects may be found, together with their parts and associated objects (like decoration)) such as pieces of furniture, home decorations, instruments of entertainment, communication, kitchen utensils (such as piano, radio- and television-set, telephone, stove, refrigerator, dish-washer, etc.) trees, plants, and stones. The normal expressions used to refer to E-objects appear typically in locative function in deep-analysis (Bloom, 1970, 67 a.o.).

Environments (quasi-individuals – rather fields of perception and action – parts or constituents of which are E-objects) such as rooms, houses, gardens, streets, etc. The syntactic functions most frequently assigned to expressions referring to environments are the same as for E-objects.

The *individual constants* of the semantic metalanguage denoting individuals will be taken as different from names or referring phrases of the object language used on occasion to refer to the individuals denoted by the formal constants. One of the reasons for this is that the referring relation between the expression (name) and what is referred to is not sufficiently stable. Apart from the fact that different particulars may sometimes be referred to by the same name, it is also the case that the same individual is referred to by different names.[10] It is therefore necessary to draw a distinction between an individual constant in the semantic metalanguage denoting a certain particular and the expressions that may be used under certain (e.g., normal) circumstances to refer to the particulars. The same distinction will be made in the following with respect to predicates of the metalanguage and the expressions of the object language used to predicate the respective attributes under certain circumstances. A possible convention for individual constants to be adapted in the following is to take A1, A2, . . ., An, . . . for primitive constants denoting A-subjects, M1, M2, . . ., Mm, . . . for M-objects, E1, E2, . . ., Ee for E-objects, and F1, F2, . . ., Fk, . . . for environments.

The set of possible words is partially characterized by the attributes (properties and relations) that may or may not be predicated of A-subjects, M-objects, and E-objects. Among the attributes there will be some that are denoted by *primitive predicates* in our semantic metalanguage.

The attributes corresponding to one-place predicates to be accounted for by a two-year-old child will be tentatively sub-classified into

External attributes (primary parts, perceptual properties and properties of manipulation, appearances, change of appearances, states etc. of A-, M-, and E-objects).

Internal attributes (localizable (=bodily) feelings, non-localizable (=global) feelings (hunger, pain, anger, . . .), intellectual states, properties and activities, controlled external activities or states etc.)

The attributes corresponding to many-place predicates are tentatively subclassified into:

Personal relations (love etc.), *position and change of position* with respect to environments, A-, M-, or E-objects (a) of self, (b) of other objects, (c) of self with other objects (transporting), *possession and change of possession* of objects, *manipulation* of M-objects (and, in certain cases, of A- and E-objects).

Certain *operators on events* will be necessary, some depending on actors, others not. Examples are to *come into being* (=to appear), to *disappear*, to *be about*, to *have just appeared*, to *be caused by*, to *be able to, required to, communicated* (among these *asserted* and *denied*).

We leave it open at this point how we are going to represent systematically in the semantic metalanguage the predicates and operators. We shall not exclude introducing several expressions of our metalanguage for the same content – in certain cases – but we shall assume in general that one of these is marked as the standard one. In contrast to this, what is predicated by a certain expression in the object language may only become determinate in definite contexts, though in many cases the possible variations that may be brought about by not too far fetched contexts may be small.

In addition to the primitive descriptive concepts and the primitive symbols denoting them we shall, as usual, assume logical notions such as logical constants, punctuation marks, parentheses, and (individual) variables.

The statement expressions in our semantic metalanguage that should be built up approximately as sentences are in Montague (1970b) (without rules A12–S16 and the corresponding semantic operations). However, the verbs should be handled in a manner corresponding to the treatment of common nouns, i.e. they should be introduced by rules corresponding to S8–S11 and F8–F11, respectively, i.e., by rules that allow us to introduce modality-tensed verbs into the sentences and to relate them to the different possible worlds. As modality tenses we shall assume the following four: *presently perceived, felt, or thought, intended, just past,* and *remembered.* Just as in the case of common nouns, we may use them to refer to some particular event (definitely or indefinitely) or to quantify away the reference by quantifiers like 'every' in the case of nouns. In modifying a verb we may either introduce a particular modality-tense or quantify it away by such adverbial quantifiers as 'always', 'sometimes', 'usually' etc. I do not have sufficient time at present to work out the details of these hints.

The internal status of an organism that determines its actions and communications is representable by a set of statements in the language of semantic representations. Depending on the types of quantifiers applied, we may partition the set of statements into the following subsets:

a. *concrete and situative statements,* i.e., statements with particular reference and modality-tense.

b. *concrete and non-situative statements,* i.e., statements where the modality-tenses are quantified away, but still contain particular reference. These statements represent the assignment of properties and relations to particulars that obtain always (i.e., invariably), usually, sometimes (i.e., may be experienced), often, or rarely. The quantifications state a statistical or normative or hypothetical *general experience about particulars.*

c. *General statements,* i.e., statements without special modality-tense or reference to particulars. These statements represent the *general experience about classes or categories of particulars.*

For the representation of the internal structure assignable to a child of two, I think it is sufficient to have only one kind of concrete and non-situative statement set (or model, in one sense of the term "model"), one kind of general model, but four concrete models corresponding to the modality tenses above for each time interval.

One further particularity should be mentioned: the particulars (individuals) of the concrete and situative model may be, but do not have to be, identical with the particulars of the concrete and non-situative model. Those particulars that are only taken account of during a certain stretch of activity or situation (and are forgotten as individuals thereafter) will be called *occasion particulars* in contrast to the particulars of the non-situative model, which are called *standing particulars.* With respect to standing particulars, we shall envisage the possibility that there may occur a kind of tension between statements of the non-situative and the situative models, such as when a certain property is a usual or normal property of a particular, but does not apply in a particular situation.

We shall assume, furthermore, that there is a function over the set of statements assigning *emotion values* to the statements (including the neutral value), and another function assigning an *awareness value* between the values: *focus* of awareness and *unconscious* presence in store.

Of particular importance in the concrete and situative model is the information stating the perception, communication, and manipulation status of the child itself. This subset of statements defines the *situative context* of the child. It contains a subset that is even more basic to a given communicative relation, it is the *communicative basis* and the *communicative status*. The communicative basis indicates for each time the communicative roles of speaker, hearer and index of time and place of utterance. The communicative role specifies the relevant statuses, attitudes and appeals with respect to the partner of communication. In contrast to this, the statements forming the internal system of the child of two does not contain, I believe, assumptions about the internal model of the adult it is communicating with. The child only vaguely takes account of the adult's previous experience of the present situation and practically not at all of what he may at present intend, need, remember, plan etc. It is with respect to this aspect that the communication of an adult with a child is radically asymmetric, since the adult in turn does take account of his assumptions about the status of the child. I believe that a child shows signs of taking into account the assumed model of the adult, when he begins to lie consciously.[11]

A preliminary analysis of the data of contexts presented by Bloom indicates that by far most of them may be represented by the statements of our semantic metalanguage. The same holds to an even higher degree for the semantic content of the expressions as far as I can decode them on the basis of the context. Nor should it be too complicated to set up rules representing the *implicational interrelations* of the system.

IV. COMMUNICATIVE FORCE

In actual speech acts the child uses his internal model as a system of orientation.[12] But he wants, moreover, to establish a *communicative force* over the communicative relation established between the persons and the environments and himself. The general categories of communicative forces to be established are:

1. expression of feelings and structuring of his own acts and perceptions
2. directing the attention of others to a fact (illocutionary force)
3. inducing others to act (perlocutionary force)
4. reacting towards acts or words of others (which are in conflict or agreement with his intended model).

An informal enumeration of more specifically described speech acts is given by the following list.

α. *Acts from Child (C) towards Adult (A)*

I. *Affectively and voluntarily determined acts*

1. C expresses his feelings such as (a) bodily feelings, e.g., hunger, thirst, heat, pain, etc., and (b) psychic states, e.g., fatigue, nervousness, tension, fear, happiness, unhappiness, etc.
2. C expresses his (a) satisfaction or (b) dissatisfaction with a given situation, event or action (not connected with A – otherwise see II, 7)
3. C expresses his wish (a) to get something, (b) to do something, (c) to get or to be somewhere, (d) to be in a certain state.
4. C expresses a request to A to the effect that A undertake a specific action helping C to obtain the fulfilment of his wishes (a–d).
5. C expresses a request to A to the effect that A should *not* undertake an action interfering with C's activities aiming at fulfilling his wishes (a–d).

II. *Role-determined speech acts*

1. C calls or addresses A
2. C expresses his love and tenderness toward A
3. C requests that A expresses his love and tenderness toward him
4. C expresses his thankfulness and affiliation to A
5. C expresses his happiness about an approval or a reward by A
6. C expresses his discomfort about A's abuse, rebuke or punishment
7. C protests against an act or a measure of A
8. C expresses his neglect of A's threats or warnings
9. C expresses his opposition to an order or an interdiction of A
10. C promises to A a certain type of conduct

Remark: Acts β II 3–11 (see below) are executed by C toward a doll in role-playing.

III. *Informational speech acts*

1. C accompanies or supports a situation, event, or act by (a) conventionally related speech, (b) by referring to or describing a certain section of it that is in the focus of his attention
2. C calls A's attention to a situation, event or act by referring to it or describing it
3. C asks A for a standard way of referring to or describing an element in the focus of his attention
4. C asks A for additional information with respect to (a) a given situation, (b) a situation described in linguistic context
5. C asks A for general rules of statements of experience and conduct
6. C reports to A on a situation experienced earlier
7. C tells an invented story to A
8. C expresses his thoughts on, or his evaluation of, a situation to A
9. C imitates or repeats something A said
10. C babbles, sings etc., i.e., plays with language and utterances.

Let me add some brief remarks on the semantic system of the adult that corresponds to the system of the child. It will be essentially of the same type, but it will contain in detail a number of propositions on the various levels not present in the child. In particular it will contain intellectual process structures for the consideration of which reactions are desirable, when given certain evidence about the state of the child and his internal model. This has already been pointed out above. From a formal point of view this does only quantitatively enrich the system, but does not change it qualitatively. To be sure, the complete system of the adult is enormously more complex, but no more complexity is needed in the communication with the child – so I claim – than just a system of about the complexity and structure outlined. As to the communicative forces to be established by the adult, the first type of pure expressing and structuring has less importance for the adult than for the child. We shall present a brief and informal enumeration of communicative forces to be established by speech acts of the adult in the following list:

β. *Acts from Adult (A) towards Child (C)*

I. *Affectively and voluntarily determined acts*
   Not common.

II. *Role-determined speech acts*

1. A calls or addresses C
2. A expresses his love and tenderness towards C
3. A requests that C expresses his love and tenderness towards him
4. A expresses his interest and care for the well-being of C
5. A requests that C expresses his thankfulness and affiliation to A
6. A approves acts of C
7. A promises a reward to C
8. A scolds C
9. A rebukes C
10. A pronounces a punishment to C
11. A threatens C
12. A warns C
13. A gives C an order to do something
14. A forbids C to do something

III. *Informational speech acts*

1. through 10. – like α III 1. through 10. (see above) with A and C interchanged. In 3. and 5. the questions will be usually test questions, whereas in 4. they may sometimes be proper requests for information.
In addition to 1. to 10. we have:

11. A reads a story to C,
12. A tells or reads verses or poems to C.

It should also be clear that most of these acts may also be performed under appropriate conditions without uttering an expression. On the other hand, in uttering an expression a speaker may perform several of these acts simultaneously.

V. SYNTACTIC CONDITIONS ON EXPRESSIONS OF A LANGUAGE

The analysis of children at about 20–24 months of age shows that from 30–50% of the utterances consist of more than one morpheme. Of these, approximately 85–90% consist of two morphemes and the rest of more than two morphemes. In other words, the utterances that may express relations between two different and specified aspects of the situation, intention, or remembrance of the child are practically all two-morpheme (or two-word) utterances at this age. An analysis of the distribution of words reveals[13] that the words may best be classified in the categories P (pivot), N (noun) and V (verb). The following arrangements of these categories occur (presented together with their frequency of occurrence) in the data of Brown *et al.* and Bloom.[14]

	Brown	Bloom	
PN	6	2	(due to a somewhat different classification than McNeill/Brown)
NN	28	31	
VN	40	39	
NV	12	18	

Three-word utterances of the following arrangements (PNN, NPN, VPN, VNN, PNV, NNV, NVN, NNN) occur with frequency 14 resp. 10 (where VNN has already frequency 7 in the Brown-data). A careful analysis of the utterances *in context* observable by an adult present in the situation of utterance (taking into account the cognitive and operational distinctions a child is able to make – as evidenced by its behaviour – and of the often unsuccessful attempts of children to express more complex relations obviously present internally in the child) reveals that there are limitations of linguistic performance that reflect "an inability to carry the full structural load of the underlying representation. Limitations in linguistic operations appear to interact with limitations in cognitive function [of apprehension and production of utterances] to influence linguistic expression [=utterance] in an as yet unspecified way." (Bloom, 1970, 169, words in square brackets are mine.)

Bloom's analysis of her data shows convincingly that in most cases it is possible to infer the semantic content intended to be expressed by the child in uttering restricted expressions *in context*. Our assumption that the semantic content may be represented in terms of the semantic metalanguage outlined above seems to be well-founded. Admittedly the inference of semantic representations draws heavily on judgments based on the adult model of syntax and semantics (Bloom, 1970, 14). However, the inference of underlying deep structural distinctions related to semantic interpretation (without further concern with semantics) seems to be particularly safe; Bloom's analysis concentrates on this problem.

We may illustrate her solution by copying a typical constituent deep-structure grammar (the one proposed for KI) containing the following five rules:

1. $S_0 \rightarrow$ Pivot $+$ N

2. $S_1 \rightarrow$ Nom (Neg)$\left\{ \begin{matrix} NP \\ VP \end{matrix} \right\}$

3. $VP \rightarrow VB\left(\left\{ \begin{matrix} NP \\ Part \end{matrix} \right\} \right)$

4. $NP \rightarrow$ (ADJ) N

5. Nom $\rightarrow \left\{ \begin{matrix} N \\ Dem \end{matrix} \right\}$

together with certain selectional restrictions for the insertion of lexical entries. (I have neglected the element 'ə' in Bloom's account.) A slight modification, substituting rule 3 by

3'. $VP \rightarrow VB\left(\left\{ \begin{matrix} Comp \\ Part \end{matrix} \right\} \right)$

3". Comp $\rightarrow$ (NP) (Prep P),

would account also for certain aspects of the more advanced stage at KII (22 months) as discussed on p. 146., *op. cit.* This grammar allows in particular a deep structure distinction of the functions subject, object, locative, attribute (by category ADJ) also in cases where the expressions uttered are only pairs of nouns. As a structural equivalent to the semantic relation (possessor-possessed object) Bloom postulates the analysis S[Nom[N[.]] NP[N[.]]]] (accepting S[Nom[N[.]] VP [VB[△] NP[N[.]]]]] as an alternative), where positions for lexical entries are marked by a point and '△' denotes a dummy.

However, the underlying structures generated by this system of grammatical rules are too complex for complete expression by the child; they exceed the limitations of surface expressions. "To account for the difference between underlying and surface structure a reduction transformation was postulated that operated to delete category constituents that dominated forms that were not expressed in surface structure – for example, the VB constituent as an intervening string in subject-object surface expressions. Kathryn was able to say 'Mommy pull' and 'pull hat' and although 'Mommy hat" did not actually occur, its occurrence could be predicted from the occurrence of such sentences as 'Mommy sock', 'Mommy diaper'." (Bloom, 1970, 71; reference is to examples (88) and (89).) Note, however, that "Mommy sock" and "Mommy slipper" in examples (79) and (78) may also express the semantic relation possessor-possessed object, as clearly shown by the context of use.

The reduction transformation postulated by Bloom is the following (in two parts)

(a)   SD: X-Ng-Y
        SC: x_1-x_2-x_3 $\Rightarrow$ x_2-x_3
(b)   SD: #-X-Y-Z, where X, Y, Z are category symbols
        SC: #-x_1-x_2-x_3 $\Rightarrow$ #-x_i-x_j, where $0 \leqslant i < j \leqslant 3$

Note that deletion operates only (a) to delete subject before negation or where the deep structure expression contains more than three lexical entries. Particles like 'it', 'on', 'off', 'away', 'no', 'now', 'here', 'outside', 'away', 'later', 'right' cannot be deleted, and a string containing, in addition to them, two lexical morphemes does not undergo reduction either.

With respect to semantic representations intended by the child in uttering the reduced expressions the communication *must* heavily rely on context (though in many cases even context is not sufficient to extract the intended content). Bloom even concludes from her research "that the emergence of syntactic structures in their [children's] speech depended on the prior development of the cognitive organization of experience that is coded by language" (Bloom, 1970, 228). The same priority of cognition is assumed by Bever for the earliest basic strategies in children (strategy A, Bever, 1970). In the case of negation, Bloom even finds support for this by the fact that children try to detect syntactic differences in the language (not actually present) for the semantic differences between nonexistence, rejection, and denial. In some cases, though, the converse is also true, viz., linguistic structuring becomes more mature than the underlying cognitive function. This happens in particular (at $2\frac{1}{2}$ years) with temporal adverbials. As reported (Bloom, 1970, 229), they occurred at appropriate positions and [sic!] the verb tense corresponded to the general temporal aspects of the adverbs. However, except for the use of "now", which was always appropriate in reference to immediate events, semantic reference was usually inaccurate or superfluous, with no inferable underlying cognitive regularity. The child appeared to have learned the syntactic function before learning the semantics of these forms.

VI. CHOICE OF COMMUNICATIVE EFFECTIVENESS

With an increase in the underlying syntactic and semantic complexity of a sentence, something had to give in its production, in view of the obligatory nature of the reduction transformation. If this is so, what determines which constituents are to be deleted and which retained? In general, I claim, there are factors of communicative effectiveness that come into play already at this early stage of human development. What is in focus and should be seen in focus by the addressee, the emphasis, the topic, etc., are already communicated very early. Later other factors are added, such as implicit presuppositions, explicitness, clarity, brevity of expression, etc., until eventually the full range of rhetorical factors is mastered.

True enough, not all of the factors may be chosen freely on the basis of communicative intention. There are, furthermore, factors determined by the developmental status of the internalized linguistic system as well as factors determined by the limits of processing in production and perception of utterances. Examples of the latter kind are mainly limitations of memory span. Interesting cases of the former enumerated by Bloom (p. 168) are:

(1) The relative recency of the appearance of the category components that dominated the deleted or retained constituents in phrase structure, such that a child having learned first to express subjects before objects and thereafter subjects before verbs or verbs before objects will tend to delete the verb in deep structure strings containing three lexemes.

(2) The child's cognizance of lexical items and the relative completeness of the indication of their functioning – e.g., the child may be able to utter "hurt" in isolation, but not having learned that it is a term insertable in a subject–verb–object deep structure, he does not use it in this cotext.

(3) In the case of negation, deletion of constituents not in the immediate scope of negation, most often subjects.

In his talk at the Olivetti Symposium, Bar-Hillel proposed as a *Gedanken-experiment* "that there were a law forbidding the use of *good will* in communication. As a consequence, everything that somebody would like to say to somebody else will have to be spelled out completely, otherwise he would be punished." (Bar-Hillel, 1970, 271). This forbids – more specifically – to take into account context, and more in particular, assumptions about the status of the internal model of the partner of communication, and therewith, of the essentially communicative nature of language use.

Even with respect to adult communication this seems to be an atrocious assumption though – as Bar-Hillel points out – this is exactly the mode in which one communicates with computers; but for communication with children such a law would have disastrous consequences: It is quite safe to predict that communication with children could not take place at all. I am, moreover, deeply persuaded that language learning would not take place. It is, therefore, only the exploitation of all cognitive, emotive and personal resources that allows the generation and application of a complicated system of rules like the one governing language use in human beings.

Technische Universität, Berlin

BIBLIOGRAPHY

Bar-Hillel, Y.: 1970, 'Communication and Argumentation in Natural Languages', in *Linguaggi*, Edizioni di Communità, Milano.
Bever, Th.: 1970a, 'The Cognitive Bases for Linguistic Structure' in J. R. Hayes (ed.), *Cognition and the Development of Language.*
Bever, Th.: 1970b, *The Influence of Speech Performance on Linguistic Structure.*
Bloom, L.: 1970, *Language Development*, MIT Press, Cambridge, Mass.
Bühler, K.: 1934, *Sprachtheorie*, G. Fischer, Stuttgart, 1965[2].
Firth, J. R. *et al.*: 1959, 'The Treatment of Language in General Linguistics', in F. R. Palmer (ed.), *Selected Papers of J. R. Firth*, Longmans, London, 1968.
Halliday, M. A. K.: 1964, 'The Users and Uses of Language', in M. A. K. Halliday *et al.*, *The Linguistic Sciences and Language Teaching*, Longmans, London.
Hintikka, J.: 1969, *Models for Modalities*, Reidel, Dordrecht-Holland.
Hockett, C. F.: 1967, *Language, Mathematics and Linguistics*, Mouton, The Hague.
Jakobson, R.: 1960, 'Linguistics and Poetics', in Th. A. Sebeok (ed.), *Style in Language*, New York, pp. 350–77.
Lamb, S.: 1966, *Outline of Stratification Grammar*, Georgetown University Press, Washington.
Lenneberg, E. H.: 1969, 'A Word between Us' in J. D. Roslanski (ed.), *Communication*, North-Holland, Amsterdam.
Lieb, H. H.: 1970, *Sprachstadium und Sprachsystem*, Stüttgart: Kohlhammer.
Lorenz, K.: 1970, *Elemente der Sprachkritik*, Suhrkamp, Frankfurt, ch. 11, 2.
Lyons, J.: 1968, *Introduction to Theoretical Linguistics*, Cambridge University Press.
Marler, P.: 1969, 'Animals and Man: Communication and Its Development', in Roslanski (ed.), *Communication.*
Marshall, J.: 1970a, 'The Biology of Communications in Man and Animals', in J. Lyons (ed.), *New Horizons in Linguistics*, Penguin Books, London.
Marshall, J.: 1970b, 'Can Humans Talk', in J. Morton (ed.), *Language with Psychology*, Logos Press, London.
McNeill, D.: 1966, 'Developmental Psycholinguistics', in F. Smith and G. A. Miller (eds.), *The Genesis of Language*, MIT Press, Cambridge, Mass.
McNeill, D.: 1969, 'The Development of Language', in P. A. Mussen (ed.), *Carmichael's Manual of Child Psychology*, Wiley, New York.
Montague, R.: 1968, 'Pragmatics', in R. Klibansky (ed.), *Contemporary Philosophy I*, pp. 102–122.

Montague, R.: 1970a, 'Pragmatics and Intensional Logic', *Synthese* **22**, 68–94.
Montague, R.: 1970b, 'English as a Formal Language', in *Linguaggi*, Edizioni di Communità, Milano.
Montague, R.: 'Intensional Verbs, Indefinite Terms and Unconceived Trees' (forthcoming).
Quine, W. V. O.: 1960, *Word and Object*, MIT Press, Cambridge.
Schnelle, H.: 1964a, 'Programmieren linguistischer Automaten', in K. Steinbuch and S. W. Wagner (eds.), *Neuere Ergebnisse der Kybernetik*, Oldenbourg, München, pp. 109–36.
Schnelle, H.: 1964b, 'CF-Grammars and CC-Automata' (mimeog.).
Schnelle, H.: 1967, *Prolegomena zur Formalisierung in der Sprachwissenschaft*, Thesis, Universität Bonn (mimeog.) I. Part 1.5; II. Part 1.3.
Scott, D.: 1970, 'Advice on Modal Logic', in K. Lambert (ed.), *Philosophical Problems in Logic*, Reidel, Dordrecht-Holland.
Sebeok, Th. A.: 1968, *Animal Communication: Techniques of Study and Results of Research*, Indiana University Press, Bloomington, Ch. 1.
Strawson, P. F.: 1970, *Meaning and Truth*, Clarendon Press, Oxford.

NOTES

[1] This is a loose way of indicating (a) one way implication between sentences or between terms as reducible to implication between sentences (as in *Lyons*, 1968, ch. 10); (b) implication (one-way and two-way) under contextual conditions.

[2] The importance of research into restricted languages has already been pointed out several times by various scholars in linguistics, though for reasons different from ours (cf. Firth, 1959; Halliday, 1964). It has been usually connected with the view that contrasts with the "monolithic hypothesis of language structure" and substitutes for it an "interconnected system of subcodes" (Jakobson, 1960, 352) or of varieties (Halliday, 1964; Hockett, 1967, 219ff), etc. For a precise analysis see H. H. Lieb (1970).

[3] E.g., for (2) to Sebeok (1968); Marshall (1970a); Marler (1969); Lenneberg (1969); and for (3) to Quine (1960), I, 4; Strawson (1970), 7; Lorenz (1970), ch. II, 2.

[4] However, the simplest systems that may be imagined and described (and sometimes are so by philosophers) do not occur, since the earliest stages gradually substitute already existing, instinctive, and fairly complex processes of communication between mother and child.

[5] As an example take the transformational theory of grammar based on generative semantics. A P-marker of deep (or semantic) structure and a P-marker of surface structure is a structural abbreviation for the fundamental complex of statements assigned to an entity on the level of semantic representation, and deep syntactic representation, respectively. This set of deep structure statements (or P-markers) is generated by grammatical rules of the basis. On the basis of other auxiliary rules – transformations plus derivational constraints – derivations may be generated. The derivations may be taken as inference rules by which statement complexes of the surface may be inferred from statement complexes in the basis. Other inferences will show how grammatical functions such as subject, object etc. are derivable from a deep structure statement complex (P-marker).

[6] Such as Montague (1968).

[7] Such as those in Hintikka (1969) or outlined in Scott (1970).

[8] Cf. description of this category in Bloom, 1970, 148.

[9] Cf. description of this category in Bloom, 1970, 167.

[10] A perspicuous case in point may be found in the language of Kathryn I as described by Bloom. KI uses both "Kathryn" (cf. examples (88), (90), (121), (123)) and "baby"

(cf. (73), (77), (83), (122)) to refer to herself, but also "baby" to refer to a certain doll (cf. (128)) as well as attributing a category of human beings (cf. (107)). Other records of children languages show that the same may happen with respect to the mother or father: in some families these may be addressed either by their function name (mommy, daddy) or their christian name.

11 Cf. analysis in Marshall (1970b).
12 Cf. Bühler (1934) in 'demonstratio ad oculos' or 'deixis' with the help of 'phantasma'.
13 (E.g., McNeill in his analysis of the data of Brown *et al.* for this early phase (1966) and (1970). In general, so far as only superficial analysis is concerned, this account is corroborated by the data of Bloom (1970).
14 Cf. McNeill (1969) . . ., Bloom, 1970, 70.

NATHAN STEMMER

SOME ASPECTS OF LANGUAGE ACQUISITION

In this paper I advance a theory that seeks to explain the learning process of a natural language.[1] The process is divided into three stages, but I shall deal here with only two of them. Due to lack of space, it will generally not be possible to enter into details and therefore only the central ideas will be expounded. Although only part of the learning process is considered, it will nevertheless be possible to deal with one of the most important aspects of human language, namely its creativity.

In the last section, the controversy between nativists and empiricists is briefly discussed.

The methodological approach of this paper (and of Thesis) may be called a Carnapian approach.[2] A distinction is made between theoretical terms (T-terms) and observational terms (O-terms). (Actually, there is only a gradual difference between them [cf. Carnap, 1966: 225ff].) It is assumed that the T-terms have no interpretation outside the theory; they receive a partial interpretation by means of correspondence rules and postulates, which directly and indirectly connect them with O-terms.

Neither in this paper nor in Thesis are the postulates and correspondence rules explicitly stated, except in a few cases. The theory is mostly informally discussed. It is expected, however, that the informal discussion may serve as a basis for a more formal treatment.

I. SPEAKING AND UNDERSTANDING

Many scientists who investigate language acquisition concentrate on only one aspect of the process: the acquisition of speech. Language, however, is not restricted to this one aspect. Children learn not only to speak a language, but also to understand it. Moreover, the understanding of a language is more fundamental than the speaking of it. The capacity for speaking a language – not babbling – presupposes a capacity for understanding the language. Before the child is able to utter proper sentences, such as "It is raining today", which have meaning and relevance in the

Yehoshua Bar-Hillel (ed.), Pragmatics of Natural Languages, 194–231. All Rights Reserved.
Copyright © 1971 by D. Reidel Publishing Company, Dordrecht-Holland.

circumstances of the utterance, he must at least be able to understand these or similar sentences.

That understanding is more fundamental than speaking can easily be shown by the fact that there are children who are not able to speak a language, but who have no difficulties in understanding it (see e.g., Lenneberg, 1962). On the other hand, there are no cases of people who are able to speak a language without understanding it.

Various authors have stressed the fact that understanding is more fundamental than speaking. Russell, for example, says (1927: 48): ". . . in the human infant as we know him, definite reactions to the words of others come much earlier than the power of uttering words himself." Similarly, Lenneberg (1962: 423) states: "It is thus likely that the vocal production of language is dependent upon the understanding of language but not vice-versa."

An objection is sometimes made against the contention that understanding precedes speaking. It is based on the fact that there are terms that are similar in different languages, terms like "Daddy" and "Mommy". In this case, the argument goes, it must be that a child utters these sounds instinctively and, by reinforcement, he learns to utter them in the appropriate circumstances.

Although I have my doubts on this point, I do not think it necessary to discuss them, as the matter has little significance here. The terms that a child may learn in this form are perhaps two, three or at the most ten, in comparison with the thousands he must first learn to understand before being able to use them in speech. There is no doubt that, except perhaps for a few terms, the child must first learn to understand and only later to speak.

I shall investigate various aspects of 'comprehension acquisition', without considering the question of how the child learns to speak. For didactical reasons it is convenient to imagine that we are investigating the language acquisition of a mute child. Note that one of the most important characteristics of human language, namely its creativity, is also realized in the language of a mute. He, too, is able to understand sentences that he has never heard before.

II. A 'UNIVERSAL' OF HUMAN LANGUAGE

Suppose that a young child is in a room in which there are several objects, among them various balls of different colours, one of which is red. Suppose now that someone says to the child "Bring the red ball", whereupon the child goes directly to the red ball and brings it. In this case, no scientist will doubt that the child must have heard at least once previously the term (sound) "red" while observing something red, and at least once the term "ball" (or "balls") while observing a ball (or balls). That is, the child has been exposed at least once to a situation in which the sound "red" has been paired with something red and the sound "ball" has been paired with the presentation of a ball. (The qualification "young" is necessary since an older child may have learned the 'meaning' of "ball" by some kind of verbal instruction. Note that in the case of "red" this last possibility is almost completely excluded.)

We shall call a situation in which a stimulus S_1 is paired with a stimulus S_2 a *pairing situation*. If S_1 is an acoustic stimulus, we shall often speak of an *acoustic pairing situation*. If in an acoustic pairing situation the acoustic stimulus belongs to the inventory of a human language, we shall frequently speak of a *verbal pairing situation*.

Using this terminology, we may say that the child of our example has been exposed, prior to receiving the above-mentioned command, to at least two verbal pairing situations. In one, the term "red" has been paired with something red and in the second, the term "ball" has been paired with a ball.

Assuming that all human languages contain simple imperatives of the kind "Bring the red ball", which children are able to understand (and to fulfil), we are now in a position to formulate the following 'universal' of human language:

U1. For all x, if x understands at t_0 a human language, then x has been exposed before t_0 to several pairing situations.

There is no direct evidence for U1. No systematic investigation has been made in order to determine whether it holds for a particular person and *a fortiori* whether it holds for all persons. Nevertheless, scientists accept U1. (I have partially confirmed this claim by asking psychologists, linguists and logicians.) There seem to be many reasons for accepting it, but it is not very easy to state them clearly. Apparently, the most important reason is the one that has been exemplified above. The act of bringing a red ball after hearing "Bring the red ball" is such a specialized type of behaviour that there remains hardly any other choice but to attribute it to previous pairing situations. Moreover, we know that, normally,

English-speaking children have had many opportunities in which to be exposed to pairings of "red" with red and of "ball" with balls before they correctly carry out commands in which these terms were used.

It is clear, however, that the fact that the child has been exposed to these two kinds of pairing situations does not completely explain the particular reaction. The child must also have learned the meanings of "bring", of "the", the meaning of the order in which the different terms have been uttered, and probably many other 'things', too. The exposure to verbal pairing situations is a necessary but usually not a sufficient condition. But at least it is this: a necessary and apparently a very important condition for language acquisition. It is this condition that we shall now study more thoroughly.

III. ASSOCIATUM

The child learns *something* by being exposed to pairing situations. Various names have been given to that which the child learns. Some say that the child learns meanings, others prefer to speak of the learning of responses. We shall introduce in this connection a relatively neutral terminology. We shall say that as a consequence of the exposure to n pairing situations ($n \geqslant 1$), the child learns *to associate an associatum* with the first stimulus S_1. This associatum depends on the second stimulus S_2 that has been used in the pairing situations. In our example, the child who has heard "red" while seeing something red and has heard "ball" while observing a ball has learned to associate two associata with these sounds. The character of the associata depends on the second stimuli, i.e., they depend on (something) red and on (a) ball.

The terms "associatum" and "to associate an associatum" are supposed to be T-terms. Hence, they have no independent interpretation. They receive a partial interpretation by means of the postulates (and correspondence rules), which connect them with O-terms.[3] In the following, I shall formulate a number of postulates whose principal function, other than providing such an interpretation, is to express an empirical theory about certain observational phenomena.

P1. If (a subject) s has been exposed to n pairings of S_1 and S_2, then, under certain appropriate conditions, s learns to associate an associatum with S_1. This associatum depends on S_2.

In this postulate the expressions "under certain appropriate conditions" and "depends" demand additional clarifications. Some will be given in this paper, others are given in Thesis, and still others have not yet been investigated. Nevertheless, I hope that the fact that a number of details are missing will not unduly derogate from the value of the postulate. P1 is directly motivated by U1, which, I suppose, is beyond discussion.

The next postulate is also directly motivated by U1. (For simplicity, it has been formulated for verbal stimuli and for young children, but it is assumed that, when appropriately modified, it also holds for other stimuli and for other subjects.)

> P2. If at time t_j, a young child reacts in a 'characteristic' form upon hearing a verbal expression, then, under certain conditions, there is a time t_i ($t_i < t_j$) at which the child has learned to associate an associatum with the expression or with some of its parts.

For example, if we observe that at a given moment a child reacts to the utterance "Bring the red ball" in a characteristic form, e.g., by bringing a red ball, then we shall usually say that the child has previously learned to associate an associatum with some parts of the utterance, e.g., with the term "red".

Here, too, we must clarify the terms "under certain conditions" and "characteristic". What we have said above holds for the first term. I shall now say a few words about the second term.

The notion 'characteristic reaction' is less exact than the notion 'predictable reaction'. Nevertheless, it is sufficiently precise to be used in psychology. In other sciences, even in physics, similar notions are used. For instance, if we observe that a leaf falls from a tree and that it touches the ground at a distance of 3.273 m from the trunk, then we consider this event as a confirming instance of Newton's law of universal gravitation. However, we are usually not able to predict the exact location on which the leaf will fall. In this case, we may call the falling of the leaf at a distance of 3.273 m from the trunk a *characteristic* effect of gravitation on the leaf but not a *predictable* effect. Admittedly, in physics it is relatively easy to create conditions that make it possible to increase the degree of predictability of certain events. But this is because the phenomena studied in physics are relatively simple. In botany, for instance, it is much more difficult. (For example, if we wish to predict the exact moment at which the leaf will fall.) And in psychology, in which the relevant factors are so many and so varied, it will be still more difficult. Nevertheless, in psychology too, it is often possible to create conditions that enable us to increase the degree of predictability of certain events. For instance, if a child is in a room in which there is an apple, it will usually not be possible to predict whether or not the child will approach and eat the apple. If he behaves in this form, we cannot say that this has been a predictable reaction to the presence of an apple, although we may call it a characteristic reaction. But if we deprive the child of food during a certain time, and if the child has eaten apples before, then it becomes possible to speak of a predictable reaction.

In my view, there is only a difference of degree between predictable and characteristic events or reactions. It is not necessary, however, to accept this position, since for our purpose it is sufficient to show that the notion 'characteristic reaction' is scientifically meaningful.

One of the means of showing this meaningfulness is by appealing precisely to U1. This 'universal' is not motivated by the observation of predictable but of characteristic reactions. The bringing of a red ball after hearing the sound-sequence "Bring the red ball" is not necessarily a predictable reaction. However, once the particular behaviour has been observed, it becomes possible to speak of a reaction to the utterance – not of a predictable but only of a characteristic reaction.

Notice that, usually, when dealing with characteristic reactions to a stimulus, it will only be possible *a posteriori* to determine whether the individual has been stimulated by the stimulus. Thus, if a normal child is in a room with an apple, we do not know *a priori* whether or not he is being stimulated by the apple. However, if he approaches the apple, then, *a posteriori*, we know that he has indeed been stimulated by the apple.

Not only with respect to commands, but also with respect to other types of verbal expressions is it possible to speak of characteristic reactions. Suppose, for instance, that someone says in the presence of a child, "In the cupboard there is a box with a ball", and we observe that the child goes to the cupboard, takes out the box, opens it, takes out the ball and plays with it. In this case, too, we will be sure that the reaction has been a characteristic reaction to the utterance of the assertive sentence. Applying U1, we can say that there is a high probability that, if the child is young, he has heard at least once the terms "cupboard", "box", and "ball" while observing the corresponding objects. Using P1 and P2 instead of U1, we may say that it is very likely that the child has been exposed to n

pairing situations in which he learned to associate certain associata with the sounds "cupboard", "box", and "ball".

The next postulate as well is motivated by U1.

P3. If at t_i, s has learned to associate with S_1 an associatum that depends on S_2, then at t_j ($t_i < t_j$), s will sometimes characteristically react when being stimulated by S_1 (either by S_1 alone or together with other stimuli). The reaction will be characteristic relative to S_2.

For example, if a child has learned to associate with "ball" the associatum b, then sometimes we may observe that the child reacts to an utterance of "ball" (either alone or together with other stimuli, e.g., together with "Bring the red . . ."). This reaction will be characteristic relative to S_2, i.e., relative to a ball.

The use of sometimes in P3 is unavoidable since it marks the difference between characteristic and predictable reactions. The child who has learned to associate associata with "cupboard", "box" and "ball" will not always react in a certain form to the utterance of "In the cupboard there is a box with a ball". Only sometimes will it be possible to observe a characteristic behaviour such as going to the cupboard.

P3 also clarifies our use of the term "depends". The fact that a child has learned an associatum that *depends* on some S will sometimes produce reactions that are *characteristic relative* to S. E.g., the child who has learned to associate with "ball" the associatum b, which depends on balls, will sometimes react to the utterance of "ball" with characteristic ball-reactions. (Notice that our use of "characteristic reaction" is systematically ambiguous. In P3 we speak of the characteristic reaction to a stimulus S_2, e.g., to a ball, while in P2 we speak of the characteristic reaction to a verbal expression that (in English) denotes this stimulus, e.g., to the sound "ball".)

Before introducing a fourth postulate, let us consider the following point. We have seen that scientists accept U1. However, there is no doubt that they accept something more. They accept that the pairing situations to which the child has been exposed and which enable him to make characteristic reactions cause certain electro-chemical processes in the child's brain. Moreover, they also agree that only while the effects of these processes persist will the child be able to form the characteristic reactions. That is, the capacity for reacting in the specified form is conditioned by the continuation of the effects of these brain processes. In our example, the exposure of the child to the pairings of "red" with red and of "ball" with ball produced certain brain processes. Only as long as the effects of these processes persist will the child be able to comply with the command "Bring the red ball". (I shall not enter into the problem of whether or not the persistence of the effects corresponds to what we might call "memory", since it does not directly affect our topic.)

Applying these considerations to our theoretical framework, we can now formulate the following postulate:

P4. Under certain conditions, the exposure of s to n pairing situations causes electro-chemical brain processes in s. If and only if these brain processes have taken place will the child associate an associatum with S_1. The subject s continues to associate the associatum if and only if the effects of the brain processes persist.

There is not much direct confirmation for P4. However, our knowledge has advanced to the point that most scientists will agree with P4 or some similar statement.

The scientific value of P4 is not yet very high. We do not know much about the electro-chemical brain processes that are caused by pairing situations and we know nothing about the differences between the processes produced by different kinds of pairing situations. E.g., we are completely ignorant about the difference between the process caused by the pairing of "red" with red and the process caused by the pairing of "ball" with ball. Nevertheless, P4 commits us to the following prediction: If sufficiently precise instruments will become available and/or if new techniques will be developed, then it will be possible to observe determinate electro-chemical brain processes as consequences of pairing situations. Moreover, we shall observe that only as long as the effects of these processes persist, will the subject make the corresponding characteristic reactions.

The four postulates connect the T-terms "associatum" and "to associate an associatum" with terms that are relatively more observational. In particular, they connect them with the terms "pairing situation", "characteristic reaction", and "electro-chemical brain processes". Consequently, the postulates provide a partial interpretation for the two T-terms. To be sure, the last connection has little value. But the other connections confer a strong empirical significance on the T-terms; they express, in a theoretical form, the 'universal' U1.

IV. MEANING

The (partial) meaning that our postulates confer on the T-term "associatum" is very similar to some of the meanings of the intuitive term "meaning". Thus, we would intuitively say that a necessary condition for a child to fulfil correctly the command "Bring a red ball" is to know at least the meanings of "red" and "ball". Moreover, we should say that, under certain conditions, situations in which "red" and "ball" are paired with something red and with a ball enable a child to learn the meanings of these terms. Or, to use a terminology more similar to ours, we should say that such pairing situations enable a child to associate meanings with acoustic stimuli. Furthermore, we might also say that such a kind of meaning-learning sometimes manifests itself in the form of characteristic reactions to verbal stimuli. And, finally, scientists would say that the learning of a meaning is reflected by some electro-chemical brain process whose effects persist at least as long as the child remembers these meanings.

The foregoing shows that it is possible to use the T-term "associatum" as an explicatum for the intuitive term "meaning". It does not mean that "associatum" is an adequate explicatum for all senses of "meaning". The introduction of an explicatum commits us only to the possibility of substituting it for certain uses of the explicandum (cf. Carnap, 1963: 933–40).

There is, however, an important difference between "associatum" and the intuitive term "meaning". Our term "associatum" is a relative term, relative to a particular individual and to a certain time-period. It is a particular individual who at some moment learns to associate an associatum with a stimulus, and he continues to associate it only during some time-period (sometimes during his whole life). On the other hand, the term "meaning" is generally not used with this kind of relativity. We normally speak of meanings without mentioning a particular individual or a particular time-period. It is in this sense that "associatum" is different from the common use of "meaning".

Actually, however, "meaning" is also implicitly used as a relative term, though in a different form from "associatum". Firstly, when speaking about meanings of terms it is implicitly assumed that the meaning is relative to some verbal community. Secondly, we know that in a verbal community meanings change with the lapse of time.

We shall introduce the theoretical expression "normal associatum relative to a community and relative to a time-period" as an explicatum for this relative use of "meaning". I shall not explicitly formulate postulates for this expression since, after making some adjustments, they can easily be obtained from our four postulates. The most important adjustments are the following. Instead of "pairing situations" we shall now speak of "normal pairing situations relative to a community". For instance, to pair "red" with something red is a normal pairing situation relative to the English community, to pair "rouge" with red is normal for a French community and to pair "red" with a net is normal for a Spanish community. A second adjustment: instead of "characteristic reactions to verbal stimuli" we shall now speak of "normal characteristic reactions to verbal stimuli relative to a (the) verbal community". E.g., to bring something red when hearing "red" may be a normal characteristic reaction for an English child, while for a Spanish child it may be to bring a net. A third change is that instead of "electro-chemical brain processes" we have now "normal electro-chemical brain processes relative to a community". Thus, the normal brain processes that correspond to the learning of an associatum to "red" are different for English children and for Spanish children.

In order to distinguish between the normal associata that are relative to a community and the associata that are relative to an individual, we shall sometimes call the latter "idiosyncratic associata".

When dealing with normal associata the time-factor will generally be ignored, as has been done already in the case of idiosyncratic associata.

The verbal pairing situations to which a small child is exposed are generally the normal pairing situations relative to the community in which the child lives. Normally, English children are subjected to the pairing of "red" with something red, while Spanish children are exposed to the pairing of a net with the same acoustic stimulus. This is the reason why it is often possible to use the term "meaning" without relating it to a particular individual. The uniformity in the pairing situations enable children of the same community to learn the *same* meanings (of terms learned during such situations). Or, in our terminology, it enables them to learn to associate the *same* associata with acoustic stimuli. (Since "associatum" is a T-term, the identity between associata is of course a theoretical issue. Only within the theory will it sometimes be possible to determine whether one idiosyncratic associatum is identical with another, whether it is identical with some normal associatum, and whether 'two' normal associata are identical. The same also holds for "meaning", if it is used in the sense of "associatum".)

V. CLASSICAL CONDITIONING

We have thus seen that, under certain conditions, a child learns something as a consequence of exposure to pairing situations. In particular, when being exposed to verbal pairing situations, he learns something that is fundamental to his comprehension acquisition. The question now arises, does this process belong to some of the processes that have been studied in connection with language acquisition? In particular, is this process some kind of conditioning, either instrumental or classical?

Many authors deal almost exclusively with instrumental conditioning in connection with language-acquisition. There is no doubt, however, that only in the learning of speech does instrumental conditioning play an important role. With respect to the learning of comprehension the situation is obviously different. In particular, the learning of meanings by pairing situations has very few similarities with this kind of conditioning.

In my opinion, and in consonance with the view of, among others, Pavlov and Bertrand Russell, if there is a process that has similar characteristics to the learning by verbal pairing situations (or by pairing situations in general), then it is classical conditioning. In classical conditioning, too, a subject is exposed to n pairing situations in which CS, the conditioned stimulus, is paired with US, the unconditioned stimulus. (I ignore in the present article more specialized aspects such as time-intervals between the presentation of the two stimuli etc.) As a result of the exposure, the individual learns something that makes him behave in a certain manner when later stimulated by CS.

Nevertheless, there is an important difference between classical conditioning and learning by pairing situations. In classical conditioning, the second stimulus, i.e., the US, is a stimulus that elicits a number of predictable reactions from the subject. For instance, a stimulus that has often been used as US is food. Now, we know that the presentation of food elicits from many organisms predictable reactions such as salivation, secretion of gastric juices, probably secretion of adrenaline and other kinds of hormones, perhaps acceleration of the pulse etc. (Frequently, these reactions are even innate.) The fact that the US elicits these reactions, together with the fact that normally they are not elicited by the CS, makes it possible to recognize clearly whether the subject has learned something by the exposure to the pairing situations. Thus, if the number of pairing situations has been sufficiently high and if some other conditions have been fulfilled, we shall be able to predict that the exposure of the subject to the CS will elicit all or part of the predictable US-reactions. (Actually, this affirmation is not completely exact. As has been demonstrated, the presentation of CS usually elicits reactions that are somewhat different from the US-reactions. They may be called "US-expectancy reactions" [see, e.g., Zener, 1937].)

This whole aspect is absent in the case of the verbal pairing situations referred to in U1 and the postulates. In these cases it is usually not possible to speak of predictable S_2-reactions. We do not know whether something red or whether a ball elicits such reactions from a child. The most that we can say is that sometimes they elicit characteristic reactions. Hence, there are no reliable tests to verify whether a child has learned something by the exposure to the pairing situations. Only in favourable cases may we obtain a characteristic reaction and, usually, even in these cases highly complex conditions will be necessary in order to elicit such reactions. For instance, normally an isolated utterance of "red" will not elicit characteristic red-reactions. Generally, "red" has to be uttered together with other verbal stimuli, e.g., together with "Bring the ... ball", to obtain a characteristic red-reaction.

But except for this difference, there is almost a complete analogy between learning by classical conditioning and learning by pairing situations. This analogy manifests itself in particular by the fact that our four postulates correspond to four obvious postulates for classical conditioning. Consider, for example, the postulates that correspond to the conditioning process in which a dog is subjected to n pairings of the sound of a bell and food. Using "X" to denote that which a subject learns in a classical conditioning process we have:

1. If a dog has been exposed to n pairings of bell and food, then, under certain conditions, he learns a certain X, where X depends on the second stimulus, i.e., on food. We shall use "X_{food}" to denote this particular X.

2. If at a given moment we observe that a dog salivates (or makes other typical food-responses) upon hearing a bell, then, under certain conditions, we shall assume that the dog has already learned X_{food}.

3. If a dog has learned X_{food} during n pairings of bell and food, then, under certain conditions, we can predict that the sound of the bell will

elicit predictable food-reactions. (Or, taking into account Zener's result, it will elicit predictable food-expectancy reactions.)

It is in this postulate that the difference is seen between classical conditioning and learning by pairing situations. In learning by pairing situations we have only characteristic reactions, which are only sometimes elicited by S_1, while in classical conditioning we have predictable reactions that, under certain conditions, are always elicited by CS.

4. Under certain conditions, the exposure to n pairings of bell and food produces electro-chemical brain processes in a dog. The dog will have learned X_{food} if and only if these processes have taken place. The effects of the learning will persist if and only if the effects of the brain processes persist.

Notice that the analogy between these postulates and the four postulates of Section III is not brought about by the specific terminology that we have used. There is no essential difference between this terminology and other terminologies that are used to describe what a subject learns in classical conditioning. For instance, it is often said that as an effect of a classical conditioning an S-R bond is established in the subject. In our example, one would say that a bell-salivation bond has been formed in the dog. If in the four postulates we write the expression "a bell-salivation bond has been formed in the dog" instead of "the dog has learned X_{food}", and if some other insignificant adjustments are made, we obtain four postulates that are acceptable to all S-R psychologists.

We thus see that the most important difference between learning by classical conditioning and learning by pairing situations is that in the former it is possible to speak of predictable reactions while in the latter only of characteristic reactions. In my view, although this is an important difference, it is not an essential one, in the sense that it should compel us to speak of essentially different processes. Predictable reactions constitute only a special case of characteristic reactions and the difference is only a methodological one (cf. Section III) – for the experimenter it is easier to work with predictable than with characteristic reactions. Consequently, in my opinion there is no essential difference between learning by classical conditioning and learning by pairing situations. This personal point of view, however, does not affect the conclusions of the present paper. They are also compatible with the position that there is an essential difference between the processes. I prefer, if possible, to reduce the number of basic processes by which an organism can learn. This is not, however, a necessary position; there is no reason why there should not exist various fundamental learning processes.

VI. SIMILARITY

Let us now deal more thoroughly with an important aspect of learning by pairing situations. Consider, again, the young child who has learned the correct meaning of "ball". (We use the expressions "to learn the correct meaning of S" or "to understand correctly S" as an abbreviation of "to learn to associate with S the normal associatum (meaning) that S has in English". Frequently, the qualification "correct" will be omitted.) According to U1, this child has been exposed to n situations in which the sound "ball" has been paired with a ball. Let us concentrate for the moment on the first stimulus, the sound "ball". There is no doubt that in the n situations the child has not heard exactly the same sound (if $n > 1$). There were surely variations in the sound, e.g., differences in pitch etc. Moreover, when the child later reacts to further utterances of "ball", e.g., when uttered in the command "Bring the red ball", the sound "ball" will certainly not be identical with the sounds heard during the pairing situations. Nevertheless, although these differences are perceptible to the child, they do not prevent him from making characteristic ball-responses when hearing "ball" as long as the differences are within a certain range. We are not interested in the dimensions of this range; of interest for us here is the fact that the stimulus need not be identical in each case, but that similarity is sufficient in order to learn correctly the meaning of the stimulus. (Notice that such an inattention to perceptible differences is also presupposed in our (meta) use of English. We use the proper name "ball" to denote a certain acoustic stimulus, which nevertheless need not be identical in all cases. Hence, the sound "ball" is really not *a* stimulus but a *kind* of stimuli.)

What holds for the first stimulus also holds for the second. Nor is a strict identity necessary here; similarity is sufficient. The child will learn the correct meaning of "ball" even though during the n pairing situations he did not see the *same* ball. As long as the balls were similar, the child may learn the correct meaning. And, in effect, different balls are similar, since they have a number of physical properties such as shape, consistency, etc. in common.

A somewhat different case is the learning of the correct meaning of the term "toy". A child may learn this meaning by n pairings of the sound with toys, e.g., with balls, trains, and dolls. In this case, too, the second stimuli must be similar for the child. Here, however, the similarity is of a different nature. It is not a similarity based on physical properties but on a common function. Balls, trains, and dolls have no significant physical properties in common. But for certain children they may have a common function. We might call it the function of 'being objects to play with'.

Thus, in order that a subject may learn something by means of pairing situations it is not necessary that the stimuli should be identical; it is enough that they are similar. (The same also holds for conditioning, see, e.g., Osgood, 1953: 350.) Furthermore, not only is similarity sufficient, but it may be based on a common function rather than on physical properties. Since these latter similarities play a fundamental role in the process of language acquisition, we shall investigate them more thoroughly.

VII. CONCRETE AND ABSTRACT (SUBJECTIVE) SIMILARITY

It is convenient to distinguish between objective similarity, i.e., the 'real' similarity that holds in the objective world, and subjective similarity, i.e., the similarity that holds for a particular s. We shall not deal with the former kind of similarity, because our main interest is subjective similarity. (Sometimes, the qualification "subjective" will be omitted.)

We shall introduce the term "subjective similarity" with the help of the term "degree of generalization". (Degrees of generalization (for s) are measured by the so called generalization gradients (which hold for s).) We define: x is (subjectively) more similar to y than to z for s if and only if for s the degree of generalization between x and y is greater than between x and z.

It is frequently possible to use the triadic predicate "x is (subjectively) similar to y for s" instead of the tetradic predicate that has just been defined. This is possible because the differences in degrees of generalization are often great enough to allow us to speak of similarity in general (between two 'things' for an s). Thus we shall say that x is similar to y for s, if for s the degree of generalization between x and y is 'psychologically significant', i.e., if x and y lie on a psychologically significant generalization gradient for s.

If a class of 'things' are similar for s, i.e., if the elements of the class lie on a (psychologically significant) generalization gradient for s, then we shall say that the class is a *generalization class* for s.

Sometimes the use of a 'sensation terminology' seems more natural. In these cases, the expression "s senses similarity (or resemblance) sensations between x and y" will be used as an alternative formulation for "x and y are similar for s".

It is possible to distinguish between two kinds of generalization gradients: species-specific and species-independent gradients. Examples of the first kind are the gradients that measure the degree of generalization between different shades of red or between different balls; they are specific to humans. In other terms, normal humans 'innately' generalize from one red shade to another and from one ball to another. We shall sometimes speak of "innate generalization gradient" instead of "species-specific generalization gradient".[4]

Species-independent gradients hold only for a specific individual or group of individuals who have undergone a similar experience. For instance, not all children generalize from one toy to another, e.g., from a ball to a doll and a train. Only those children who have had a certain experience, e.g., who have played with these objects, are able to generalize between these toys. Similarly, not all persons generalize between a chair and a table. Only those who live in a specific culture and who have had a certain experience with these objects, e.g., who have used them in certain indoor activities, will generalize between these pieces of furniture. We shall often speak of *acquired* or *learned* instead of species-independent generalization gradients.

It is now possible to distinguish between two kinds of similarity sensations, innate and acquired, which correspond to the two types of generalization gradients. E.g., normal children sense an *innate* similarity between red objects whereas only specific children sense an *acquired* similarity between different toys. In other terms, for humans there is an innate (subjective) similarity between red objects, whereas for certain persons there is an acquired (subjective) similarity between different toys.

Similar distinctions will be made between generalization classes. We shall speak of innate generalization classes, which are valid for a species, and of acquired generalization classes, which are valid only for some s or for some community.

We have seen above that in the case of an acquired similarity, it is frequently possible to point to a function that is common to the members of the acquired generalization class. In the case of toys, for example, we can speak of their playing function. It is this common function that often makes it possible to sense the acquired similarity sensation.[5] Therefore, only the individuals who know the function of certain objects will sense a resemblance between them. E.g., only children who are acquainted with the function that toys fulfil will sense a similarity between them. Similarly, only the persons who know that a chair and a table have a common function, i.e., the function 'to be used in certain indoor activities' will sense an (acquired) resemblance between these objects.

Innate similarity, on the other hand, is generally based on a physical property common to the elements of an innate generalization class. For example, the objects that constitute the innate generalization class 'balls' have a number of physical properties in common. Therefore, all normal members of a species are able to perceive the similarity between them.

Following Hull (1943: 194), we shall sometimes use "abstract (subjective) similarity" instead of "acquired or learned or species-independent similarity". Instead of "innate or species-specific similarity" the expression "concrete or physical (subjective) similarity" will often be used, provided it is the human species that senses the innate similarity. (Hull speaks in the last case of common sense similarity.)

Applying these definitions we see that the similarity between balls or between red objects is a concrete similarity – it holds for the human species – while the one between different toys, or pieces of furniture, or clothes or weapons, is an abstract similarity; it is based on a common function.

Our definitions of "abstract" and "concrete" should not be interpreted as a claim that this is the only correct use of these terms. The intention is to introduce two explicata that, in my opinion, are adequate for certain uses of these terms in natural language.

Not only humans but animals, too, can acquire generalization gradients. Suppose that a dog is sometimes fed from a round plate and sometimes from a square box. It is very likely that, for such a dog, these two objects will lie on a generalization gradient. He will generalize from the plate to the box and vice versa. This gradient, however, is not species-specific. Normal dogs do not make such generalizations. Only those who have undergone a certain experience and 'know' the function of both objects, the function, say, of serving as a basis for food, will sense a similarity between the two objects. Since these objects lie on an acquired generalization gradient, it follows that the similarity that the dog senses between the plate and the box is an acquired or abstract similarity; it is based on a common function.

Pavlov (1927: 55–6) mentions an experiment that can easily be interpreted as the acquisition of a similarity sensation between three stimuli. A dog was subjected to three types of pairing situations in which the sound of a buzzer, the sound of a metronome and a tactile stimulus were paired with food (acid). As a result of this pairing, the three stimuli became 'food signals' for the dog. (They acquired the capacity of eliciting food-responses.) Later, one of these stimuli was inhibited and it was observed that the inhibition generalized to the other two stimuli. Thus, this particular dog, after having undergone a certain experience, made a generalization that is not a normal one (for dogs). Hence, the corresponding generalization gradient is not innate but acquired. Speaking of similarity, the dog acquired an abstract similarity sensation with respect to the three stimuli. This sensation was based on the common function of being 'food signals' that they acquired for the dog.

Humans have a great capacity for acquiring similarity sensations. This fact is of the highest importance, since it enables them to learn highly complex 'things'. In particular, it is important for the process of language-acquisition, because, as we shall see, in this process acquired similarity sensations play a fundamental role. We shall now investigate how the exposure to pairing situations enables a child to acquire such sensations.

Suppose that a child has learned the normal meanings of "Mommy", "Daddy", and "Uncle John" by being exposed to appropriate pairing situations. Now, it is clear that these terms (sounds) have no innate similarity for children; they do not lie on a species-specific generalization gradient for humans. However, as a consequence of the pairing situations in which these sounds have been paired with persons, they have now acquired a common function for the child; the function of denoting persons.[6] This common function enables the child to sense an acquired similarity between sounds which are devoid of physical similarity. The so called 'semantic generalization phenomenon' shows that we may expect a significant generalization between such 'person terms'.

Let us take another example. Suppose that a child has learned to associate the sounds "ball", "train", and "doll" with their normal associata (in English). Again, these sounds have no similarity for normal humans. However, as a result of being paired with toys, these 'toy terms' become similar for the child. This similarity is based on the common function that the sounds have acquired for such a child; the function of denoting toys.

We thus see that the exposure to pairing situations has (at least) two consequences. It causes the individual to associate an associatum with the first stimulus and it also permits him to acquire similarity sensations between stimuli that are not physically (innately) similar.

VIII. CONTEXTUAL PAIRING SITUATIONS

We shall now analyse a more complex case of comprehension acquisition. Suppose we observe that a young child reacts in some characteristic manner to the utterance of "Daddy holds the ball" and in a different manner, but also characteristic, to the utterance of "Daddy throws the ball". In this case, scientists will agree that the child has already heard the term "Daddy" while observing his father and the term "ball", while observing a ball. Moreover, they will also agree that he has heard at least once some derived form of the verb "to hold", while observing a 'holding situation' (i.e., a situation in which something holds something else), and at least once some derived form of the verb "to throw", while observing a 'throwing situation'.

Let us concentrate on the pairing situations in which the derived form of "to hold" has been paired with holding situations. For simplicity, we assume that the term that the child has heard in the situations has been "holds". As a consequence of the exposure to these situations the child learns, under certain conditions, to associate a particular associatum (meaning) with the term "holds". This associatum depends on the second stimulus with which the term has been paired, i.e., it depends on a holding situation (or a holding aspect). Hence, once the child has learned to associate this associatum with "holds", he may sometimes react with a characteristic 'holding-reaction' to utterances in which this term occurs. E.g., when hearing "Daddy holds the ball", he may stop searching in the cupboard and go to his father.

In general, the four postulates of Section III apply to the learning process of "holds"; it is based (at least) on the exposure to pairing situations. Nevertheless, it is very plausible that there will be an important difference between this process and the processes by which a child learns the meanings of terms like "ball" or "red". The difference is connected with the 'certain conditions' of P1. When learning the meaning of "holds" it will normally not be sufficient for the child to hear an isolated utterance of this term paired with a holding situation. It will be necessary that the term be uttered within some verbal context, i.e., together with other terms. For example, he may hear "holds" within the sentence "Mommy holds the train". Moreover, it will also be necessary that the child should already understand most 'context terms'. In our example, the child must already understand "Mommy" or "train".

These conditions seem not to be necessary in the cases we have considered until now. Although it is highly probable that, when the child learned the meanings of terms like "ball" or "red", he had in fact heard them within some verbal context, he *could* have learned them in an isolated form. The reason is that such terms denote objects (or aspects) that constitute 'strong' or 'important' stimuli for normal children. (That there are terms that a child learns before knowing the meanings of the context terms follows from the fact that there must be a given moment in a child's life in which he begins his comprehension acquisition.)

On the other hand, it is very unlikely that a child is able to learn the meaning of "holds" in an isolated form. A holding aspect seems not to be sufficiently prominent to be correctly grasped by n pairing situations in which the single term "holds" is paired with a holding situation (unless perhaps n is very high). Hence, as stated above, it is plausible to assume that the child must hear "holds" within some verbal context in order to learn its correct meaning. Moreover, he must already understand most of the context terms.

We shall call the pairing situations in which a child learns the meaning of a term that he *could* have learned in isolated form "isolated pairing situations", even when in practice the term was uttered within some verbal context. When the utterance of the verbal context is a necessary one, we shall speak of "contextual pairing situations". In these latter processes it is fundamental that the child should already understand part of the context terms. It is thus clear that only in a second stage is it possible to learn by means of contextual pairing situations, since they presuppose a prior process in which the meanings of the context terms have been learned.

We shall thus assume that the child is learning the meaning of "holds" by means of contextual pairing processes. In concrete, we assume that the child has been exposed to the pairing of the sound-sequence "Mommy holds the train" with a 'Mommy holds the train' situation. (For simplicity, I assume that for the child the expression "the train" constitutes a single stimulus and that in the n pairing situations in which he learned its meaning, only utterances of this particular combination were paired with appearances of a train.) According to our postulates it follows that, under certain conditions, the child will learn to associate an associatum (meaning) with the sound-sequence "Mommy holds the train". The associatum will depend on the second stimulus of the pairing situation, i.e., on the 'Mommy holds the train' aspect. As a consequence of the exposure, the child will now be able to associate this associatum with further utterances of the *same* sound-sequence. (This may be shown by characteristic 'Mommy holds the train'-reactions to these utterances.)

But it is evident that one cannot yet say that the child knows the meaning of "holds". A minimal requirement is that the child should be able to understand not only this particular sentence, but also other sentences in which "holds" occurs, sentences such as "Daddy holds the ball". In other words, he must at least be able to generalize from "Mommy holds the train" to "Daddy holds the ball". In what follows we shall see that if the child has already learned the meanings of the person terms and of the toy terms that occur in these sentences, he will be able to make this generalization. (Note that this implies that the child already masters a creative language; he understands a sentence that he has never heard before.)

Let us now investigate more carefully the pairing situations in which "Mommy holds the train" has been paired with a 'Mommy holds the train' situation. In these situations, the child has heard a sound-sequence in which the first term has been a person term, the second, the term "holds", and the third, a toy term. In other words, he has heard an utterance of the form "P holds T" where "P" denotes a person term and "T" a toy term. This utterance has been paired with a corresponding 'P holds T' situation, i.e., with a situation in which the denotatum of "P" holds the denotatum of "T".

Now, we recall that, usually, the stimuli to which an individual is exposed during n pairing situations are not strictly identical but only similar (for the individual). This means, then, that the learning of an associatum, as described in our postulates, is usually not a consequence of the pairings of n *identical* stimuli with other n identical stimuli, but of the pairings of n *similar* stimuli with other n similar stimuli. Hence, the individual does not learn to associate an associatum with one stimulus, but with a class of similar stimuli, and this associatum does not depend on *the* second stimulus S_2, but on the class of similar stimuli that constitutes the second stimulus in the pairing situations.

By applying these considerations to our present case, it follows that the child, who has been subjected to n pairings of utterances of the form "P holds T" with the corresponding 'P holds T' situations, has learned to associate a particular associatum with the first *kind* of (similar) stimuli. That is, he associates this associatum with all the utterances that for him are similar to (hence not necessarily identical with) the utterances that he has heard during the n pairing situations. This associatum depends on the second *kind* of stimuli. That is, it depends on corresponding 'P holds T' situations.

It now follows that, if for the child the sentence "Daddy holds the ball" is similar to "Mommy holds the train", he will correctly understand the former sentence; the associatum that he will associate with it will be the normal one (in English). Namely, it will be an associatum that depends on a situation in which the denotatum of the person term holds the denotatum of the toy term. In concrete, he will associate "Daddy holds the ball" with an associatum that depends on the situation in which the father of the child holds the ball.

The question now is: Is the sentence "Daddy holds the ball" similar, for the child, to "Mommy holds the train"? Or, in general, are sentences of the form "P holds T" similar for the child? The answer is that if the child already understands the person and the toy terms that occur in these sentences then they may be similar for him.

There is, of course, no *physical* similarity between person terms nor between toy terms. We recall, however, that when the child learned the meanings of these terms, they *acquired* a similarity for him (see end of the last section). Hence, our question is: Are combinations of similar stimuli similar (for an individual)?

Now, we know that for many organisms, in particular for humans, combinations of different stimuli constitute *a* stimulus. (See, e.g., the section on multiple-sign learning in Warren, 1965.) But since generally we do not have *a* stimulus but only a *kind* of (similar) stimuli, this really means that for many organisms a combination of different *kinds* of stimuli constitutes *a* stimulus. However, to be a stimulus for an s means that the instances of the stimulus are similar for s, i.e., s generalizes from one instance to another. Therefore, if for a child each of the components of the combination "P holds T" forms a *kind* of stimuli, the combination itself will be *a* stimulus for him.[7] He will be able to generalize from one instance to a second; he will be able to sense a resemblance between the instances.

It thus follows that a child who already understands person and toy terms is able to generalize from the sentence "Mommy holds the train" to other sentences that for him have the pattern "P holds T". In particular, he is able to generalize to the new sentence "Daddy holds the ball", provided the term "Daddy" is similar for him to "Mommy", e.g., if both are person terms for him, and provided "the ball" is similar for him to "the train", e.g., if both are toy terms for him. In this case, then, the child will be able to associate with this sentence the same (kind of) associata that he associates with "Mommy holds the train". Namely, the (kind of) associata that depend on a situation in which the denotatum of the person term holds the denotatum of the toy term.[8]

IX. CREATIVITY

We have thus seen that a child, as a consequence of exposure to different kinds of pairing situations, learns to understand sentences that he has never heard before; he acquires a creative language. In these processes, a fundamental role is played by the acquired similarity sensations, which enable a child to generalize between stimuli that are devoid of physical similarity. Before continuing with our main topic, let us briefly consider some aspects of this creativity.

The creativity of human languages is not an unrestricted one. A child does not understand every new sentence he hears. At least the following two conditions must be fulfilled:

(a) The child must already know the meanings of the components of the sentence.[9] E.g., normally English children do not understand the sequence "Bring the red pelota" because they do not know the meaning of the last sound.

(b) The new sentence must be similar to some sentence that the child already understands. E.g., normally English children do not understand the string "Red the ball bring".

Thus, not only must the child know the meanings of the components of a new sentence, but this sentence must have some pattern with which he is already familiar.

It seems that nativists do not completely accept the second condition. E.g., Chomsky (1968: 10) states,

... The normal use of language is innovative, in the sense that much of what we say in the course of normal language use is entirely new, not a repetition of anything that we have heard before and not even similar in pattern – in any useful sense of the term "similar" and "pattern" – to sentences or discourse that we have heard in the past.

Now, we have just given a very simple example that shows that a child cannot understand *any* combination of 'old' terms. The combination must indeed be similar in form or pattern to some sentence that is already understood by the child.

Against this Chomsky would surely argue that this use of "similar", "form", and "pattern" is not scientifically meaningful. And, apparently, the reason would be that there is hardly ever a physical similarity between different sentences. This, of course, is true. We have seen, however, that in psychological processes not only physical but also acquired similarities intervene; similarities based on common functions. And there is no doubt that the notion 'acquired similarity' is scientifically meaningful, since it has been introduced with the help of the term "acquired generalization gradient", which describes a perfectly observable phenomenon.

Acquired similarity plays an essential role in the process by which a child learns to transfer meanings to new sentences. A child may be able to understand "Daddy holds the ball" after having heard "Mommy holds the train". But this is possible because the first sentence has the same pattern as the second (for certain children). Both are of the (non-physical) form "P holds T". If the sound-sequence has another form, say, the form "Holds P T" (e.g., "Holds the ball Daddy"), the situation is different. Since such sequences are not similar (for the child) to the sequences with which he already associates an associatum, he will not be able to associate an associatum with them; he will not understand them.

But even if the sequence has the form "P holds T", it may happen that the child will not understand it. This will occur if, for the child, there is no similarity between the person term or the toy term of the particular utterance and the person or toy terms that he has heard during the *n* pairing situations. Only the child who has acquired the necessary similarity sensations will be able to generalize from one sentence of the pattern "P holds T" to another sentence of this pattern. More exactly, only for him will the two sentences have the (non-physical) pattern "P holds T".

There are of course much more complex cases of acquired pattern similarities and we shall later deal with some of them. However, even this relatively simple case is sufficient to show how children may learn something creative, something that is apparently beyond the capacities of the most developed animals.

X. ANIMAL LANGUAGE

We have seen that the exposure to pairing situations, together with the faculty of acquiring similarity sensations, enables a child to learn a creative language. The question now arises, since animals are also able to learn 'something' by being exposed to pairing situations and since they, too, are able to acquire similarity sensations, why do they not learn some creative language?

Many animals are able to learn primitive kinds of languages, or, to use a more neutral terminology, they are able to learn 'signal systems'. They may learn such a system by being exposed to pairing situations, either artificially in a laboratory or naturally by observing accidental pairings of stimuli. For instance, there are dogs that have learned that the sound of a bell is a sign of food and that the sound of a buzzer is a sign of an electric shock. There are, of course, many different signal systems that animals can learn. Thus, in one laboratory the rule may be that a bell is a signal for food, while in another laboratory the animal may have to learn the 'semantical rule' that a buzzer signals food.

Some species are able to learn more complex signal systems. Apes, in particular, have such a capacity as is shown for instance in Premack (1970). Nevertheless, the difference between the signal system that Premack's chimpanzee acquired and the language that small children acquire is so great that it is still justified to ask why small children are able to learn something that no animal can learn.

It is difficult to give a conclusive answer. There are strong indications, however, that suggest that it is a consequence of the fact that a number of crucial capacities are far more developed in humans than in animals. In particular, the following capacity differences seem to play a fundamental role:[10]

1. For humans, very subtle aspects of the environment may constitute stimuli. For instance, Miller (1959: 247) states:

One of the factors which make the mental processes of man so much 'higher' than those of animals may be a greater capacity to respond selectively to more subtle aspects of the environment as cues – especially to aspects such as triangularity, numerosity, and other relations and patterns which are commonly referred to as 'abstract'.

2. Humans have a highly developed memory. In particular, they have a high capacity to remember the different functions of different objects.

3. Humans have a great capacity to perceive as *a* stimulus different combinations of stimuli, while at the same time to remember the function of each component.

4. Humans have a very high capacity to acquire similarity sensations (based on common functions).

By using these well developed capacities, a child is able to perceive very subtle aspects of situations, e.g., small differences between verbal stimuli such as between "ball" and "balls". Moreover, he remembers many functions that 'things' have, e.g., the different functions of spoons and forks, the different 'semantic' functions of the sounds "spoon" and "fork", and, as we shall see, many other highly specialized functions that sounds and sound-combinations fulfil in a language. These capacities explain why a child is able to learn such a complex skill as human language.

Instead of attributing language acquisition to such well developed capacities, a number of authors prefer to attribute it to a special property, a 'second substance whose essence is thought' as Cartesians might say, which can only be detected in humans (see, e.g., Chomsky, 1968: 5).

Now, it is clear that if we are going to attribute a second substance to any organism that can learn something that another cannot, then humans will surely have to be assigned not just a second substance but one of a much higher order. There are many species that show enormous differences between the 'things' that they are able to learn.

It may be argued, however, that in the present case the difference between the achievements is so great that it becomes necessary to postulate some new substance, or, in a more modern terminology, some completely new innate dispositions. This argument will be discussed in the last section.

Before leaving the present topic, let me point out that if there is a significant point of contact between human language and some animal language, then it is with artificial signal systems and not with naturally occurring communication systems. The reason is clear. Natural communication systems are highly species-specific. Human languages, on the other hand, are essentially species-independent. Of course, the innate dispositions that enable a child to acquire a human language are species-specific. However, the language that he learns is species-independent; it depends completely on the particular language that is spoken in his community. Similarly, the innate dispositions that enable an animal to learn some signal system are species-specific. The particular system that it may learn, however, is not; it depends completely on the laboratory in which it has been trained or on the accidental pairing situations that it has observed.

XI. SEMANTICAL WELLFORMEDNESS

We have thus seen that a child may learn to understand sentences of the form "P holds T" after having been exposed to the pairing of, e.g., "Mommy holds the train" with a corresponding situation. However, we still cannot say that this child already knows the correct meaning of the term "holds". It is not sufficient that he understands sentences where "holds" appears between a person and a toy term; he must also understand other types of combinations. E.g., he must at least be able to understand sentences like "The hook holds the coat". We shall now see that the child is indeed able to make this type of generalization as well.

In Section VIII we have attributed to "Mommy holds the train" the form "P holds T". It is clear, however, that this has been an arbitrary decision. We have hereby classified the term "Mommy" as a person term and the term "the train" as a toy term. Admittedly, by assuming this classification it has been possible to explain how the child understands "Daddy holds the ball", since we know that the child is able to sense a resemblance between different person terms and also between different toy terms. Hence, he can generalize from the former to the latter sentence. There is no reason, however, why the child should make just the same classification. To generalize from "Mommy holds the train" to "Daddy holds the ball", the child can use other similarity sensations as well. And it is plausible that he will use the similarity sensations that are directly relevant to the new term that he has learned, the term "holds". In particular, he may use the acquired similarity between terms that (for him) denote objects that can be in an active holding position and the acquired similarity between terms that denote objects that can be in a (corresponding) passive holding position. If the child uses these sensations, then he may sense the (acquired) similarity that exists between the pairs ⟨"Mommy", "the train"⟩, ⟨"Daddy", "the ball"⟩, and ⟨"the hook", "the coat"⟩. Each pair has acquired for the child the common function of denoting two objects that can be in an active and a corresponding passive holding position. Hence, in this case he will be able to understand "The hook holds the coat" by generalizing from the (for him) similar "Mommy holds the train". In general, he will be able to understand all the sentences of the form "X holds Y", if the pair ⟨"X", "Y"⟩ has acquired for him the above-mentioned function.

Notice, however, that if the child uses these similarity sensations, he will probably not understand the sequence "The newspaper holds the house". With respect to the capacity of 'holding something', the pair ⟨"the newspaper", "the house"⟩ is not similar to pairs such as ⟨"Mommy", "the train"⟩; a newspaper cannot hold a house.

We thus see that the exposure to pairing situations, besides enabling the child to understand sentences that he has never heard before, also teaches him to distinguish between semantically wellformed and semantically deviant sequences. The former are those sequences that he understands, the latter those that he does not understand.

XII. SYNTACTICAL WELLFORMEDNESS

But at a given moment the child learns something else. He learns that there are (at least) two types of semantically deviant sequences. The sequences of one type have an important property in common with semantically wellformed sequences, while those of the second type are devoid of this property. Consider, for instance, the sequences "The newspaper holds the house" and "Holds the ball Daddy". The child does not understand either of them since they are not similar (for him) to the sentences uttered during the pairing situations. Nevertheless, *we* know (or feel) that the former, though semantically deviant, is nevertheless syntactically wellformed, while the latter is not. Hence, at some stage, the child must also learn to distinguish between syntactically wellformed and syntactically deviant sequences. Loosely speaking, we can say that the child has to learn that (in English) sentences uttered with an 'assertive intonation' may have the form 'Noun + Verb + Noun' but not the form 'Verb + Noun + Noun'.

Now, as a matter of fact, many 'assertive' sentences that the child has heard have been of the first form while no assertive sentence has been of the latter form. Theoretically, he is thus able to distinguish between the two types of sentences. But here the question arises, how does the child know that these sentences have such a form? How does he know whether some sound is a noun or a verb or whether it belongs to some other category? Moreover, many sounds belong to more than one category.

Thus the second question is: How does the child know whether some sound is playing the role of a noun within some sentence, or whether it has some other function?

The answer to these questions is that a child who has been exposed to the pairing situations described above is in a position to have acquired this knowledge. He comes to know that some terms belong to one category, e.g., to the category 'nouns', and that other terms belong to some other category, e.g., to the category 'verbs'. Using 'similarity terminology', we can say that the child is able to sense a specific similarity sensation between nouns, and another similarity sensation between verbs. He learns to sense these (acquired) similarity sensations by observing the properties and functions that terms have in the language to which he is exposed. For instance, nouns have a number of properties and functions that distinguish them from other kinds of terms. E.g., a noun can often receive a plural (in English); it often denotes three-dimensional objects (while verbs often denote actions of such objects); it is sometimes preceded by an article; it has a specific position in certain sentences (e.g., it may occupy the first and the last place in "holds"-sentences) etc.

Thus the child, by living in an environment in which a language is used in determinate circumstances and under determinate conditions, learns that relative to his language certain classes of terms have certain common properties and functions, while other classes have other common properties and functions. In exactly the same way as the child who, by living in a certain culture in which toys are used, learns that certain objects have a specific function in his environment. Of course, the linguistic functions are very subtle and highly specialized; however, they are as objective as the playing function of toys.

Once the child has observed these properties and functions he will be able to sense an acquired similarity between terms having the same properties and functions. Using 'category-terminology', we may say he will have the capacity to classify different terms in different syntactical categories. For instance, he will be able to know whether some term is a noun, or a verb, or whether it belongs to some other category. Consequently, he will be able to recognize whether some sound-sequence has the form 'Noun + Verb + Noun' or the form 'Verb + Noun + Noun'.

Syntactical categories are based on highly sophisticated linguistic properties and functions. Therefore, only organisms with a relatively high intelligence can acquire similarity sensations that correspond to such categories. Semantical categories, on the other hand, are much easier to learn since they are based on the properties and functions of denotata. (Of course, not all semantical properties are easy to learn, because there are denotata that have highly complex properties and functions.) Hence, the exposure to simple pairing situations enables a child to classify terms in semantic categories. E.g., he may classify terms according to whether they denote persons, or toys, or animate objects, or three-dimensional objects, or properties, actions, and functions of such objects etc.

We thus see that in the first stage of language acquisition the child is already able to acquire similarity sensations that correspond to semantical categories. This fact is of the highest importance, since the child can use the semantical categories as a basis for the syntactical categories that he has to learn. And, indeed, many syntactical categories are built on such a basis, for instance, the categories 'animate', 'human', 'countable', 'noun' etc. Of course, the semantical categories undergo a great number of adjustments when becoming syntactical categories, since these are determined by additional properties and functions. However, the child can, and it is likely that he will, use the semantical categories as a kind of nucleus around which he constructs the syntactical categories.

The second question we had to answer was: How does the child know to which syntactical category a particular utterance of some term belongs?

This problem is part of the general problem of ambiguity. How does the child (and we) know whether the meaning of a certain sound "light" is connected with weight or rather with illumination? He knows it by paying attention to the context, linguistic or situational, in which the term occurs. One context determines one meaning, another a second meaning, and a third context may leave it undetermined. (This process is similar to 'conditional' conditioning in which the subject learns that when a stimulus S occurs together with a stimulus A it 'means' something, and when it occurs together with a stimulus B it means something else.)

The same method is used by the child for resolving syntactical ambiguities; he pays attention to the whole context. For instance, if the child already knows that the first term of an assertive "holds"-sentence is often a noun and (almost) never a verb, then he will be able to know that in "The ring holds the key", the sound "ring" has a different syntactic function than in the sequence "The boys ring the bell".

Let me indicate in a very general way how children learn to use notions such as 'noun phrase', 'verb phrase' etc. We have seen above that a child, by being exposed to pairing situations, does not only learn the meanings of single terms, but also of term-combinations such as "P holds T". In a similar form he also learns the meanings of other kinds of term-combinations, e.g., of "the house which is white", "the red table" etc. This allows him to classify such combinations into semantical categories. Moreover, after observing how these combinations are used within the whole language, the child is also able to classify them into syntactical categories. For instance, the above-mentioned combinations have a number of properties and functions that are characteristic of terms that belong to the category 'noun'. E.g., they denote (inanimate) three-dimensional objects; they can be subject to a plural transformation; they can occur after "holds" in sentences such as "John holds . . ." etc. Hence, by being exposed to pairing situations and by observing his language, the child learns to classify not only single terms, but also term-combinations in syntactical categories.

In this form, then, the child learns to distinguish sequences of the pattern 'Noun Phrase + Verb Phrase + Noun Phrase' from sequences having the pattern 'Verb Phrase + Noun Phrase + Noun Phrase'. Therefore, he is able to distinguish not only between the 'ungrammatical' sequence "Holds the ball Daddy" and the grammatical sequence "The newspaper holds the house", but also between the former sequence and the grammatical sequence "The newspaper holds the house that is white".

XIII. INNATE IDEAS

We have investigated only some aspects of comprehension acquisition, and even these only very superficially. Many important aspects have not even been touched. For instance, we have dealt only with learning of meanings by means of pairing situations. We know, however, that most meanings are not learned by such processes. Usually, when a person learns the meaning of some term (or the 'meaning function' of some term), the objective situation that he is observing is not directly relevant to the learning process. But, for lack of space, I shall not deal with these topics.

This last section will be devoted to investigate some aspects of the controversy between nativists and empiricists.

There are various points in which there is apparently a divergence between the two schools, but I believe the following aspect to be one of the most basic. For nativists, the human language phenomenon shows that there is an essential difference between humans and animals. E.g., Chomsky (1968: 62) writes:

As far as we know, possession of human language is associated with a specific type of mental organization, not simply a higher degree of intelligence . . . it is an example of true 'emergence' – the appearance of a qualitatively different phenomenon at a specific stage of complexity of organization.

On the other hand, consistent empiricists accept what we might call the "continuity thesis", which denies such an 'emergence'. Let me quote here part of Carnap's clear formulation of the thesis:

As a specific argument against the doctrine of *emergentism*, which has been adopted even by some empiricists, I should like to emphasize in this context the philosophically important fact that scientific investigations demonstrate ever more clearly a *continuity* in the evolution of man. We may think, e.g., of the development of quasi-organic entities from inorganic substances, further of viruses, one-cell organisms, higher organisms, and finally human beings. All empiricists have abandoned the earlier belief that there is a fundamental difference, a 'difference in kind', between man and the other animals, and between organisms and the organic world (1963: 883–4).

With respect to language acquisition, the continuity thesis suggests the following proposition:

There is no qualitative difference between the innate dispositions that enable humans to learn some human language, and the innate dispositions that enable higher organisms to learn certain 'things'.

In other terms, according to empiricists, language acquisition does not show that humans have a 'specific type of mental organization' that is qualitatively different from the mental organization of animals.

In order to be able to compare the two positions we must know something about the character of the qualitative difference that is postulated by nativists. One of the points that is frequently mentioned in this connection is the issue of innate ideas. Such ideas are supposed to be of a higher type of mental organization, indicating thus the appearance of a true emergence. It is clear, however, that innate ideas constitute an emergence only if it can be shown that humans have them whereas animals do not have them. But this has by no means been demonstrated. On the contrary, almost all reasons that have been given for attributing innate ideas to humans are also reasons for attributing them to animals. For instance, Descartes says, "Because we already possess within us the idea of a true triangle . . . we, therefore, when we see the composite figure, apprehend not it itself, but rather the authentic triangle" (cf. Chomsky, 1968: 72).

We know, however, that there are animals that are also able to recognize triangles and to distinguish them from other figures. Therefore, there is no reason for not crediting them also with the 'idea of a true triangle'. Of course, empiricists would prefer another terminology; they would prefer to speak about innate *dispositions* to behave in a certain way or of innate dispositions that make it possible to learn something in a determinate form. But this is only a difference in terminology.

The same also holds for Leibnitz's analogy of the block of marble. The reasons that are valid for rejecting a *tabula rasa* in humans are also valid for rejecting them in animals.

One of the consequences of the innate ideas approach is Humboldt's contention that "one cannot really teach language but can only present the conditions under which it will develop spontaneously in the mind in its own way" (cf. Chomsky, 1965: 51). But we can use exactly the same formulation to describe how animals may learn different signal systems. Thus, we may say that one cannot teach an animal a particular signal system, but can only present the conditions under which the system will develop spontaneously in its mind. Again, this is not a terminology that empiricists like to use. However, the fact that it is applicable to animals shows that this phenomenon is no indication of a qualitative difference.

In a similar form, Chomsky's statement (1965: 27) that "the child approaches the data with the presumption that they are drawn from a language of a certain antecedently well-defined type, his problem being to determine which of the (humanly) possible languages is that of the community in which he is placed" can be applied to animals as well. Thus, we may say that the dog learning a signal system approaches the data with the presumption that they are drawn from a particular signal system, his problem being to determine which of the (dogly) possible signal systems is that of the laboratory in which it is placed.

That there is no practical difference between innate ideas and innate dispositions is shown, in particular, by the nativist's conclusion that innate ideas do not function unless appropriate stimulation takes place (see, e.g., Chomsky, 1968: 70). There is no doubt that the corresponding claim that certain innate dispositions do not function unless appropriate stimulation takes place can be accepted by all empiricists.[11]

There seems, then, to be no doubt that innate ideas alone are not sufficient for indicating a qualitative difference between humans and animals. I believe, however, that it is possible to interpret the nativist's thesis in the following form:

(a) The processes by which animals learn cannot account for the learning of a creative language.

(b) Since humans are able to learn a creative language, they must have a special sort of innate dispositions that allow them to learn by other kinds of processes.

For instance, Chomsky (1965: 57–8) says, "empiricist speculations ... have not provided any way to account for, or even to express the fundamental fact about the normal use of language, namely the speaker's ability to produce and understand instantly new sentences ...".

However, in the foregoing sections we have seen that learning of a creative language does not demand processes that are qualitatively different from those used by animals. After a child has acquired certain similarity sensations, he may learn a creative language as a consequence of exposure to pairing situations. In our terminology, such an exposure enables him to associate the normal associatum with new sentences (see Section VIII). But animals also can acquire similarity sensations and they, too, learn to associate associata as a result of the exposure to pairing situations. (Animals are also able to make characteristic (and predictable) reactions to posterior presentations of the first stimulus S_1.) Therefore, the acquisition of a creative language does not presuppose essentially different learning processes.

Admittedly, in language acquisition the acquired similarity sensations are very subtle and the same must be said of those aspects of the pairing situations that play the role of S_1 and S_2. But subtlety points at a gradual difference; it is not a sign of a qualitative difference. Consequently, since there is no qualitative difference between human and animal learning processes there is no reason for assuming such a difference between human and animal innate dispositions.

It seems that one of the most important reasons that made nativists postulate 'higher mental faculties' is their disregard of semantic factors in language acquisition. For instance, Chomsky, when considering the possibility that such factors may be helpful in language acquisition, states, "the exact relevance of [semantic information] to the problem at hand has never been clarified" (1965: 203).

There is no doubt, however, that semantic information indeed plays an important role in language acquisition. Thus, in the last section we have seen that the learning of complex syntactical categories may be facilitated by the prior learning of semantic categories.

We shall now analyse another case that shows that the consideration of semantic factors frees us from the need of postulating 'innate knowledges'. One of Katz's (1966) arguments against empiricists is that a child demonstrates knowledge of certain kinds of linguistic features to which he has never been exposed. He gives the example of the 'you' feature, which underlies imperatives but which, usually, is not explicitly present in such sentences. Now, Katz advances an explanation that might be used by empiricists to account for this implicit knowledge, "the empiricist might argue that he can account for the semantic effect of an absent feature such as the 'you' subject of imperatives on the basis of inductive generalization, because some imperatives, such as ["You help the man"], explicitly contain the word" (p. 256). Katz shows that this explanation is not valid.

But I believe that Katz is mistaken when assuming such an empiricist explanation. In the present case, an empiricist will not appeal to some verbal utterance that the child might have heard. He will explain the child's implicit knowledge by the fact that the *situations* in which imperatives are used usually contain a second person. In other terms, an 'imperative situation' is in general a situation in which (at least) two persons are present or are assumed to be present. Hence, once the child has learned the meaning of imperatives like "Bring the red ball", he knows that besides the speaker, there is normally also a hearer present, namely, the implicit 'you' of imperatives.

We thus see that if one seriously considers semantic factors in language acquisition, one does not need to wonder about innate knowledges.

The neglect of semantic factors is particularly striking in the discussions about the LAD (language acquisition device) with which humans are equipped. It is correctly stated than one output of the device (among others) is grammatical competence. When describing the input, however, only verbal utterances are usually mentioned, and in the few cases where semantic experiences are named, they are practically ignored afterwards. But as is *demonstrated* by the universal U1, the input does not consist solely of verbal stimuli, but very often of verbal stimuli *paired with objects, actions, aspects, situations etc.* Once this evident fact is taken into account, no reasons remain for attributing to the human LAD properties that are not found in animals. Of course, there are important capacity differences (see Section X), but these are differences in degree and not in quality.[12]

Before concluding let us briefly discuss two further nativist claims. The first is that the grammar that a child acquires "has empirical consequences that extend far beyond evidence" (Chomsky, 1968: 23). But, if grammar extends beyond evidence, why is it that the sequences "Ball the bring red" and "Holds the ball Daddy" are not grammatical for English children? There is no *a priori* reason why such sequences should not be grammatical. On the contrary, there are natural languages where wellformed (assertive) sentences 'correspond' to the second sequence. Hence, if an English child considers these sequences as deviant, it can only be attributed to the fact that the language that he hears in his community has *observable* properties that distinguish such sequences from wellformed ones. And, indeed, we have seen that with respect to the last sequence, English children *observe* that assertive sentences have often the form 'Noun Phrase + Verb Phrase + Noun Phrase' but almost never the form 'Verb Phrase + Noun Phrase + Noun Phrase'.

The second nativist claim is that there is no *a priori* justification why the empiricist explanation should have preference over other kinds of explanations. E.g., Chomsky (1968: 22) argues, "Although there is nothing inherently unreasonable in an attempt to account for knowledge and use of language in these [empiricist] terms, it also has no particular plausibility or a priori justification."

Against this claim I should like to argue that an empiricist approach had indeed an *a priori* plausibility. This plausibility is a consequence of the continuity thesis. We know that many human properties and dispositions have their analogues in animals (although there are often important differences in degree between them). Now, if language acquisition presents us with highly specialized learning processes that demand highly specialized innate dispositions, then the method suggested by the continuity thesis is to investigate first whether these dispositions have their analogues in animals. Only if they cannot be found does it become necessary to look for essentially new properties and dispositions.

Bar-Ilan University, Ramat Gan.

BIBLIOGRAPHY

Carnap, R.: 1956, 'The Methodological Character of Theoretical Concepts', in H. Feigl and M. Scriven (eds.), *Minnesota Studies in the Philosophy of Science*, Vol. 1, Univ. of Minnesota Press, Minneapolis.

Carnap, R.: 1963, 'Replies and Expositions', in A. Schilpp (ed.), *The Philosophy of Rudolf Carnap*, Open Court, La Salle, Ill.

Carnap, R.: 1966, *Philosophical Foundations of Physics*, Basic Books, Inc., New York.

Chomsky, N.: 1965, *Aspects of the Theory of Syntax*, M.I.T. Press, Cambridge, Mass.

Chomsky, N.: 1968, *Language and Mind*, Harcourt, Brace & World, Inc, New York.

Fodor, J. A.: 1966, 'How to Learn to Talk: Some Simple Ways', in F. Smith and G. A. Miller, *The Genesis of Language*, M.I.T. Press, Cambridge, Mass.

Hull, C. L.: 1943, *Principles of Behavior*, Appleton-Century, New York.

Katz, J. J.: 1966, *The Philosophy of Language*, Harper & Row, New York.

Lenneberg, E. H.: 1962, 'Understanding Language without Ability to Speak: A Case Report', *J. Abnormal Soc. Psychol.* **65**, 419–25.

Miller, N. E.: 1959, 'Liberalization of Basic S-R Concepts: Extensions to Conflict Behavior, Motivation and Social Learning', in S. Koch (ed.), *Psychology: A Study of a Science*, Vol. 2, McGraw-Hill, New York.

Osgood, C. E.: 1953, *Method and Theory in Experimental Psychology*, Oxford Univ. Press, New York.

Pavlov, I. P.: 1927, *Conditioned reflexes*, Oxford Univ. Press, London.

Premack, D.: 1970, 'The Education of Sarah', *Psychology Today* **4**, 54–8.

Russell, B.: 1927, *Philosophy*, W. W. Norton & Co., New York.

Stemmer, N.: 1971, 'Innate ideas and quality spaces', *Semiotica* **3**, 234–40.

Warren, J. M.: 1965, 'Primate Learning in Comparative Perspective', in A. M. Schrier, H. F. Harlow, and F. Stollnitz (eds.), *Behavior of Nonhuman Primates*', Vol. 1, Academic Press, New York.

Zener, K.: 1937, 'The Significance of Behavior Accompanying Conditioned Salivary Secretion for Theories of the Conditioned Response', *Amer. J. Psychol.* **50**, 384–403.

NOTES

[1] The present paper is based on my Ph.D. Thesis, 'An empiricist theory of language acquisition' (henceforth: Thesis), submitted to the Hebrew University of Jerusalem.

[2] See, e.g., Carnap (1956, 1966).

[3] Usually, no distinction will be made here between postulates and correspondence rules.

[4] There are a number of problems involved in equating species-specific with innate dispositions, but in order not to complicate matters too much, I shall not enter into them here.

[5] In this paper I ignore the acquisition of similarity sensations as a consequence of identical labelling or of other kinds of linguistic processes.

[6] The following definition is assumed: x *denotes* y for s, if and only if s associates x with an associatum that depends on y. If x denotes y for s, then we shall say that y is the *denotatum* of x for s. Notice that "to denote (for s)" and "denotatum (for s)" are T-terms.

[7] I am making here the plausible assumption that such a combination is not too complex to be perceived by a normal child as *a* combination.

[8] In Section XI we shall see that it is likely that the generalization will not be based on the (acquired) functions "to be a person term" and "to be a toy term" but on some other functions.

9 It is sometimes sufficient to know the meanings of some of the components. This pheno-menon is studied in Thesis under the category of partial definitional processes.

10 These capacities are not necessarily independent. It is thus possible that some of them are only manifestations of one fundamental capacity.

11 The relations between innate ideas and innate dispositions are more extensively dealt with in Stemmer (1971).

12 Fodor (1966) recognizes that semantic factors may be relevant, but he does not take them into account practically. Thus he states, "The difficulty with relying upon 'seman-tic' considerations in explaining language learning is not, then, that such considerations are known to be irrelevant, but simply that we do not know how to describe them in any very revealing way" (p. 110). (It is curious that scientists have preferred to postulate an 'emergent' LAD, instead of trying to improve the description of a factor that is already present in the very beginnings of language acquisition.)

SYNTHESE LIBRARY

Monographs on Epistemology, Logic, Methodology,
Philosophy of Science, Sociology of Science and of Knowledge, and on the
Mathematical Methods of Social and Behavioral Sciences

Editors:

DONALD DAVIDSON (Rockefeller University and Princeton University)
JAAKKO HINTIKKA (Academy of Finland and Stanford University)
GABRIËL NUCHELMANS (University of Leyden)
WESLEY C. SALMON (Indiana University)

‡NICHOLAS RESCHER et al. (eds.), *Essays in Honor of Carl G. Hempel. A Tribute on the Occasion of his Sixty-Fifth Birthday.* 1969, VII+272 pp. Dfl. 50,—

‡PATRICK SUPPES, *Studies in the Methodology and Foundations of Science. Selected Papers from 1911 to 1969.* 1969, XII+473 pp. Dfl. 72,—

‡JAAKKO HINTIKKA, *Models for Modalities. Selected Essays.* 1969, IX+220 pp. Dfl. 34,—

‡D. DAVIDSON and J. HINTIKKA (eds.), *Words and Objections: Essays on the Work of W. V. Quine.* 1969, VIII+366 pp. Dfl. 48,—

‡J. W. DAVIS, D. J. HOCKNEY and W. K. WILSON (eds.), *Philosophical Logic.* 1969, VIII+277 pp. Dfl. 45,—

‡ROBERT S. COHEN and MARX W. WARTOFSKY (eds.), *Boston Studies in the Philosophy of Science.* Volume V: *Proceedings of the Boston Colloquium for the Philosophy of Science 1966/1968.* 1969, VIII+482 pp. Dfl. 60,—

‡ROBERT S. COHEN and MARX W. WARTOFSKY (eds.), *Boston Studies in the Philosophy of Science.* Volume IV: *Proceedings of the Boston Colloquium for the Philosophy of Science 1966/1968.* 1969, VIII+537 pp. Dfl. 72,—

‡NICHOLAS RESCHER, *Topics in Philosophical Logic.* 1968, XIV+347 pp. Dfl. 70,—

‡GÜNTHER PATZIG, *Aristotle's Theory of the Syllogism. A Logical-Philological Study of Book A of the Prior Analytics.* 1968, XVII+215 pp. Dfl. 40,—

‡C. D. BROAD, *Induction, Probability, and Causation. Selected Papers.* 1968, XI+296 pp. Dfl. 54,—

‡ROBERT S. COHEN and MARX W. WARTOFSKY (eds.), *Boston Studies in the Philosophy of Science.* Volume III: *Proceedings of the Boston Colloquium for the Philosophy of Science 1964/1966.* 1967, XLIX+489 pp. Dfl. 70,—

‡GUIDO KÜNG, *Ontology and the Logistic Analysis of Language. An Enquiry into the Contemporary Views on Universals.* 1967, XI+210 pp. Dfl. 41,—

*EVERT W. BETH and JEAN PIAGET, *Mathematical Epistemology and Psychology.* 1966, XXII+326 pp. Dfl. 63,—

*EVERT W. BETH, *Mathematical Thought. An Introduction to the Philosophy of Mathematics.* 1965, XII+208 pp. Dfl. 37,—

‡PAUL LORENZEN, *Formal Logic.* 1965, VIII+123 pp. Dfl. 26,—

‡GEORGES GURVITCH, *The Spectrum of Social Time.* 1964, XXVI+152 pp. Dfl. 25,—

‡A. A. ZINOV'EV, *Philosophical Problems of Many-Valued Logic.* 1963, XIV+155 pp. Dfl. 32,—

‡MARX W. WARTOFSKY (ed.), *Boston Studies in the Philosophy of Science.* Volume I: *Proceedings of the Boston Colloquium for the Philosophy of Science, 1961–1962.* 1963, VIII+212 pp. Dfl. 26,50

‡B. H. KAZEMIER and D. VUYSJE (eds.), *Logic and Language. Studies dedicated to Professor Rudolf Carnap on the Occasion of his Seventieth Birthday.* 1962, VI+256 pp. Dfl. 35,—

*EVERT W. BETH, *Formal Methods. An Introduction to Symbolic Logic and to the Study of Effective Operations in Arithmetic and Logic.* 1962, XIV+170 pp. Dfl. 35,—

*HANS FREUDENTHAL (ed.), *The Concept and the Role of the Model in Mathematics and Natural and Social Sciences. Proceedings of a Colloquium held at Utrecht, The Netherlands, January 1960.* 1961, VI+194 pp. Dfl. 34,—

‡P. L. R. GUIRAUD, *Problèmes et méthodes de la statistique linguistique.* 1960, VI+146 pp. Dfl. 20,—

*J. M. BOCHEŃSKI, *A Precis of Mathematical Logic.* 1959, X+100 pp. Dfl. 23,—

SYNTHESE HISTORICAL LIBRARY

Texts and Studies
in the History of Logic and Philosophy

Editors:

N. KRETZMANN (Cornell University)
G. NUCHELMANS (University of Leyden)
L. M. DE RIJK (University of Leyden)

‡KARL WOLF and PAUL WEINGARTNER (eds.), *Ernst Mally: Logische Schriften.* 1971, X+340 pp. Dfl. 80,—

‡LEROY E. LOEMKER (ed.), *Gottfried Wilhelm Leibnitz: Philosophical Papers and Letters.* A Selection Translated and Edited, with an Introduction. 1969, XII+736 pp. Dfl. 125,—

‡M. T. BEONIO-BROCCHIERI FUMAGALLI, *The Logic of Abelard.* Translated from the Italian. 1969, IX+101 pp. Dfl. 27,—